# Cambridge English

OFFICIAL
PREPARATION MATERIAL

James Styring
Nicholas Tims
Series Editor: Annette Capel

# Prepare!

## STUDENT'S BOOK
### Level 7

**Cambridge University Press**
www.cambridge.org/elt

**Cambridge English Language Assessment**
www.cambridgeenglish.org

Information on this title: www.cambridge.org/9780521180368
© Cambridge University Press and UCLES 2015

First published 2015

Printed in Dubai by Oriental Press

A catalogue record for this publication is available from the British Library

ISBN 978-0-521-18036-8 Student's Book
ISBN 978-1-107-49801-3 Student's Book and Online Workbook
ISBN 978-1-107-49800-6 Student's Book and Online Workbook with Testbank
ISBN 978-0-521-18038-2 Workbook with Audio
ISBN 978-0-521-18039-9 Teacher's Book with DVD and Teacher's Resources Online
ISBN 978-0-521-18042-9 Class Audio CDs
ISBN 978-1-107-49798-6 Presentation Plus DVD-ROM

# Contents

| VOCABULARY 2 | WRITING | LISTENING AND SPEAKING | EXAM TASKS | VIDEO |
|---|---|---|---|---|
| Spelling | An essay (1)<br>Organising essays | | Reading and Use of English part 7<br>Writing part 1 | Creative minds |
| Verb + preposition, e.g. *apologise for*, *cope with*, *laugh at* | | **Listening** The boy who wore a skirt to school<br>**Speaking** Interviews<br>Introducing an opinion | Speaking part 1 | Fashion |
| Verb + *to* infinitive, e.g. *agree to do something*, *advise someone to do something* | An informal letter or email | | Reading and Use of English part 6<br>Writing part 2 | |
| Phrasal verbs: Health, e.g. *cut down on*, *get over* | | **Listening** Talking about stress<br>**Speaking** Offering help | Reading and Use of English part 4<br>Listening part 3 | |
| Expressing frequency, e.g. *from time to time*, *rarely* | An article (1) | | Reading and Use of English part 2<br>Writing part 2 | |
| Adverbs: Type and position | | **Listening** Everyday situations<br>🔵 **Word profile** *thing*<br>**Speaking** Favourite things<br>Generalising | Reading and Use of English part 1<br>Listening part 1 | |
| Time phrases, e.g. *before long*, *in no time* | A story | | Reading and Use of English part 5<br>Writing part 2 | Stories |
| *as if* / *as though* | | **Listening** A new skate park<br>**Speaking** Comparing photographs<br>Comparing and contrasting | Reading and Use of English part 7<br>Listening part 2<br>Speaking part 2 | Where we live |
| Adjective and noun suffixes | An essay (2)<br>Comparing and contrasting | | Reading and Use of English part 3<br>Writing part 1 | |
| Extended meanings of words | | **Listening** A radio phone-in<br>**Speaking** Surprising news<br>Expressing surprise<br>🔵 **Word profile** *expect* | Reading and Use of English part 6<br>Reading and Use of English part 4<br>Listening part 4 | Surprises! |

5

# Welcome to *Prepare!*

## Learn about the features in your new Student's Book

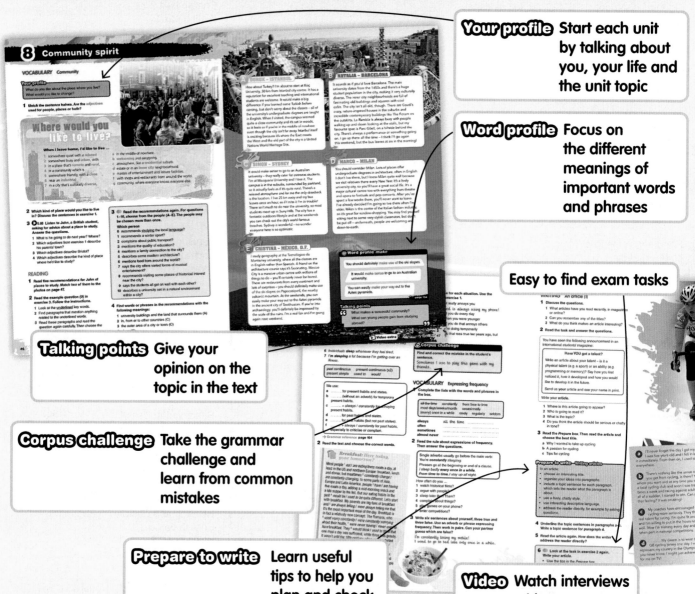

**Your profile** Start each unit by talking about you, your life and the unit topic

**Word profile** Focus on the different meanings of important words and phrases

**Easy to find exam tasks**

**Talking points** Give your opinion on the topic in the text

**Corpus challenge** Take the grammar challenge and learn from common mistakes

**Prepare to write** Learn useful tips to help you plan and check your writing

**Video** Watch interviews with teenagers like you

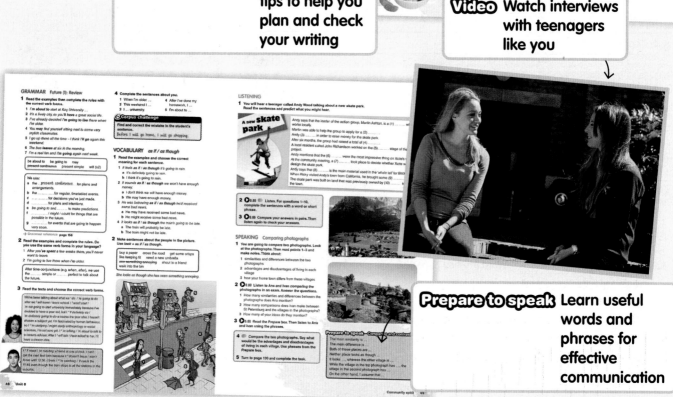

**Prepare to speak** Learn useful words and phrases for effective communication

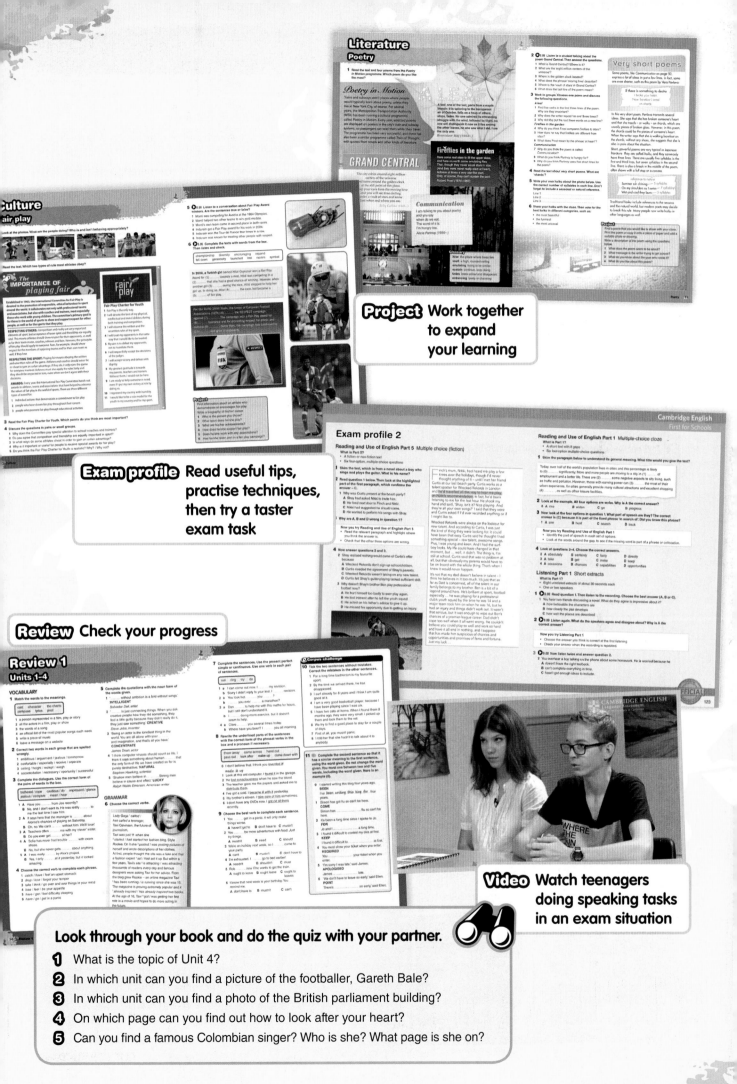

**Project** Work together to expand your learning

**Exam profile** Read useful tips, practise techniques, then try a taster exam task

**Review** Check your progress

**Video** Watch teenagers doing speaking tasks in an exam situation

## Look through your book and do the quiz with your partner.

1 What is the topic of Unit 4?
2 In which unit can you find a picture of the footballer, Gareth Bale?
3 In which unit can you find a photo of the British parliament building?
4 On which page can you find out how to look after your heart?
5 Can you find a famous Colombian singer? Who is she? What page is she on?

# 1 Creative minds

## VOCABULARY  Online, films, music, media

### Your profile
What do you spend the most time doing?
*watching TV or films*  *reading books*
*using the internet*  *listening to music*

**1** Read the quiz and note down your answers.
Check the meaning of the words.

## MEDIA QUIZ

1 Have you got a website, or **blog**, or
do you record a podcast?
2 How often do you **post comments** on websites?
3 Have you ever **reviewed** a movie or TV show
online?
4 Which actor plays your favourite film or TV
**character**?
5 Can you remember a good **scene** from a film
you've seen recently?
6 Does your favourite film have an
all-star **cast** or unknown actors?
7 Have you ever bought the **soundtrack** to a
movie or TV series?
8 Do you think you have a good singing **voice**?
9 Have you ever **composed** or written a piece
of music yourself?
10 Do you ever learn the **lyrics** to songs that
are in **the charts**?
11 Have you ever **formed** a band? What
instrument do you play?
12 Do you read modern **bestsellers**, or do you
prefer the **classics**?
13 What's your favourite **series** of books?
14 Are there film **versions** of any books
you like?

**2** Discuss the quiz questions.
A: *Have you got a website, or blog, or do you record a podcast?*
B: *I've got a blog. It's about computer games. But I've never recorded a podcast.*

**3** Match the creative jobs to the definitions.

| critic | director | editor | novelist | TV presenter |

Someone who …
1 reviews things and shares their opinion about them.
2 corrects and changes text in a book.
3 tells the actors in a film or play what to do.
4 writes fictional books.
5 introduces a show.

**4** ▶ 1.02 You will hear five people talking about their jobs. Match each speaker to a job in exercise 3.

**5** ▶ 1.02 Listen again and make notes about each job. Then discuss the questions below.
1 Which job do you think is the easiest/hardest? Why?
2 Which job do you think is the most interesting? Why?

## READING

**1** Read the questions. Then read text A about a talented young person. Which two questions relate to text A?
**Which person**
1 was inspired by a famous book?
2 discovered a talent after watching a film?
3 took up a new hobby in order to do something well?
4 used a video website to enter a competition?
5 provided information about their private life that was well received?
6 was confident that their work would be taken seriously?
7 had a parent who was initially unsupportive of their idea?
8 benefited from a highly unusual form of education?

**2** ⬤ Read the whole article. For the remaining questions in exercise 1, choose from the people (B–D). The people may be chosen more than once.

**3** Complete the sentences with the highlighted words in the texts.
1 The Olympics is a chance to see many athletes at the ........... of their career.
2 Lucy is ........... she can sing, but her voice is awful!
3 They ........... a competition to design their website.
4 Do people like Emerson and Nancy give you the ........... to get creative?
5 Mark has the ........... to be a great singer.

# FOUR TO WATCH:
## YOUNG, TALENTED AND CREATIVE

**A JACKIE EVANCHO** It was while watching the musical version of *Phantom of the Opera* on TV that Jackie Evancho found her passion for music. She started singing the songs around her home and revealed a surprisingly mature singing voice. Jackie started entering local singing contests and after seeing the reaction of audiences, her parents realised her potential. From there, Jackie's life changed dramatically. Her mum started uploading Jackie's performances to the web to share with her ever-increasing numbers of fans. Jackie used the clips to enter an audition for the TV show, *America's Got Talent* and won a place on the show! Although she wasn't quite good enough to win the show – she finished in second place – it was an incredible achievement. Since the show, she's worked as a professional singer. She's released several albums, toured the US and even starred in a Hollywood thriller.

**B NANCY YI FAN** When Nancy Yi Fan moved to the US from China, aged seven, she spoke hardly any English. She learned by reading classics, she says. It took her two years to write her first novel, *Swordbird*. When she had finished it, she emailed a copy to several leading publishers in the US. Without an agent, book proposals are rarely read, but Nancy believed in her ability to succeed. And she did – a year later, at the age of 12, she was a published novelist with a bestseller. Now, Nancy has not only completed all three books in the *Swordbird* series, but also translated them into Chinese herself.
The inspiration for Nancy's series came from a dream and her love of birds. The story is about a world full of birds, at war over a lack of food. Nancy even trained in martial arts in order to write the fight scenes more accurately.

**C EMERSON SPARTZ** As a child, Emerson Spartz read a lot. Instead of having to help around the house, he and his brother were told to read biographies of successful people. At just 12, Emerson persuaded his parents to let him leave school and teach himself at home. Very few children of his age do this, but it quickly proved successful for him.
While Emerson was reading the first novel in the Harry Potter series, he came up with the idea of *Mugglenet* – a website and online forum for Potter fans. He launched the website when he was still just 12. Over the next five years, Emerson and his parents watched in amazement as the website grew to receive, at its peak, 50 million visits every month. Emerson even wrote a book for fans on the famous wizard. Now Emerson is running his own company, Spartz Media. The company owns over 20 popular websites especially aimed at young people.

**D TOM CASSELL** Tom Cassell is an entrepreneur who has turned a hobby into a living. A massive fan of computer gaming, Tom had the idea of filming a game and commenting on the action while he was playing. But just as popular as Tom's comments on the game itself, were the details he gave about what he was up to personally. At first, Tom's father wasn't convinced the project would be successful. However, when one video got 3,000 views in a day, he changed his mind. It took three years, but Tom's online video channel now has millions of viewers. He travels widely, promoting his videos and is a well-known figure in the video-gaming world. For Tom, this is just the beginning. 'I've got three ultimate goals in life – a job in the games industry, to travel the world and create my own house. I'm going to build my own dream gaming house.'

**EP Word profile** *not*

My day-to-day work's not half as exciting as people think.

She wasn't quite good enough to win the show.

I have to be up at four, … not to mention being in bed by eight the previous evening.

page 132

**Talking points**

" Do you think people are naturally creative, or can they learn to be creative?

What other qualities do young people need in order to succeed? "

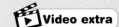

## GRAMMAR    Simple, continuous or perfect

**1** Match the examples to the meanings.

1 *Since the show, she's **worked** as a professional singer.*

2 *When she **had finished** it, she emailed a copy to several leading publishers in the US.*

3 *Now Emerson **is running** his own company.*

4 *The company **owns** over 20 popular websites.*

5 *While Emerson **was reading** the first novel, …*

6 *He **launched** the website when he was still just twelve.*

a  an action in progress in the present

b  an action in progress in the past

c  an action that started in the past and continues into the present

d  a fact or state in the present

e  a single completed action in the past

f  a past action which links back further in the past

**2** Complete the rules with *continuous*, *perfect* or *simple*.

We use the:

a present or past ............ for permanent states and for regular or completed actions.

b present or past ............ for actions or states that are in progress or unfinished.

c present or past ............ for actions or states that connect two time periods.

→ **Grammar reference   page 148**

**3** Choose the correct sentence or response. Can you explain your choices?

1 We didn't have time to speak to Jack for long.
   a  When we arrived, he had left.
   b  When we arrived, he was leaving.

2 I did nothing yesterday.
   a  I spent the entire day sleeping.
   b  I've spent the entire day sleeping.

3 What are you up to at the moment?
   a  I often review films online.
   b  I'm reviewing a film online.

4 I'm looking forward to the next book in the series.
   a  I read all the others.
   b  I've read all the others.

5 This actor is often in police thrillers.
   a  Yes, he's playing lots of characters like this.
   b  Yes, he plays lots of characters like this.

### Corpus challenge

Find and correct the mistake in the student's sentence.

*My worst experience was when I have lost my house key.*

**4** Choose the correct verbs.

One day, while Kishan Shrikanth [1] *travelled / was travelling* to school, he saw some young children selling newspapers. He asked his dad why the children weren't at school. His dad [2] *explained / had explained* that many of the children were probably homeless. This conversation [3] *inspired / has inspired* Kishan to write a short story. The story was developed into a film script and at the age of just ten, Kishan [4] *directs / directed* the film himself.

Kishan, who is known as Master Kishan in India, [5] *was already / has already been* an actor at the time. He [6] *appeared / had appeared* in over 20 films and 1,000 episodes of Indian soap operas. His film about homeless children [7] *made / had made* Kishan the youngest film director in the world.

Since directing his first film, Kishan [8] *has won / had won* several awards for his work. When he [9] *doesn't work / isn't working* on a film, he studies film-making and special effects and [10] *dreams / is dreaming* of winning an Oscar, like his hero, the director Steven Spielberg.

## VOCABULARY    Spelling

**1** Choose the correct spellings.

1 It quickly proved *succesful / successful* for him.

2 She revealed a *suprisingly / surprisingly* mature singing voice.

3 Nancy *believed / beleived* in her ability to succeed.

4 *Although / Althought* she wasn't quite good enough to win the show, it was an incredible achievement.

5 The company owns over 20 popular websites *especially / expecially* aimed at young people.

**2** Match the types of spelling mistakes to the misspelled words in exercise 1. Write the correct spellings.

a  single consonant instead of a double: *successful*

b  wrong letter: ............

c  letters in wrong order: ............

d  missing letter(s): ............

e  extra letter: ............

**3** Underline and correct the spelling mistakes. What type of spelling mistakes are they?

1 I would prefer more of a choise in school subjects.

2 Nowadays it's rarely necesary to use public phones.

3 I was bored from the beginning and couldn't wait untill it was over.

4 We were delighted to recieve the award.

5 The government isn't doing enough about the enviroment.

6 I don't know wether that bed will be comfortable.

## WRITING An essay (1)

**1** **Discuss the questions.**

1  What creative subjects do you do at school?
2  Do you spend as much time on creative subjects as academic subjects?

**2** **Read the task. What is the essay question?**

In your English class you have been talking about different school subjects. Now your English teacher has asked you to write an essay.

Write an essay using **all** the notes and giving reasons for your point of view.

**Subjects such as drama and music are just as important as maths and languages. Do you agree?**

**Notes**
Write about:

1  which subjects are important in your country
2  what subjects are useful for a career
3  ................. (your own idea)

**3** **Read the *Prepare* box and the jumbled paragraphs of the essay. Match the paragraphs to the plan.**

### Prepare to write – Organising essays

You can use four paragraphs to write an opinion essay about a statement or question.

- **Paragraph 1**: an introduction, possibly a statement about the current situation
- **Paragraph 2**: one or more arguments for or against the statement, possibly with an example from your own knowledge or experience
- **Paragraph 3**: one or more contrasting arguments, possibly with an example from your own knowledge or experience
- **Paragraph 4**: a conclusion, your opinion of the statement

**A** To sum up, it is clearly necessary for everyone to study academic subjects but, at the same time, creative subjects are often ignored by schools. They deserve a more significant role in children's education.

**B** This is an interesting question which many people hold strong opinions about. In most schools in my country, students have far more lessons in subjects like maths and languages than creative subjects such as drama and music. Furthermore, many students study no creative subjects after the age of 15.

**C** However, others feel that without music and drama, students may never get to express their creative sides. They might never discover their talent for singing, playing musical instruments or acting. Many of the highest academic achievers have a creative side. For instance, Einstein loved music as much as he loved physics.

**D** Most people agree that academic subjects are important. Almost everyone will need maths and foreign language skills in their future working life. In contrast, few people will be lucky or talented enough to earn a living as a professional musician or an actor.

**4** **Which of the highlighted expressions in the essay introduces:**

**a**  a general opinion?  **d**  an example?
**b**  an additional idea?  **e**  the conclusion?
**c**  a different idea?

**5** **Read the task and answer the questions.**

In your English class, you have been talking about the role of education. Now your English teacher has asked you to write an essay.

Write your essay using **all** the notes and giving reasons for your point of view.

**Schools should teach practical skills, such as managing money and applying for jobs, as well as academic subjects. Do you agree?**

**Notes**
Write about:

1  the importance of academic subjects
2  the difficulty of learning practical skills
3  ................. (your own idea)

1  Do you agree or disagree with the statement?
2  What arguments support the statement?
3  What arguments are against the statement?
4  What are your conclusions?

**6** **Write your essay.**

- Use your answers to the questions in exercise 5.
- Organise your essay into the paragraph plan in the *Prepare* box.
- Use the expressions in exercise 4.
- Check your spelling and grammar.
- Write 140–190 words.

## VOCABULARY  Adjective + preposition

**Your profile**

What do you take into account when you buy clothes?
*fashion   price   tradition or culture   your personality*

**1** ▶1.03 **Read what four young people say about fashion. Match the sentence halves of the extracts. Listen and check.**

### Emma

1  I'm aware of what's in fashion
2  I'm easily impressed by designer labels.
3  I'm pretty adventurous with

a  my taste in clothes, but I'd never wear fur.
b  My favourite is Prada.
c  because I read blogs like models.com.

### Ahmed

4  I'm addicted to clothes shopping.
5  I do need to be cautious about spending
6  I'm absolutely hopeless at making

a  decisions about clothes.
b  I just can't stop.
c  too much though.

### Dan

7  I'm not all that bothered about what
8  You shouldn't be critical of the way
9  I've never been mean about a friend's

a  dress sense. People can be very sensitive about their appearance.
b  others think of my dress sense. I just wear whatever I like.
c  others dress. It's up to individuals to choose how they want to look.

### Sara

10  There's no point in being loyal to a
11  I certainly wouldn't be jealous of a friend
12  I'm fairly decisive about what to buy.

a  I don't waste time worrying about what else might be available.
b  just because they had an expensive brand of trainers.
c  particular brand. You should feel free to wear anything that looks good.

**2** ▶1.03 **Answer the questions. Listen again and check.**

1  Where does Emma buy most of her clothes?
2  What did Ahmed have to do when he accidentally spent too much?
3  Why does Dan like wearing conventional clothes?
4  What does Sara think of brands and labels?

**3** **Which statements in exercise 1 are true for you? Discuss your answers.**

A: '*I'm aware of what's in fashion because I read blogs.*' That's true for me.
B: *No, it isn't true for me.*

## READING

**1** **Look at the photo of a clothing stall at Camden Lock Market. Would you enjoy shopping here? Why? / Why not?**

**2** **Read the text quickly. Which 'Big Question' are all five people answering?**

1  Do people worry too much about fashion?
2  Does fashion actually matter?
3  Are you aware of the latest fashions?

**3** **Are the sentences true or false according to the text? Correct the false sentences.**

1  One particular colour has always been associated with girls. (Matteo)
2  It is worth paying more for a good brand of trainers. (Halia)
3  People might make fun of you for wearing fashionable trainers. (Halia)
4  I try not to judge people by what they wear. (Musa)
5  Your clothes can change your mood. (Isabel)
6  Cheap clothes can look as good as more expensive fashion items. (Isabel)
7  Clothes can tell other people about the wearer. (Hannah)

**4** **Replace the underlined phrases with the highlighted words in the text.**

1  Your earrings are <u>absolutely beautiful</u>.
2  I like wearing <u>interesting and unusual</u> clothes.
3  I like fairly <u>traditional, ordinary</u> clothes, nothing too unusual.
4  Your jacket has loads of pockets. It looks very <u>practical and useful</u>.
5  He was wearing a suit in a <u>popular, well-designed</u> style.

# THE BIG

## QUESTION: .................?

**OF COURSE,** but I'm more worried about other people's terrible dress sense! I've been reading an article about the history of fashion. It made some good points, like who says blue is for boys and pink is for girls? In fact, 100 years ago, pink was a boys' colour and blue was for girls! And what about skirts for men? They're comfortable and functional, but men in the West never wear them.

We tend to think of fashion as fast-moving, but it actually changes super-slowly. Men have been wearing shirts, ties and suits for centuries. Similarly, women's dress has changed very little during the past few hundred years, except for the introduction of trousers in the 1950s. You see some weird stuff on the catwalks, but in real life clothes are boring. I reckon it's time for a fashion revolution!

*Matteo, 16, Verona*

**NOT REALLY.** I can't stand labels. Everyone at my school wants designer labels, but I can't understand why people are willing to pay hundreds of euros for top brands when cheaper ones are really no different! It's hard to know what to do at school! If you have cheap clothes, people might tease you, but if you have really expensive clothes, there's always the worry that someone might try to steal them. The point is, logos and brands cause all kinds of problems.

*Halia, 17, Thessaloniki*

**NO.** I'm pretty relaxed about my clothes and I certainly don't depend on anyone's advice about what to wear. I tend to go for a conventional look, clothes that feel great and that you can wear anywhere. I've been relaxing at home, so I'm wearing something casual: a pair of old Levis and a tennis shirt with a pocket on the chest. I appreciate classic design, but I don't think clothes matter that much. Underneath the mask, we're all human beings and we're all individuals. I sometimes find myself making judgements about people based on their clothes, but I quickly stop myself. It's important to ignore someone's appearance and concentrate on the person inside.

*Musa, 17, Ankara*

**YES.** Clothes actually make me happy – up to a point! I have clothes to suit every mood, occasion and season. Fashion is important because it helps people to express their individuality and identity. 'High' fashion – the clothing supermodels wear on the catwalk – is associated with Paris, Milan, New York, London, but every country has developed its own fashion industry and its own look. There's no point in spending loads of money on fashion. Most good malls sell clothes that are inspired by the catwalk, so you can still buy clothes that look stunning but they cost ten times less. With fashion, there's something for everyone.

*Isabel, 17, Santiago*

**I THINK IT DOES, ACTUALLY.** Some people aren't interested in how they look, but everyone wears *some* form of clothing and their clothes make a statement. I think clothes matter because your choice of clothes influences how others think of you. Take me, for example. I'm really into 'alternative' clothing. I avoid chain shops in malls. I go for small, independent shops and second-hand clothes from markets. I collect badges. I've been looking for some 1950s American badges but they're all much too expensive. So what do my clothes say about me? They say I'm an individual. I think independently. I'm original. I have my own style. What do your clothes say about you?

*Hannah, 16, Glasgow*

## EP Word profile *point*

It made some good points.

Clothes actually make me happy – up to a point.

There's no point in spending loads of money on fashion.

The point is, logos and brands cause all kinds of problems.

page 132

## Talking points

" Why do you think that some people are so concerned about fashion?

Do you think that clothing can affect a person's mood? How?

In what ways do you think the clothes someone wears show their personality? "

**Clothing stall, Camden Lock Market, London**

▶ Video extra    Addicted to fashion    **15**

## GRAMMAR    Present perfect simple and continuous

**1** **Match the examples to the rules.**

1 Men **have been wearing** shirts, ties and suits for centuries.

2 Every country **has developed** its own fashion industry and its own look.

3 Women's dress **has changed** very little during the past few hundred years.

4 I**'ve been relaxing** at home, so I'm wearing something casual.

> We use the present perfect simple for:
>
> **a** a past action with a present result.
>
> **b** an action that happened in a time period that is not yet complete.
>
> We use the present perfect continuous for:
>
> **c** an action that started in the past and is still continuing.
>
> **d** an action (still continuing or just completed) that explains a present situation.

→ Grammar reference **page 149**

**2** **Match the pairs of sentences.**

1 *Vogue* magazine has published …

2 *Vogue* magazine has been publishing …

   **a** only one super-long magazine – with 916 pages!

   **b** fashion magazines since 1892.

3 My wardrobe's almost empty. I've been getting rid …

4 I used to have loads of jackets, but I've got rid …

   **a** of them all, sorry.

   **b** of lots of old clothes recently. It's a nice feeling!

5 Anna works for Gucci. She has been designing …

6 Anna works for Gucci. She's designed …

   **a** handbags for 15 years.

   **b** hundreds of beautiful bags.

**3** **Complete the sentences. Use the present perfect simple or continuous form of the verbs.**

1 I'm cold. We ................. outside without jackets. (sit)

2 Stella McCartney ................. some of fashion's most interesting designs. (produce)

3 I haven't put your clothes outside to dry yet. It ................. all afternoon. (rain)

4 Look! I ................. some new shoes! (buy)

5 I ................. your blog all week. It's brilliant. (read)

6 'You're late!' 'I'm sorry. I ................. in the queue.' (wait)

**4** **Make five sentences with the present perfect simple or continuous form of the verbs in the box. Compare your sentences.**

> blog    buy    chill out (with)    learn
> live (in)    play    watch    wear

I haven't been blogging for long. I think I wrote my first about three months ago.

### Corpus challenge

**Find and correct the mistake in the student's sentence.**

I am thinking of you since I arrived in Athens.

## VOCABULARY    Verb + preposition

**1** **Complete the sentences with the phrases in the box.**

> apologised for    compared with    cope with
> depending on    do without    ~~heard of~~    laugh at

**people wearing onesies**

0 I haven't .....heard..of.. 'onesies'.

1 You still haven't ............ losing my scarf.

2 I hate it when people ............ my uniform.

3 Clothes these days are very comfortable ............ a century ago.

4 I hate ............ my parents for money to buy clothes.

5 Maria can't ............ going to crowded shopping centres.

6 I can't ............ buying new clothes at least once a month.

**2** **Ask and answer questions using verb + preposition phrases.**

A: *Is there anything that you can't do without?*

B: *I definitely can't do without my sunglasses.*

# LISTENING

**1** You will hear part of a TV chat show. Look at the picture and discuss what the people might talk about.

**2** ▶1.04 Listen and check.

**3** ▶1.04 Listen again and answer the questions.

1 What new dress regulations did Chris Bennett's school introduce?
2 Why did the school decide to ban shorts?
3 What did the rules about school clothing fail to mention?
4 Where do men wear clothes that are similar to skirts?
5 How did the school respond when Chris wore a skirt?
6 When did the school agree to a debate on the subject?
7 What point did the school make in the debate?
8 What was the result of the debate?

**4** Discuss the questions.

1 Do you think schools and colleges are right to ban some items of clothing? Why? / Why not?
2 What are the good and bad points about uniforms in schools and at work?

# SPEAKING  Interviews

**1** ▶1.05 You will hear Sophia and Pavel doing an interview. Read the interview questions, then listen. Which question does the interviewer not ask?

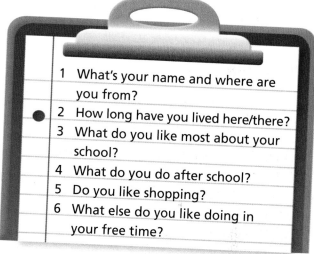

1 What's your name and where are you from?
2 How long have you lived here/there?
3 What do you like most about your school?
4 What do you do after school?
5 Do you like shopping?
6 What else do you like doing in your free time?

**2** ▶1.05 Read the *Prepare* box. Who uses each phrase? Listen again and write S (Sophia) or P (Pavel).

## Prepare to speak – Introducing an opinion

To be honest, …
To tell the truth, …
I guess …
Frankly, …
I would say …

**3** Prepare for a short interview about yourself.
- Make notes on your answers to the questions in exercise 1.
- Add a few extra ideas for each answer.
- Review the questions. Think about what tenses and relevant vocabulary you can use for each answer.

**4** 🔵 Work in pairs. Interview each other.
- Ask the questions from exercise 1. You can add other questions during the interview.
- Answer using phrases from the *Prepare* box.

# Culture
## Fashion design

**1** Match the pictures to the words in the box. Then read the text. What are the British Fashion Awards?

> high heels   menswear   miniskirt   slogan

## The BRITISH FASHION Awards

Once a year, the British Fashion Council rolls out the red carpet for the British Fashion Awards – a star-studded event to honour the nation's most talented, creative designers.

The BFC held its first awards ceremony in 1984 with the introduction of its Designer of the Year Award. The first winner was a young designer named Katharine Hamnett, who created T-shirts with bold, controversial slogans, such as 'Stop and Think' and 'Make Trade Fair'. Five years later, when the BFC decided to add more categories, the British Fashion Awards were born.

Along with the year's best designer, the ceremony honours the best menswear and the best accessories, such as shoes, hats and jewellery. There is also an award for the Best Brand, which Victoria Beckham won in 2011 for her self-named company. Every year there is also an award for Outstanding Achievement to recognise designers who have made an impact on the global fashion industry. In 2012, this award went to Manolo Blahnik for his spectacular designs of high-heel shoes and other footwear.

The BFAs also include Emerging Talent Awards for the most promising new designers of ready-to-wear collections, menswear and accessories. Fittingly, there is also an award for the year's best fashion model, with past winners including supermodels Kate Moss and Agyness Deyn.

### BFA TRIVIA

◉ Mary Quant, who invented the miniskirt in the 1960s, entered the BFA Hall of Fame in 1990 for her lifetime contribution to fashion.

◉ Alexander McQueen was named Designer of the Year four times between 1996 and 2003.

◉ Kim Jones has won the BFA for the best menswear on four different occasions, in 2006, 2009, 2011 and 2012.

**2** Read the sentences. Are they true or false? Correct the false sentences.

1 The BFA is an annual awards ceremony.
2 The first British Fashion Awards were in 1989.
3 There are only awards for fashion designers.
4 Manolo Blahnik designs shoes.
5 Mary Quant won a special award in 1990.

**3** Answer the questions with information from the text.

1 How many awards did the BFC give in 1984?
2 Which designer won the Best Brand award in 2011?
3 What awards are there are for new designers?
4 In which category has Agyness Deyn won an award?
5 Who won the Designer of the Year award four times?
6 Who won the Best Menswear award in 2009?

**4** Read the success stories of two rising stars. Complete them with the words in the boxes.

**Text A**

| animal | brand | British | own |
| --- | --- | --- | --- |
| simple | uniforms | | |

**Text B**

| founded | customers | house |
| --- | --- | --- |
| furniture | comfortable | bright |

**5** In pairs, discuss the questions.

1 What do you think it takes to become a successful designer?

2 Stella's father is very famous. Do you think this helped her career? Why? / Why not?

3 Do you think fashion designers should use any animal products?

**6** ▶1.06 Listen to a podcast about the British designer Christopher Raeburn. Take notes.

**7** ▶1.06 Use your notes to choose the correct words. Listen again and check.

1 Christopher Raeburn uses a lot of *artificial* / *recycled* materials for his fashion designs.

2 Raeburn is famous for *reusing* / *designing* military uniforms for his collections.

3 He finished art school in *2006* / *2008*.

4 Raeburn *has* / *doesn't have* his own company.

5 He makes clothes for *men* / *men and women*.

6 His designs are usually *not practical* / *simple*.

7 Raeburn's clothes are made in *Asia* / *the UK*.

## SUCCESS STORIES

**A** Stella McCartney first became famous as the daughter of Paul McCartney, a member of the (1) ................. band, The Beatles. However, Stella is now well known as a talented fashion designer. Her clothes are cool and modern, with clean, (2) ................. lines and she never uses (3) ................. products like leather or fur.

Stella showed her first collection in 1995 and established her (4) ................. fashion house six years later. Her (5) ................. includes womenswear, as well as accessories and sportswear. For the 2012 Olympics, Stella designed (6) ................. for the British athletes, although some people thought they were too unconventional.

**B** Jonathan Saunders, a designer from Scotland, is an up-and-coming name in British fashion. Famous for combining (7) ................. colours and bold prints, Saunders' clothes are also (8) ................. and easy to wear. His most famous (9) ................. include women like Michelle Obama and the actress Sienna Miller. Jonathan studied (10) ................. and textile design before entering the world of fashion. At first, he created prints for famous designers, like Alexander McQueen. Then he (11) ................. his own Jonathan Saunders brand in 2003. In addition to running his business, Jonathan also designs clothing for the Pollini fashion (12) ................. in Italy.

### Project

Write a profile of a fashion designer. Answer the questions below.

1 Where is the designer from?

2 What do his/her designs look like?

3 When did he/she start in fashion?

4 Does he/she have a personal brand?

5 Has he/she won any fashion awards?

# in the mind

## Abstract nouns

s are you naturally good at?
What skills or sports have you learned to be good at?

**1** ▶1.07 **Read the paragraph about a podcast. Choose the correct abstract nouns. Listen and check.**

> ## THE Debate
>
> Is there finally ¹ *agreement / fortune* in the debate over ² *intelligence / nature* vs nurture?
> Are we born with a personality that never changes and with a fixed amount of ³ *intelligence / development*? In other words, is our ⁴ *agreement / fortune* in life dictated by our genes – the 'nature' argument? Or do we start life as a blank sheet? Does our social and intellectual ⁵ *fortune / development* come from our life experiences – the 'nurture' view?
> New research appears to suggest that both sides in the debate might be right.

**2** ▶1.08 **Listen to Sara and Ahmed talking about 'THE Debate'. Are the sentences true or false?**

1 Ahmed has already listened to 'THE Debate'.
2 According to the podcast, everyone has the genes to become a professional footballer.
3 You need the right genes and the right environment to be successful.
4 According to the podcast, people can become more intelligent by working hard.

**3** ▶1.08 **Complete the sentences with the abstract nouns in the box. Listen again and check.**

> belief    concentration    creativity
> determination    luck    success

1 They discussed what you need to achieve ............ in life.
2 You need the ............ to be born with the right genes.
3 That was a common ............ in the past.
4 You could be born with the ............ to be a great artist.
5 Students who have the ............ to study hard, can actually become more intelligent.
6 If you really try to improve your ............ , you can develop different parts of your brain.

**4** **Complete the sentences with the correct abstract nouns from exercises 1 and 3.**

1 Have you got the ............ to work hard and be successful?
2 I'm sure you'll win. I wish you good ............ !
3 Are good exam results really a proof of ............ ?
4 Reading helps to improve your ............ .
5 She is lovely. It's in her ............ to be kind.

**5** **Discuss the questions.**

1 What is your opinion about the nature vs nurture debate?
2 What do you think are signs of intelligence?

## READING

**1** **Look at the photos and read the title of the article. In what ways are humans smarter than other species? Read the article quickly and check your ideas.**

**2** **Six sentences have been removed from the article. Read sentences A–G and notice the underlined words. What do you think the words might refer to?**

A Some psychologists have trained <u>one</u> to recognise over 1,000 nouns!
B However, research suggests that <u>they</u> can't put individual words together to form sentences.
C <u>It</u> was using a rock to crack open a shellfish.
D It is the moment when <u>they</u> realise that an image in a reflection is actually of themselves.
E <u>It</u> has got a bigger brain, but brain size doesn't equal intelligence.
F This happens whether or not <u>they</u> belong to the same family.
G <u>The latter</u> involves being able to imagine what it must be like to be in another's situation.

**3** **Read the example answer. Notice how the underlined words can help you to decide on the correct answer.**

*1G: 'The latter' refers to 'empathy' two lines before the gap. 'Empathy' is also mentioned in the sentence following the gap.*

**4** ⬤ **Choose from sentences A–F the one which fits each gap (2–6). Use the underlined words to help you decide. There is one extra sentence which you do not need to use.**

**5** **Find the 12 animal species in the text. In what ways are they intelligent?**

**6** **Find the eight** highlighted **nouns in the article. Which ones are abstract nouns?**

# HUMANS: THE **SMARTEST** SPECIES?

**Many animals are said to be bright** and some live up to this reputation in surprising and charming ways: whales can sing, dolphins enjoy showing off with balls and rubber rings, parrots can pick up language and, apparently, an octopus has even learned to take the lid off a jar! This demonstrates a certain amount of determination, but does it mean animals are actually intelligent, like humans?

There are five commonly-recognised signs of intelligence: 1) the ability to make and use a tool, 2) problem-solving, 3) the ability to communicate and understand, 4) the capacity for abstract thought (for example, adding numbers up) and 5) psychological qualities such as self-awareness and empathy. The former of these psychological qualities is the ability to realise that you are an individual who is separate from other individuals. **1** G Most children start to show basic signs of empathy from a very early age.

Our ancestors started using stone tools more than 2.5 million years ago. Scientists used to believe that only humans possessed this skill, but nowadays we know that some animals also use tools. Chimpanzees can make unusual ones, from brushes to collect ants, to pointed sticks for use as weapons. Brown bears rub stones against their fur to remove dirt and dead skin. Even a tropical fish was filmed recently using a tool! **2**

Both understanding and producing language are obvious signs of intelligence. Although a dog can't talk, it can understand commands. **3** It can also understand verb + noun commands in English, like *Touch the ball!*

or *Pick the bone up!* including combinations of verb + noun that it hasn't heard before. This is similar to the understanding of a human child aged two.

Most animals can communicate with each other by singing, barking and so on. When parrots hear human language, they can pick it up and repeat it, often to great comic effect. **4** Some chimpanzees can 'talk' to humans using sign language, but what they can say is fairly limited. Only humans can use complex language with grammar.

There is an interesting test for self-awareness – the mirror test. For humans, the 'mirror stage' occurs at about 15–18 months old. **5** To test this with animals, scientists draw a coloured spot on an animal's face. An animal that recognises itself in a mirror always tries to touch or remove the spot. Most animals can't recognise themselves in the reflection in a mirror – not even dogs. Only elephants, dolphins and great apes (chimpanzees, gorillas and orang-utans) realise they are looking at themselves in a mirror.

Perhaps the hardest intelligence test of all is for empathy. Empathy is extremely rare in animals, but elephants are said to display it. They are aware of others in the group and care for them when they are ill, and adults work together to protect young ones. **6** Elephant behaviour such as this is fascinating, but the chimpanzee is by far the cleverest animal overall. Some baby chimps have even beaten *people* in a memory test of numbers on a computer screen! But even though chimpanzees are good at problem-solving and abstract thought, they can't light fires, cook food, make clothes or send rockets into space, which makes humans the smartest species on earth.

**EP Word profile *smart***

Humans: the smartest species?

I need a smart jacket for my interview.

I wish I had a smart phone.

page 132

**Talking points**

" In which ways are human beings <u>not</u> the smartest species?

To what extent do humans depend on animals?

Does mankind show animals enough respect? How? / Why not? "

## GRAMMAR   The grammar of phrasal verbs

**1** Underline the phrasal verbs in the examples.

1 *Some animals live up to this reputation in charming ways.*
2 *Dolphins enjoy showing off.*
3 *They care for them when they are ill.*
4 *They have the capacity for adding numbers up.*
5 *When parrots hear human language, they can pick it up and repeat it.*

**2** Match the phrasal verbs in exercise 1 to the types of phrasal verb in the rules.

> There are four types of phrasal verb:
> **a** phrasal verbs without an object
> *Our car broke down last night.*
> **b** separable phrasal verbs with an object
> *I switched off the TV.*
> *OR I switched the TV off.*
> *I switched it off.*
> (NOT *I switched off it.*)
> **c** inseparable phrasal verbs with an object
> *Can you deal with this problem?*
> *Can you deal with it?*
> (NOT *Can you deal this problem/it with?*)
> **d** inseparable three-part phrasal verbs
> *I'm looking forward to the weekend.*

→ Grammar reference **page 150**

**3** Read the email. Choose the correct phrasal verbs. In one answer, both options are possible.

I have some bad news about my visit. I'm really sorry but I need to ¹ *put off it / put it off* again. It's my best friend's birthday party the same weekend and I'm helping to organise the party. I have to be there and I can't really ² *get it out of / get out of it.* It's such a pity, I've been ³ *looking forward to it / looking it forward to.* I'm sorry to ⁴ *let down you / let you down.* I've even bought my train tickets. I can't get a refund, so I'll have to ⁵ *throw them away / throw away them,* which is a bit annoying! Are you free 30th May? I think I can get away then. I'd love you to ⁶ *show around me / show me around* the city. Maybe you could ⁷ *book us in / book in us* at a restaurant. I will come next time, I promise! By the way, ⁸ *pass on my thanks / pass my thanks on* to your brother for the                 book he lent me.

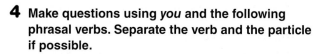

**4** Make questions using *you* and the following phrasal verbs. Separate the verb and the particle if possible.

0 you / ever hand in / homework / late
  Have you ever handed homework in late?
1 put off / revising
2 get on with / everyone in your family
3 clear up / at home
4 join in / team sports
5 look forward to / summer holidays

**5** Ask and answer the questions you wrote in exercise 4.

## VOCABULARY   Verb + *to* infinitive

**1** Read the examples. Which verb can't be followed by an object?

1 *I've persuaded my friends to lend me some money.*
  *I've persuaded my friends not to worry about me.*
2 *Do you want me to stay a little longer?*
  *Do you want to stay a little longer?*
  *I don't want to stay any longer.*
  *I don't want you to stay any longer.*
3 *They tend to go shopping on Saturdays.*
  *They tend not to go shopping on Sundays.*

**2** Complete the table with the verbs in the box. Use a dictionary to help.

> advise   ~~agree~~   ask   beg   encourage
> expect   force   help   hope   intend
> persuade   plan   pretend   refuse
> remind   tend   want   warn

| Never with an object | *agree* |
|---|---|
| Sometimes with an object | |
| Always with an object | |

**3** Discuss the questions.

1 When was the last time you refused to do something?
2 How would you persuade a friend to help you with a job?
3 What are you planning to do this weekend?
4 What do you intend to do when you leave school?

# WRITING   An informal letter or email

**1** Discuss the questions.

 1  What new skills have you learned recently?

 2  What is the best way to learn a new skill?

**2** Read the task, then read Dan's email. Has Dan answered all Raj's questions?

---

You have received an email from your friend, Raj.

> Can you help me with my class project? I have to write about the ways in which people learn a new skill. Please tell me about a skill you have learned recently. How have you developed this skill? What aspects of it have you found difficult? Would you recommend other teenagers to take up the same skill?
>
> Thanks, Raj

Write your **email**.

---

Hi Raj

It's great to hear from you. Actually, I got a lifeguard qualification earlier this year, so now I'm spending most Saturdays down at the beach. We're there to help swimmers and surfers who get into difficulties and this could be pretty scary without any training, right?

Anyway, to get qualified, I did a course at my local pool. I reckon I'm a strong swimmer and I've always been quite fit, so the physical parts of the course were fine, but I found all the stuff on first-aid techniques really challenging. I'm fine with it all now though and I've picked up loads of practical tips from the more experienced guys I'm working with.

You need to be 15 for lifeguard training. Plus you must be in good shape. The thing is, other people will be relying on your strength and fitness in risky situations and you can't let them down.

Keep in touch

Dan

**3** Read the *Prepare* box. Then read Dan's email again. Find:

 **a**  an opening expression

 **b**  a closing expression

 **c**  four phrasal verbs

 **d**  four other examples of informal language

## Prepare to write — Informal letters and emails

In informal letters and emails:

- use an informal opening expression
  *How nice to get your news!*
  *It's great to hear from you.*
  *Thanks for your email.*
- use informal expressions to add ideas
  *To start with …   Also …   Plus …*
- use informal language and phrasal verbs
  *I reckon …   The thing is …*
- use contracted forms
  *don't, can't, wouldn't*
- use an informal closing expression
  *Take care   Write soon   Love   Keep in touch*

**4** Find informal sentences and expressions in the email to match the formal sentences and expressions below.

 1  It was very pleasing to receive your email.

 2  Our job is to assist swimmers and surfers who experience difficulties.

 3  This could be rather daunting without training.

 4  It is also important that you have a good level of fitness.

**5** Dan has not answered the final question in the task. Write a fourth paragraph to Dan's email, answering this question.

 *I'd recommend becoming a lifeguard because…*

**6** Read the task and plan your answer.

---

You have received a letter from your English-speaking pen friend, Niki.

> Can you help me with my school project? I need to find out about people's earliest memories. What are your most important childhood memories? Why do you think you have remembered them? Which recent experiences would you like to be able to recall in the future?
>
> Write back soon!
> Niki

Write your **letter**.

---

**7**  Write your letter to Niki.

- Answer all of Niki's questions.
- Use the tips in the *Prepare* box.
- Check your grammar and spelling.
- Write 140–190 words.

## VOCABULARY  Stress

**1** ▶1.09 **Listen to eight situations and match them to the pictures.**

**2** Match the words and phrases to the pictures.

> faint   feel dizzy   get in a panic
> go over and over something in your mind
> have an upset stomach   have difficulty sleeping
> lose your temper / get bad-tempered
> lose your appetite

**3** Discuss the questions.

1 When was the last time you lost your temper?
2 Do you ever get into a panic about exams?
3 Have you ever had difficulty sleeping? When?

## READING

**1** Read the headings for an article on stress. Do you agree or disagree? Compare your answers in pairs.

a Stress is for adults, not people my age.
b A bit of stress helps me to get things done.
c I know how to deal with stress.
d It's not my fault that I get stressed.
e Everyone gets stressed from time to time. It's no big deal.

**2** Read the article quickly. Match the headings in exercise 1 to Parts 1–5 of the article. Use the sentence(s) in bold at the end of each paragraph to help you choose the heading that follows.

**3** Read the article again. Complete the sentences with either two or three words.

1 The article suggests that most teenagers have fewer reasons ............ than adults.
2 The author believes that stress is about more ............ deadlines.
3 Hormones released in stressful situations can both ............ our energy levels.
4 The article strongly recommends finding time in your day-to-day life ............ and also to relax.
5 Psychologists advise people to try and see ............ stressful situations.

# UNDER PRESSURE?

**1** _a) Stress is for adults, not people my age._

Which of these two types of people are more stressed: a parent who has to go to work to earn money to pay bills and bring up a family, or a teenager who has to go to school to study? Surveys report that 75% of adults say they feel stressed on at least three occasions every week. However, an astonishing 85% of teenagers between 14 and 17 say the same thing. What's more, a third of the girls and half of the boys believe the pressure is there every single day. In this age group, the three most frequent causes of stress are schoolwork, parents and problems with friends. **But isn't this just part of life?**

**2** .....................................................................................

Very few of us would say we never get stressed. But what does stress mean to you? Is it a piece of work you need to finish for school? Perhaps it's a class you mustn't be late for. If stress was just about deadlines, we would probably be able to keep it under control. However, for most people it's bigger than this. And it can be a very big deal. But could we get rid it from our lives? **Do we actually want to?**

**3** .....................................................................................

When we are stressed, our body responds to the danger by releasing chemicals called _hormones_. They temporarily increase our heart rate and boost our energy levels. Thousands of years ago we used this energy to avoid getting eaten! So, in small doses, many find stress can motivate them. But constant stress can have the _opposite_ effect, leading to feelings of anxiety. At this point, hormones actually lower our energy levels and we risk suffering from a whole range of health problems. **So how do we avoid this situation?**

**4** .....................................................................................

Most of us know the basics of how to handle stress: we should take regular exercise and eat healthily. Sleep is also important. According to some reports, teenagers ought to get over nine hours every night! Do you? But fighting stress needn't be boring. You must also make some time in your schedule for fun, preferably with friends, and also a little quiet time, relaxing by yourself. Spend time around positive people, who don't get you down. Look into volunteering – helping other people can help you feel less stressed. And if you're getting in a panic, stop what you are doing and take several deep breaths. Pause for a moment and think about all the good things in your life. **So have you tried that? Is everything (or everyone) still stressing you out?**

**5** .....................................................................................

A common belief is that our stress comes from all the things we have to do because of _other_ people. However, some psychologists believe it's more helpful to think of stress as how we _react_ to the things that stress us. The reason is that these things are beyond our control, but we _can_ control how we react to them. So another way of fighting stress is to look for the positive in situations. When your parents say you can't go away for the weekend, think of it as an opportunity to do something at home. You don't have to do something you hate – choose something you enjoy but don't always have time to do. And is that difficult homework due in next week? You do have to do it, yes. You can't control it. **But maybe you could see it as a challenge rather than a chore.**

## EP **Word profile** _control_

The instructor had to use his controls to stop the car.

The reason is that these things are beyond our control, but we _can_ control how we react to them.

I almost lost control of the car.

page 133

## Talking points

" Do you think teenagers get stressed as much as adults?
What do you think is the best way to deal with stress? "

## GRAMMAR   Modals (1): Necessity and obligation

**1** Read the examples and complete the rules with some of the bold verbs.

1 You **don't have to** do something you hate.
2 We **should** take regular exercise.
3 Teenagers **ought to** get nine hours of sleep.
4 Fighting stress **needn't** be boring.
5 I **need to** finish this work for school.

> We use:
> **a** ............ or *ought to* for advice.
> **b** ............ for necessity.
> **c** ............ (*haven't got to*) or *needn't* for lack of obligation.

→ Grammar reference **page 151**

**2** ⬤ Complete the second sentence so that it has a similar meaning to the first sentence, using the word given. Use between two and five words.

0 It would be a good idea if I went to bed early tonight. SHOULD
I ...*should go to*... bed early tonight.
1 Clare knew that she had to be home by ten. NECESSARY
Clare knew that ............ for her to be home by ten.
2 My tennis coach says that I must attend additional training sessions. NEED
My tennis coach says that ............ training sessions than before.
3 You are under no obligation to attend the extra classes. HAVE
You ............ attend the extra classes.
4 Our school makes us wear a uniform. HAVE
We ............ a uniform at school.

**3** Read the examples and complete the rules with the bold verbs.

*Teenagers **have to** study.*
*You **mustn't** be late for class.*
*You **must** make time to have fun.*
*You **can't** go out.*

> We use:
> **a** ............ or ............ for obligation.
> **b** ............ or ............ for prohibition.
> **c** ............ or ............ when the obligation or prohibition comes from ourselves.
> **d** ............ or ............ when the obligation or prohibition comes from someone else.

**4** Choose the correct verbs. When both answers are possible, can you explain the difference in meaning?

1 Simon *needs / must* control his temper more.
2 You *mustn't / don't have to* use my things without asking first!
3 She told me in secret so you *mustn't / don't have to* say a word.
4 Everyone *must / has to* deal with stress sometimes.
5 I haven't done any exercise for ages. I *must / have to* do some this week.

### ⊙ Corpus challenge

**Find and correct the mistake in the student's sentence.**

The bicycle is cheaper than the car and you mustn't spend any money on petrol.

**5** Complete the sentences with your own ideas.

1 I really should …
2 At school we don't have to …
3 Tomorrow I must …
4 Every day I have to …
5 Students mustn't …
6 My parents say I can't …

## VOCABULARY   Phrasal verbs: health

**1** Read the examples and match the bold phrasal verbs to the meanings.

1 *You mustn't **stay up** so late!*
2 *It's taken me weeks to **get over** this flu.*
3 *Arguing with my friends really **gets** me **down**.*
4 *I'm trying to **cut down on** sweet things.*
5 *We all **came down with** food poisoning in the evening, so we couldn't go out.*
6 *If I stand up very quickly, I sometimes **pass out**.*

**a** eat or drink less or reduce something
**b** make someone feel unhappy
**c** get better after an illness or an unhappy event.
**d** faint or become unconscious
**e** become ill
**f** remain awake later than usual

**2** Complete the sentences with the correct form of the phrasal verbs in exercise 1. Then discuss the questions.

0 What kinds of things ...*get*.. you ...*down*...?
1 How often a week do you ............ past midnight?
2 Does it take you a long time to ............ arguments with good friends?
3 Do you know anyone who ............ at the sight of blood?
4 Have you ever ............ an illness because you've been outside in the cold for too long?
5 Would you like to ............ anything in your diet?

## LISTENING

**1** ▶ **1.10 You will hear Emma talking about stress. Read the sentences carefully. Then listen and decide which sentence is true for Emma.**

A I don't really suffer from stress.

B Schoolwork and family get me stressed the most.

C I have a range of ways to deal with stress.

D The future is my biggest cause of stress.

E Exercise is my main way of fighting stress.

F I don't like how I behave when I'm stressed.

G I followed someone's advice on a technique for dealing with stress.

H Arguing with my brother makes me stressed.

**2 Now read what Emma said. Find and underline the part that tells you the right answer.**

It's not a big deal, but I do get stressed – almost always over exams. The first thing that happens is I lose my appetite and partly because of that, I reckon, I get a bit bad-tempered. I do a variety of things to keep the stress under control – I talk to my parents about whatever's worrying me, I avoid staying up late, I even do a bit of sport. And all these things help. Within a day I've usually got over whatever it is, or I've moved on to something else. I try not to let things get me down in general.

**3 Read the reasons why A–D in exercise 1 are true or not true for Emma. Work in pairs and decide why E–H are not true.**

A Not true. Emma says she does get stressed.

B Not true. Exams stress her, but she only mentions talking to her parents.

C True. Emma says she does a variety of things to keep the stress under control.

D Not true. She doesn't mention the future.

**4** ▶ **1.11 ⬤ You will hear four more teenagers talking. For questions 2–5, choose from the list A–H in exercise 1 what each speaker says. Use the letters only once. There are three extra letters which you do not need to use.**

| | | | | |
|---|---|---|---|---|
| Speaker 1 | C | 1 | Speaker 4 | 4 |
| Speaker 2 | | 2 | Speaker 5 | 5 |
| Speaker 3 | | 3 | | |

## SPEAKING   Offering help

**1** ▶ **1.12 Listen to the conversation. What is Dan going to do for Sara?**

**2** ▶ **1.12 Listen again and complete the phrases.**

| like | need | sure | shall |
|---|---|---|---|

1 ........... I take the games for you?

2 Are you ............ ? That'd be fantastic, thanks.

3 I'll text you when I leave here, if you ............ .

4 Thanks, but there's no ............ .

**3** ▶ **1.13 Listen to a conversation between Dan and his mother. Answer the questions.**

a Who offers to help who?

b What offers are made?

c What does Mrs Fisher really want Dan to do?

**4** ▶ **1.13 Read the *Prepare* box, then listen again. Which phrases do Dan and Mrs Fisher use?**

### Prepare to speak — Making offers

**Making offers**

Would you like me to …?

Let me …

Shall I …?

I'll … if you like.

**Refusing offers**

It's OK, I can do it myself.

No, don't worry. I can manage that.

Thanks, but there's no need.

**Accepting offers**

It'd be great if you could.

Are you sure? That'd be fantastic, thanks.

**5 Write down all the things you need to do this week. Which of them could someone else help with?**

**6 Work in pairs. Then change roles.**

**Student A**   Tell Student B about your list.

**Student B**   Make offers to Student A.

**Student A**   Respond to the offers appropriately.

A: *I've got to finish a project, get some new trainers and get a birthday present for my dad.*

B: *Let me help you with your dad's birthday present.*

A: *It'd be great if you could.*

# Biology
## The heart

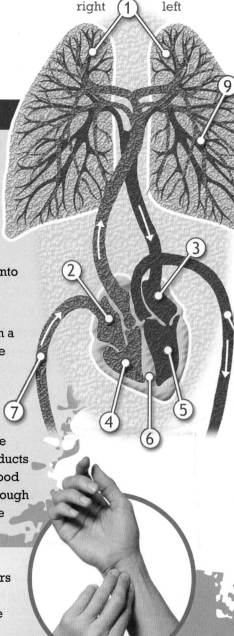

right ① left

**1** Read the text. Then label the diagram with the words in the box.

| capillaries | left artery | left atrium | lungs |
|---|---|---|---|
| right artery | right atrium | septum | vein | ventricle |

## YOUR CIRCULATORY SYSTEM

### Heart structure and function

Your heart is a natural pump that pushes blood around your body. It has two sides that are divided by a thick wall called the septum. Both sides are divided into two closed spaces called chambers. The upper chamber is the atrium and the lower chamber is the ventricle.

The right atrium receives blood from your body. This blood is deoxygenated – it does not carry very much oxygen ($O_2$). First, the right atrium pumps the blood to the right ventricle. Then the right ventricle pumps it to the lungs where it picks up new oxygen from the air that you breathe.

The left atrium receives oxygenated blood from the lungs and pumps it into the left ventricle. Then the left ventricle pumps the blood around the rest of your body. This blood carries oxygen to all of your body's other cells.

### Arteries, capillaries and veins

Blood circulates through your body in a closed system of tubes called arteries and veins. The arteries carry blood away from the heart and divide into branches of smaller tubes.

The smallest tubes, called capillaries, are thinner than a human hair. The walls of the capillaries are so thin that oxygen can pass through them and into the cells of your body. Your cells also release carbon dioxide ($CO_2$) and other waste products into the blood. Then the blood flows back to your heart through the veins carrying away the waste products.

### Check your pulse

- Your heart beats about 100,000 times a day, or 35 million times a year! Check your heart rate by feeling the pulse in your wrist. Use the fingers of your other hand. Don't use your thumb because it also has a pulse.
- Your heart is a double pump. When you check your pulse, you'll notice two beats close together. The first beat is made by the left and right atrium together. The second is made by the left and right ventricles.

**2** How does blood move through the circulatory system? Number the parts in order, starting with the lungs.

a ............ left ventricle
b ............ capillaries
c ............ left atrium
d ............ right ventricle
e ............ right atrium
f .....1..... lungs
g ............ arteries
h ............ veins

**3** Answer the questions with information from the text in exercise 1.

1 What separates the right and left sides of the heart?
2 Which ventricle pumps out deoxygenated blood?
3 Where does your human blood become oxygenated?
4 Why can oxygen go through the walls of capillaries?
5 What tubes carry waste away from the body's cells?
6 Which beats first: the right ventricle or right atrium?

### Glossary

**atrium** an upper chamber of the heart (plural *atria*)
**carbon dioxide ($CO_2$)** a waste gas that your body produces
**cell** the smallest living part of your body
**oxygen ($O_2$)** a gas that your body needs to live
**release** let something go out or away
**ventricle** a lower chamber of the heart

**4** Read the text. Match four of the sections to the pictures.

# Do you 💙 your heart?

**1** **Feed your heart.** Your heart needs protein to build new muscle. Be sure to eat healthy, protein-rich foods, like fish, white meat, eggs, beans, nuts and seeds. Avoid eating too much red meat – it contains a lot of fat.

**2** **Have your 'five a day'.** Try to eat five servings of fruit and vegetables every day. They contain vitamins and minerals that your heart needs to work properly. The rest of your body will also thank you!

**3** **Maintain a healthy weight.** Be careful not to overeat. When you carry too much extra weight, your heart has to work harder than necessary. However, being too thin isn't good for you either. Keep a healthy balance!

**4** **Avoid fatty and salty food.** Don't eat too much fat or salt. Some fat builds up in your arteries and veins, causing heart disease. Too much salt makes your body retain water, which increases your blood pressure.

**5** **Lead an active lifestyle.** Your heart is a powerful muscle, but it needs regular exercise to stay strong and healthy. You should do at least 30 minutes of exercise a day to give your heart a workout. So get moving!

**5** Read the text in exercise 4 again. Then read the sentences. Give yourself a score for each sentences from 1 (= never) to 5 (= always). Discuss your answers with a partner.

1 I feed my heart with carbohydrates and proteins.
2 I have five servings of fruit and vegetables a day.
3 I try to maintain a healthy, balanced body weight.
4 I avoid food that has a lot of unhealthy fat or salt.
5 I lead an active lifestyle by doing sport and exercise.

**6** ▶ 1.14 **Listen to an interview. Make notes on what Karen eats and how much exercise she does. What does the dietician say about Karen's diet and lifestyle?**

## Project

How well do you care for your heart? Write a paragraph about your lifestyle.

1 How can you improve your eating habits?
2 What sport do you enjoy doing?
3 Do you exercise or go to a gym?
4 Does school cause a lot of stress for you?
5 Does anyone in your family smoke?
6 Is the air clean in your town or city?

# Review 1
## Units 1-4

## VOCABULARY

**1** Match the words to the meanings.

> cast    character    the charts
> compose    lyrics    post

1 a person represented in a film, play or story
2 all the actors in a film, play or show
3 the words of a song
4 an official list of the most popular songs each week
5 write a piece of music
6 leave a message on a website

**2** Correct two words in each group that are spelled wrongly.

1 ambitious / arguement / jealous / tommorrow
2 confortable / especially / receive / seperate
3 ceiling / height / reciept / wiegh
4 accomodation / necessary / oportunity / successful

**3** Complete the dialogues. Use the correct form of the pairs of words in the box.

> bothered / cope    cautious / do    impressed / glance
> jealous / compare    mean / hear

1 A Have you ............ from Joe recently?
  B No, and I don't want to. He was really ............ to me the last time I saw him.
2 A It says here that the manager is ............ about Alonso's chances of playing on Saturday.
  B Oh, no. We can't ............ without him. We'll lose!
3 A Teachers often ............ me with my 'clever' sister.
  B Do you ever get ............ of her?
4 A Sofia has never had trouble ............ with exam stress.
  B No, but she never gets ............ about anything.
5 A I was really ............ by Alex's project.
  B Yes, I only ............ at it yesterday, but it looked amazing.

**4** Choose the correct verb to complete each phrase.

1 *catch / have / feel* an upset stomach
2 *drop / lose / forget* your temper
3 *take / think / go* over and over things in your mind
4 *lose / feel / be* your appetite
5 *have / get / feel* difficulty sleeping
6 *have / go / get* in a panic

**5** Complete the quotations with the noun form of the words given.

1 '............ without ambition is a bird without wings.' **INTELLIGENT**
   *Salvador Dali, artist*

2 '............ is just connecting things. When you ask creative people how they did something, they feel a little guilty because they didn't really do it, they just saw something.' **CREATIVE**
   *Steve Jobs, inventor*

3 'Being an actor is the loneliest thing in the world. You are all alone with your ............ and imagination, and that's all you have.' **CONCENTRATE**
   *James Dean, actor*

4 'I think computer viruses should count as life. I think it says something about human ............ that the only form of life we have created so far is purely destructive.' **NATURAL**
   *Stephen Hawking, scientist*

5 'Shallow men believe in ............ . Strong men believe in cause and effect.' **LUCKY**
   *Ralph Waldo Emerson, American writer*

## GRAMMAR

**6** Choose the correct verbs.

Lady Gaga [1] *called / has called* a teenager, Tavi Gevinson, the future of journalism.
Tavi was just 11 when she [2] *started / had started* her fashion blog, Style Rookie. On it she [3] *posted / was posting* pictures of herself and wrote descriptions of her clothes.
At first, people thought the site was a fake and that a fashion expert [4] *set / had set* it up. But within a few years, Tavi's site [5] *is attracting / was attracting* thousands of readers every day and famous designers were asking Tavi for her advice. From the blog grew Rookie – an online magazine Tavi [6] *has been running / is running* since she was 15.
The magazine is proving extremely popular and it [7] *already inspired / has already inspired* two books. At the age of 16, Tavi [8] *got / was getting* her first role in a movie and hopes to do more acting in the future.
It's hard not to be impressed by Tavi – she [9] *didn't even finish / hasn't even finished* school yet!

**7** Complete the sentences. Use the present perfect simple or continuous. Use one verb in each pair of sentences.

> run   ring   try   do

1 a I can come out now. I ............ my revision.
  b Sorry I didn't reply to your text. I ............ revision.
2 a You look hot. ............ you ............?
  b ............ you ever ............ a marathon?
3 a Dan ............ to help me with this maths for hours, but I still don't understand it.
  b I ............ doing more exercise, but it doesn't seem to help.
4 a Clare ............ you several times today.
  b Where have you been? I ............ you all morning.

**8** Rewrite the underlined parts of the sentences with the correct form of the phrasal verbs in the box and a pronoun if necessary.

> threw away   came across   hand out
> pass out   look after   ~~make up~~   come down with

0 I don't believe that. I think you <u>invented it</u>!
  *made it up*
1 Look at this old computer. I <u>found it</u> in the garage.
2 He <u>lost consciousness</u> when he saw the blood.
3 The teacher gave me the papers and asked me to <u>distribute them</u>.
4 I've got a cold. I <u>became ill with it</u> yesterday.
5 My brother's eleven. I <u>take care of him</u> sometimes.
6 I don't have any DVDs now. I <u>got rid of them</u> recently.

**9** Choose the best verb to complete each sentence.

1 You ............ get in a panic. It will only make things worse.
  A haven't got to   B don't have to   C mustn't
2 You ............ be more adventurous with food. Just try things.
  A mustn't   B need   C should
3 We're on holiday next week, so I ............ come to your party.
  A can't   B mustn't   C don't have to
4 I'm exhausted. I ............ go to bed earlier!
  A needn't   B shouldn't   C must
5 Rob ............ now if he wants to get the train.
  A ought to leave   B ought leave   C ought to leaves
6 I know that next week is your birthday. You ............ remind me.
  A don't have to   B mustn't   C can't

**⊙ Corpus challenge**

**10** Tick the two sentences without mistakes. Correct the mistakes in the other sentences.

1 For a long time badminton is my favourite sport.
2 By the time we arrived there, he has disappeared.
3 I surf already for 8 years and I think I am quite good at it.
4 I am a very good basketball player, because I have been playing since I was six.
5 I have two cats at home. When I found them 8 months ago, they were very small. I picked up them and took them to the vet.
6 We try to find a good place to stay for a couple of days.
7 First of all, you musn't panic.
8 I told her that she hadn't to talk about it to anybody.

**11** ⬤ Complete the second sentence so that it has a similar meaning to the first sentence, using the word given. Do not change the word given. You must use between two and five words, including the word given. Here is an example (0).

0 I started writing this blog four years ago.
  **BEEN**
  I've *been writing this blog for* four years.
1 Simon has got flu so can't be here.
  **COME**
  Simon has ............................. flu so can't be here.
2 It's been a long time since I spoke to Jo.
  **FOR**
  Jo and I ............................. a long time.
3 I found it difficult to control my skis at first.
  **KEEP**
  I found it difficult to ............................. at first.
4 You must show your ticket when you enter.
  **REQUIRED**
  You ............................. your ticket when you enter.
5 'I'm sorry I was late,' said James.
  **APOLOGISED**
  James ............................. late.
6 'We don't have to leave so early,' said Ellen.
  **POINT**
  There's ............................. so early,' said Ellen.

## VOCABULARY   History

**Your profile**

Which periods of history have you studied at school?
Which parts of history do you find interesting? Why?
What do you know about the history of your local area?

**1** Read the quiz questions and guess the meaning of the **words**.

**2** ▶1.15 Answer the questions in pairs. Listen and check. What extra information do you hear? Make notes.

**3** Discuss the questions.

1 In which decade and century were you born? What about your parents?
2 How different would your life be without the internet? What would you have to do differently?
3 Which other inventions have had the biggest impact on you? And on society? Why?

## READING

**1** Read the example answer (0) in the first paragraph of the text. What other word could you use instead of *if*?

**2** ● Read the first paragraph again. For questions 1–8, think of the word which best fits each gap. Use the ideas below to help.

- Look at the words before and after each gap.
- Use only **one** word in each gap.
- There may be more than one correct answer.

# History quiz

**1** On which continent did our earliest **ancestors** live?
 **a** Africa   **b** America   **c** Asia

**2** Which **civilisation** came first?
 **a** Ancient Greece
 **b** the Roman Empire
 **c** the **Kingdom** of Egypt

**3** Which **tribe** of women from an ancient **myth** gave their name to a South American river?
 **a** the Amazons
 **b** the Centaurs
 **c** the Titans

**4** In which **century** was the car invented?
 **a** 18th century
 **b** 19th century
 **c** 20th century

**5** In 1900, which country had the most **citizens**?
 **a** Russia   **b** India   **c** China

**6** Which city had the most **inhabitants** in 1900?
 **a** New York   **b** London   **c** Tokyo

**7** In which **decade** was television first broadcast to the public?
 **a** 1930s   **b** 1950s   **c** 1970s

**8** When was the internet **launched** publicly?
 **a** 1975   **b** 1995   **c** 2005

**3** Read the questions and discuss possible answers.

1 What alternatives can you think of to an eight-hour sleep?
2 How did sleeping habits change after the invention of artificial lighting?
3 How do the sleep patterns of different cultures and different age groups compare?
4 What is a 'siesta'?
5 What is a 'body-clock'?

**4** Read the rest of the text and check your answers.

**5** Complete the sentences with the highlighted words in the text.

1 How long do you ............ sleep at night?
2 He was physically and ............ hurt by the terrible experience.
3 I never realised, but it ............ that we are at the same school.
4 Can't you remember to bring your own phone? You're ............ asking if you can borrow mine.
5 I'm not tired. Let's ............ a bit later.

# A GOOD NIGHT'S SLEEP?

What happens (0) ....*if*.... you wake up in the middle of the night? Do you have difficulty falling asleep again? Perhaps you're someone (1) ........... becomes frustrated because you can't get back (2) ........... sleep straightaway.

Then you might begin to get (3) ........... a panic about being tired the next day, or even about any problems you have, going over and over things in your head. Or perhaps you've woken up after a nightmare and the negative images are still in your mind. Whatever your sleeping habits, in (4) ........... 21st century being awake at night is generally regarded as problematic. This is logical of course: there's (5) ........... point in being awake when everyone else is asleep. And if you end up being awake all night, you'll be (6) ........... tired to cope the following day. (7) ........... in most parts of the world a 'good night's sleep' means more or less eight hours (8) ........... interruption, it turns out that the concept of an eight-hour sleep is fairly recent.

**Naturally,** history textbooks only tend to record memorable accounts of wars and empires, of love and death, or bravery and determination. Sleep is something we take for granted, so it isn't mentioned. However, some historians noticed references to a 'first sleep' and a 'second sleep' in documents covering several centuries and countries. The first sleep started after sunset and lasted until around midnight. Then people would lie awake for a while and chat or pray. Some neighbours even used to take the opportunity to visit each other between sleeps. After a few hours, they would have their second sleep, until dawn. In countries with long hours of daylight in summer, this often meant starting work as early as four or five o'clock in the morning.

**Artificial lights** weren't common until a few centuries ago. Only the rich could afford candles and without electricity, nobody could do anything outdoors when it was dark. By the end of the 18th century, lighting had become more widespread as cities installed gas streetlights and domestic gas lamps appeared. All of a sudden, most people had lights and could stay up late if they wanted to. By the time electric lighting was introduced just a century ago, the two-sleep pattern had disappeared.

**It's a pity** we lost the two-sleep habit because believe it or not, being awake for a period at night is both natural and healthy. It follows the body's natural energy and sleep rhythms. It is beneficial psychologically too: the period between the two sleeps was the perfect time to think about the day and to take it easy. The nearest we get to it these days is the 'siesta', the half-hour mid-afternoon sleep still enjoyed in some parts of the world.

**The two-sleep** habit used to be quite widespread, but it wasn't universal. Sleep patterns vary between different cultures and depend partly on how much daylight different places have. Some cultures don't have a fixed time for sleeping, but have much more informal sleep patterns, where individuals sleep for short periods throughout the day or night, whenever they feel tired.

**Sleep patterns** also vary according to age. While older adults and pre-teens are happy with early mornings in general, teenagers have a habit of staying up all night and getting up later. In many modern families, parents are always complaining that teenagers won't get up in the mornings, while teens are constantly finding excuses to stay up late. Really, it shouldn't matter. Getting up late isn't lazy and neither is getting an early night. Maybe we should all take into account what our body clock is telling us and sleep when our body tells us it's time to do so.

## EP Word profile *take*

Sleep is something we take for granted.

They used to take the opportunity to visit each other.

It was the perfect time to take it easy.

Maybe we should take into account what our body clock is telling us.

page 133

## Talking points

" What is 'a good night's sleep'?
What might be the advantages and disadvantages of more informal sleep patterns?
What difficulties might someone have if they work at night and sleep all day?
Do you like the idea of living in a 24-7 society? "

## GRAMMAR  Present and past habits

**1** Read the examples, then complete the rules with the correct verb forms.

1 *Between sleeps, people **would lie** awake and chat.*
2 *The two-sleep habit **used to be** quite widespread.*
3 *They **used to take** the opportunity to visit each other.*
4 *My brother **was always waking** me **up** early when I was younger.*
5 *Teenagers **are constantly finding** excuses to stay up late.*
6 *Individuals **sleep** whenever they feel tired.*
7 *I**'m sleeping** a lot because I'm getting over an illness.*

> past continuous     present continuous (x2)
> present simple    *used to*    *would*

> We use:
>
> a  ............ for present habits and states.
> b  ............ (without an adverb) for temporary present habits.
> c  ............ + *always/constantly* for annoying present habits.
> d  ............ for past habits and states.
> e  ............ for past habits (but not past states).
> f  ............ + *always/constantly* for past habits, especially to criticise or complain.

→ **Grammar reference  page 152**

**2** Read the text and choose the correct words.

### Breakfast: Here today, gone tomorrow?

Most people ¹ *eat / are eating* three meals a day, at least in the US and northern Europe: breakfast, lunch and dinner, but mealtimes ² *constantly change / are constantly changing*. In some parts of Asia, Europe and Latin America, people ³ *have / are having* five meals a day, adding a mid-morning snack and a late supper to the list. But our eating habits in the past ⁴ *would be / used to be* quite different. Let's start with breakfast. My parents are big fans of breakfast and ⁵ *are always telling / were always telling* me that it's the most important meal of the day. Breakfast is in fact a relatively new concept. The Romans, who ⁶ *used worry constantly / were constantly worrying* about their health, ⁷ *were never having / never used to have* breakfast. They ⁸ *would think / used to think* that one meal a day was sufficient, while three was greedy. It wasn't until the 18th century, when people started working in factories, that workers ⁹ *used to need / were needing* a big breakfast before they went to work. Habits ¹⁰ *still change / are still changing* now. People often ¹¹ *don't feel / aren't feeling* hungry first thing, or they are in a rush, and more and more people nowadays ¹² *would miss / are missing* breakfast. Perhaps, after a few hundred years of popularity, 'breakfast' is going to disappear again.

**3** Write a sentence for each situation. Use the grammar from exercise 1.

0 something that really annoys you
  *My best friend is always using my phone!*
1 something that you do every day
2 a habit from when you were younger
3 something that you do that annoys others
4 something you're doing temporarily
5 a fact about you that was true ten years ago, but not any longer

> **O Corpus challenge**
>
> **Find and correct the mistake in the student's sentence.**
> *Sometimes I use to play this game with my friends.*

## VOCABULARY  Expressing frequency

**1** Complete the lists with the words and phrases in the box.

> ~~all the time~~    constantly    from time to time
> most days/weeks/month    occasionally
> (every) once in a while    rarely    regularly    seldom

| always | *all the time* ............ | ............ |
|---|---|---|
| often | ............ | ............ |
| sometimes | ............ | ............ |
| almost never | ............ | ............ |
| | ............ | |

**2** Read the rule about expressions of frequency. Then answer the questions.

> Single adverbs usually go before the main verb:
> *You're **constantly** sleeping.*
> Phrases go at the beginning or end of a clause.
> *I sleep badly **every once in a while**.*
> ***From time to time**, I stay up all night.*

How often do you …
1 watch historical films?
2 argue with people?
3 sleep later than 11am?
4 complain about things?
5 play games on your phone?
6 enter competitions?

**3** Write six sentences about yourself, three true and three false. Use an adverb or phrase expressing frequency. Then work in pairs. Can your partner guess which are false?

*I'm constantly losing my mobile!*
*I used to go to bed late only once in a while.*

# WRITING An article (1)

**1** Discuss the questions.

1 What articles have you read recently, in magazines or online?

2 Can you remember any of the titles?

3 What do you think makes an article interesting?

**2** Read the task and answer the questions.

> You have seen the following announcement in an international students' magazine:
>
> ### Have YOU got a talent?
>
> Write an article about your talent – is it a physical talent (e.g. a sport) or an ability (e.g. programming or memory)? Say how you first noticed it, how it developed and how you would like to develop it in the future.
>
> Send us **your** article and see your name in print.
>
> Write your **article**.

1 Where is this article going to appear?

2 Who is going to read it?

3 What is the topic?

4 Do you think the article should be serious or chatty in tone?

**3** Read the *Prepare* box. Then read the article and choose the best title.

a Why I wanted to take up cycling

b A passion for cycling

c Tips for cycling

## Prepare to write – Writing articles

In an article:
- choose an interesting title.
- organise your ideas into paragraphs.
- include a topic sentence for each paragraph, which tells the reader what the paragraph is about.
- use a lively, chatty style.
- use interesting descriptive language.
- address the reader directly, for example by asking questions.

**4** Underline the topic sentences in paragraphs a–c. Write a topic sentence for paragraph d.

**5** Read the article again. How does the writer address the reader directly?

**6** ⬤ Look at the task in exercise 2 again. Write your article.
- Use the tips in the *Prepare* box.
- Check your grammar and spelling.
- Write 140–190 words.

**a** I'll never forget the day I got my first bike. I was five years old and I fell in love with it immediately. From then on, I used to cycle everywhere.

**b** There's nothing like the sense of freedom you get from cycling, is there? You can go where you want and at any time you want. I joined a local cycling club and soon I was training three times a week and racing against adult riders. Then, all of a sudden, I started to win. Can you imagine that feeling? It was amazing!

**c** My coaches have encouraged me to take cycling more seriously. They think I have a real talent for racing. I'm quite fit and competitive and I'm willing to put in the hours needed to do well. Now I'm training every day and I've already taken part in national competitions.

**d** .............. My dream is to wear the Team GB cycling jersey one day. I would love to represent my country in the Olympic Games. And you never know, I might just achieve it. Watch out for me on TV!

# 6 Strong emotions

## VOCABULARY  Expressing emotions

**Your profile**

Which of these emotions have you experienced recently? Why did you feel this way?
*fear  happiness  anger  worry  satisfaction*

**1** Match the questions to the pictures.

  **a** Do you go to school in the morning feeling **bright** and **cheerful**?

  **b** Are you generally an **optimistic** or **pessimistic** person?

  **c** Have you ever been **scared** while watching a film or TV show?

  **d** Have you ever felt **furious** with someone, but not said anything?

  **e** What environmental problems are you most **concerned** about?

**2** Complete the table with the **adjectives** in exercise 1.

| | |
|---|---|
| **Fear** | |
| **Anger** | |
| **Worry** | |
| **Happiness** | *bright, cheerful* |
| **Unhappiness** | |

**3** Ask and answer the questions in exercise 1.

**4** ▶1.16 **Listen to Sara, Ahmed, Emma and Dan. How are they feeling? Choose the correct words and complete the sentences.**

  1 Sara's **fed up with / anxious about** …

  2 Ahmed's **bad-tempered about / anxious about** …

  3 Emma's **relieved about / over the moon about** …

  4 Dan's getting **depressed / irritated** because …

  5 Emma's **down about / content with** not …

  6 Dan's **petrified of / fed up with** some kind of …

**5** Add the **words** in exercise 4 to the table in exercise 2. Use a dictionary to help you.

**6** Discuss when you last felt …

  • relieved about something

  • over the moon about something

  • fed up with someone

  • irritated by something

  • anxious about something

## READING

**1** Read Part A of the article, ignoring the gaps. Which fears are mentioned?

**2** ⬤ **Read Part A of the article again and decide which answer (A, B, C or D) best fits each gap.**

| | A | B | C | D |
|---|---|---|---|---|
| **0** | beginning | birth | start | origin |
| **1** | universal | complete | shared | united |
| **2** | phases | stages | times | points |
| **3** | develop | grow | expand | progress |
| **4** | unique | rare | unlikely | small |
| **5** | emerge | reveal | cause | find |
| **6** | take | have | fix | keep |
| **7** | condition | impact | hit | implication |
| **8** | up | over | into | on |

**3** Read Part B of the article. Write the correct names.

  1 Who was abandoned in a public place?

  2 Who recently had a bad experience at a friend's house?

  3 Whose parents thought their fear was normal?

  4 Who has been accepted for further education?

  5 Who almost got into trouble with the law because of their phobia?

  6 Whose phobia has made them more sociable?

**4** Match the highlighted words in the text to the meanings.

  1 having your attention taken away from something

  2 making you worried or upset

  3 very large in amount or degree

  4 stupid

  5 likely to cause death

# When fear becomes phobia . . .

 **A** Fear is something we all experience from (0) ..B.. and for good reason: without it we would find it difficult to survive. It is thought to be the earliest emotion, evolving millions of years ago.

Some fears, such as a fear of heights, are (1) ............ to almost all mammals. Other fears, like a fear of mice, are specific to humans and in this case possibly result from (2) ............ when these rodents carried deadly diseases.

As we (3) ............ older, our fears change. Under the age of seven, fears frequently include monsters or the dark. By ten, children fear events that are real – though extremely (4) ............ to happen – like murder or war. For teenagers, social fears begin to (5) ............ , such as looking foolish in front of friends.

The vast majority of us are able to (6) ............ our fears under control. However, for others a fear can get out of control and have a significant (7) ............ on their lives.

When this happens, a fear has turned (8) ............ a phobia.

**B** Psychologists recognise over 500 phobias, from Ablutophobia (fear of washing) to Zoophobia (fear of animals).

## CASE STUDY 1

### NYCTOPHOBIA

**As a child,** Jacob Elson used to be terrified of the dark. Until the age of eight, he spent most nights in his parents' room and insisted on leaving a light on. His parents never suspected a problem – after all, such fears are common among young kids. But Jacob has never got used to sleeping in the dark and is now 16. He still sleeps with a light on, which is fine, of course. However, Jacob's *nyctophobia* can occasionally make everyday life difficult.

'I was at a birthday party last week. Someone turned the lights out while the candles on the cake were being lit,' Jacob says. 'Even though I knew there was no danger, I got extremely upset.'

Jacob can't explain the reasons behind his phobia. However, many phobias result from a distressing experience in childhood.

## CASE STUDY 2

### AUTOPHOBIA

**Seventeen-year-old** Claudia Jennings believes that her *autophobia* – the fear or being alone – comes from an incident when she was ten. She and her mum were shopping in a department store. Suddenly her mum got an urgent phone call from work and became distracted. She left the shop quickly and simply forgot her daughter was with her. Obviously Claudia was in tears until her mum returned and she's suffered from autophobia ever since.

Although Claudia hasn't entirely got over her fear, she's now used to her autophobia and has several strategies she uses to cope with it. 'Reading or listening to music definitely help. Plus I deliberately make lots of friends so I'm almost always with someone.'

Both nyctophobia and autophobia are common. But other phobias are quite unusual – and, in some cases, possibly difficult to believe.

## CASE STUDY 3

### SCOLIONOPHOBIA

**Psychologist Nigel Gove** says scolionophobia has been recognised since the 1960s. Children who suffer from this will feel extreme anxiety about going to school – with symptoms such as headaches and feeling physically sick. For over three years, William Carr experienced just this. At one point, the school threatened to take William's parents to court for keeping their child at home. When his parents demonstrated that William was studying at home, the school eventually agreed to help. Now, after a period of psychological treatment, William is a typical 18 year old and is about to leave home for university.

'One of the worst things about that time was the fact that my school didn't believe me,' says William. 'They thought I was trying to get out of studying – when, in fact, I've always enjoyed learning.'

**ing points**

Why do you think some people suffer from phobias such as *scolionophobia*?

Do you think fear is a useful emotion? Why?

## GRAMMAR  *be/get used to*

**1** Read the examples and the rules. What kinds of words can follow *be/get used to*?

1 *Although Claudia hasn't entirely got over her fear, she's now* **used to her autophobia**.

2 *Jacob has never* **got used to sleeping** *in the dark*.

> **a** We use *be/get used to* to talk about how familiar something is for someone.
>
> **b** If you *are used to* something, you are familiar with it. You have experienced it often enough for it to seem normal to you and it is no longer strange.
>
> **c** If you *get used to* something, you become familiar with it.

→ Grammar reference  **page 153**

**2** Choose the correct words.

1 I feel exhausted. I*'m not / don't get* used to staying up so late.

2 At first we found it hard, but now *we're / we get* used to speaking English in class all the time.

3 I can't *be / get* used to that website now they've redesigned it. It's so confusing!

4 It took me several days to *be / get* used to the time change when we went to the US on holiday.

5 Our school starts at 7.30 so I've always *been / got* used to getting up early.

6 I'm *being / getting* used to our new teacher, but I still miss our old one.

**3** Imagine a friend from another country is coming to live in your country. What will they have to get used to? Write sentences. Use the ideas below and your own ideas.

> daily routine    food    people    TV

*You might find it difficult to get used to our sense of humour.*

**Corpus challenge**

Find and correct the mistake in the student's sentence.

*I am used to eat this kind of food.*

**4** Read the examples. Which example describes a past habit or state?

1 *She's* **used to being** *alone now*.

2 *I* **used to be** *terrified of spiders*.

**5** Complete the second sentence so that it has a similar meaning to the first sentence, using *used*. Use between two and five words.

1 In the past, I was petrified of dogs.
   I ......................................................... petrified of dogs.

2 My new school no longer feels strange to me.
   I ......................................................... my new school.

3 Josie is no longer worried about sleeping in the dark.
   Josie ............................................... in the dark now.

4 In the past, I was afraid of heights.
   I ......................................................... afraid of heights.

5 Did Mark become accustomed to the cold weather in Finland?
   Did Mark ...................... the cold weather in Finland?

## VOCABULARY  Adverbs: type and position

**1** Match the examples to the types of adverbs.

1 *Fears* **frequently** *include monsters or the dark*.

2 *He slept* **in his parents' room**.

3 *I was at a birthday party* **last week**.

4 *Jacob can't explain the reasons behind his phobia.* **However,** *many phobias …*

5 *She left the shop* **quickly**.

6 *Reading or listening to music* **definitely** *help*.

**a** adverbs of time

**b** frequency adverbs

**c** adverbs of certainty

**d** adverbs of manner

**e** adverbs of place

**f** connecting adverbs (which link to a previous sentence)

**2** Where in a sentence (beginning, middle or end) are the adverbs in exercise 1 usually used?

**3** Write the sentences with the adverbs in the correct positions. More than one answer is sometimes possible.

1 He can sing. (beautifully)

2 I have been afraid of insects. (never)

3 I'll get used to it. (probably)

4 I had an upset stomach. I had difficulty sleeping. (as a result)

5 I get anxious about homework. (from time to time)

6 I've been getting bad-tempered. (lately)

7 If we leave now, we'll be home. (by nine)

8 She left home. (a few minutes ago, definitely)

9 We have lunch. (always, at midday)

10 They were laughing. (loudly)

## LISTENING

**1** You will hear people talking in five different situations. Read the questions. Underline the key words that might help you get the correct answers.

1 You hear a <u>student</u> talking about her <u>degree</u>. What does she think about studying <u>psychology</u>?
   **A** It's more <u>enjoyable</u> than she thought it would be.
   **B** She finds the <u>research</u> <u>fascinating</u>.
   **C** It's going to be very <u>useful</u> for her <u>career</u>.

2 You overhear a conversation between two friends. Why does the boy think his parents will be annoyed?
   **A** There are a lot of passwords on his phone.
   **B** He's missed the bus.
   **C** They keep warning him about losing things.

3 You hear a girl leaving a voicemail message for her friend. Why is she calling?
   **A** to find out what a test will cover
   **B** to suggest doing some revision together
   **C** to check some dates she's not sure about

4 You overhear two friends talking about a school project. What does the teenager say about his project?
   **A** He's feeling optimistic about its progress.
   **B** He's concerned he's not going to finish it in time.
   **C** He's finding it difficult to understand the subject.

5 You hear a father talking to his daughter on the phone. How is he feeling now?
   **A** furious
   **B** concerned
   **C** relieved

**2** ▶1.17 ● **Listen. For questions 1–5, choose the best answer (A, B or C).**

**3** ▶1.17 **Listen again and check your answers.**

---

### EP Word profile *thing*

I just want to forget the whole thing.

The thing is they're always telling me not to put stuff down.

It's a good thing you told me to put that password on it.

The main thing for me is that I'm actually into what I'm studying.

page 134

---

## SPEAKING Favourite things

**1** ▶1.18 **Listen to Ahmed and Sara talking about their best and worst days of the week. Which person is more like you?**

**2** ▶1.18 **Who says these phrases? Listen again and write A (Ahmed) or S (Sara).**
   1 What normally happens is …
   2 Virtually every Monday …
   3 As a rule, I …
   4 Nine times out of ten, …
   5 with the exception of …

**3** ▶1.19 **Listen to Emma and Dan. Complete the sentences.**
   1 Two of Emma's favourite subjects are ................. .
   2 Emma gets on really well with the ................. .
   3 Dan rarely does his homework on ................. .
   4 Dan has a bit of a phobia of ................. .

**4** ▶1.19 **Read the *Prepare* box, then listen again. Which phrases do Emma and Dan use?**

### Prepare to speak — Generalising

**Generalising**
Ninety percent of the time …
What normally happens is …
Nine times out of ten, …
Generally speaking, …
On the whole, …
As a rule, …
For the most part, …
Virtually every Monday, …

**Exceptions**
One exception is …
… with the exception of …

**5** **Work in pairs. Interview each other. Use phrases from the *Prepare* box.**
   1 Which is your best/worst day of the week? Why? What normally happens on this day?
   2 Which is your best/worst time of the year? Why? What generally happens at this time?
   3 What's your favourite lesson at school? Why?
   4 Describe a typical weekend for you.

# Culture
## Colours around the world

**1** Work in pairs. Do the colour quiz and discuss your answers.

**1** When British people are angry, they say they . . . .
   a) see blue   b) see red   c) see green

**2** In Spain, many people think the colour yellow is . . . .
   a) unlucky   b) fashionable   c) depressing

**3** Green is considered a lucky colour in . . . .
   a) China   b) Malaysia   c) Ireland

**4** In European countries, purple is associated with . . . .
   a) royalty   b) money   c) health

**5** Which colour apart from red and yellow is often used for warning signs?
   a) pink   b) blue   c) orange

**6** Objects that absorb all the colours of light look . . . .
   a) black   b) grey   c) white

**7** The most popular colour around the world is . . . .
   a) green   b) brown   c) blue

**8** In English, a 'grey area' is something . . . .
   a) exciting   b) uncertain   c) frightening

**2** Read the text. Check your answers to the quiz in exercise 1.

# colour CONNECTIONS

## Cool

**BLUE** is the typical colour of clear skies and water. It's considered to be a relaxing, calm colour and it's often associated with peace. Perhaps for that reason, blue is the world's most popular colour. On the negative side, blue suggests cold temperatures, as well as low energy. In English, for example, people who are sad or depressed say they 'feel blue'.

**GREEN** is the colour of plants, so it's often associated with life and growth. In Ireland, people think it's a lucky colour and in Japan, it represents eternal life. However, green also has negative meanings in English. It's the colour of envy – 'the green-eyed monster' – and people's faces 'turn green' when they feel sick.

**PURPLE** is a fairly unusual colour in nature. Some minerals are purple and there are plants with purple flowers, but they aren't common. In Europe, purple has been the colour of royalty since ancient times, when purple dye for clothing was rare and very expensive. It was often made from a special type of shellfish.

## Warm

**RED** is the colour of blood, so it's often associated with life, energy and strong feelings. For example, many people's faces turn red when they are feeling nervous, embarrassed or excited. In English, people also say they 'see red' when they feel angry. Red objects jump out at us because they appear to be closer than they really are.

**YELLOW** is the colour of sunlight, so it's often associated with warmth and happiness. It's also the most intense colour, which means bright shades of yellow can be irritating, like too much sunlight. Yellow is unlucky in some countries, such as Spain, while in India, it's associated with wealth and business.

**ORANGE** is a combination of lively red and cheerful yellow, making it a bright colour that catches our attention. It's also the colour of healthy foods, like oranges, carrots and pumpkins. Because of its high visibility, orange is often used for warning signs and for emergency equipment, like lifejackets.

## Neutral

**BLACK** is neutral because it absorbs all the colours of light. It's associated with darkness and night, as well as mystery and the unknown. In many countries, black is a serious colour, associated with death and sadness, but also with elegance and authority.

**BROWN** is the colour of earth, wood and autumn leaves which makes it a neutral, reassuring colour. It's also the colour of many foods, such as bread, nuts and chocolate. However, many people consider brown plain and boring, especially for clothes.

**WHITE** is the colour of fresh snow, so it's often associated with cleanliness and purity. In the US, it's the typical colour of wedding dresses. However, white also suggests emptiness and in some countries, like Japan, it's linked to death and mourning.

**GREY** is the colour of foggy days, when we can't see clearly. Grey is between black and white, making it the most neutral colour. In English, the phrase 'grey area' is used to describe things that are ambiguous.

**3** Read the text in exercise 2 again. Discuss the following situations with a partner using information from the text.

1 You want to open a health-food restaurant in the UK. Which colours would you use to decorate it?

2 You are creating an advertisement for an American bank. Which colours would be best to use?

3 You want to make signs that will catch people's attention at your school. Which colours would be most effective?

4 You are decorating an expensive clothing shop. Which colours would you use?

**4** ▶1.20 **Listen to four people talking about the significance of certain colours in their country and complete the chart.**

| Interview | Country | Colour(s) | Significance/Use |
|---|---|---|---|
| 1 | | | |
| 2 | | | |
| 3 | | | |
| 4 | | | |

**5** Work with a partner. Which colours have the greatest significance in your country and why?

**6** Read the following pairs of sentences. Study the underlined colour phrase in the first sentence. Then choose the correct meaning in the second sentence.

1 Sam <u>saw red</u> when I told him. He was really *happy / angry*.

2 This is a <u>green</u> company. It's very *ecological / unsuccessful*.

3 You're looking a bit <u>blue</u>. *Have you been away? / What's wrong?*

4 The rules are there <u>in black and white</u>. They *could / couldn't* be clearer.

5 Last week, <u>out of the blue</u>, I got a call from Daniel. I was really *miserable / surprised*.

**7** Make a list of colour phrases in your own language. Write explanations in English.

**Project**

Write advice about colours for tourists who visit your country.

1 Explain any special colour associations in your culture.

2 Are there any colours that tourists should not wear?

3 Explain some important colour phrases in your language.

4 What colour phrases should tourists avoid?

# 7 Telling stories

## VOCABULARY  Verbs of movement; sounds

**Your profile**

Which genres of story do you like and dislike? Why?
*comedy    horror    murder mystery    fantasy
romance    science fiction*

**1** Match the pictures to sentences 1–6. Then write
the infinitives of the verbs.

1 She **leant** forward and **tapped** him on the shoulder.
2 The door **burst** open and Sue **bounced** in.
3 She **rushed** across the street, **shaking** with fear.
4 He was **kneeling** down when suddenly someone
**slapped** him on the back.
5 She **charged** towards the man, yelling 'STOP!'
6 The door **swung** open and Sue **wandered** in.

**2** ▶ 1.21 **Listen and decide which verb describes
the sounds the people make.**

mumble    mutter    sigh    whisper    whistle    yell

**3** Match the sentence halves.

1  She leant over and
   whispered
2  I was yelling for hours
3  He sighed
4  Jim muttered that
5  Liz and Kay mumbled
   an excuse
6  Martin began to whistle

a  when he saw mess
   in the kitchen.
b  a tune he'd heard on
   the radio.
c  about forgetting their
   homework.
d  before anyone came
   to help me.
e  something in his ear.
f  it wasn't fair!

## READING

**1** You are going to read an extract from a novel.
Look at the picture and read the extract quickly.
What genre do you think this story is?

**2** ⬤ For questions 1–5, choose the answer
(A, B, C or D) which you think best fits
according to the text. Before you choose your
answers, read the tip next to each question.

1  According to the first paragraph,
   how did Holmes behave on
   Thursday morning?
   A He calmly read the newspaper
     with Watson.
   B He was eager to get on with his
     music studies.
   C He commented positively on their
     peaceful way of life.
   D He was unable to sit still due to
     a feeling of anxiety.

   TIP: Read
   paragraph 1.
   Underline the
   words which
   give you the
   answer.

2  The word 'stroll' in line 27 means
   to move
   A noisily and aggressively.
   B quietly and secretively.
   C surprisingly quickly.
   D extremely slowly.

   TIP: Read the
   sentences
   before
   and after
   the word
   carefully to
   work out the
   answer.

3  Why does Holmes complain
   when Watson mentions the thefts
   in London?
   A because he thinks Watson has
     got the facts wrong
   B because all of these cases have
     already been solved
   C because he believes his skills
     are wasted on such crimes
   D because the weather has
     caused a big increase in theft

   TIP: Read the
   conversation
   between
   Holmes
   and Watson
   about
   criminals.

4  What does 'it' refer to in line 40?
   A a murder
   B a reason
   C a meeting
   D an appointment

   TIP:
   Underline
   words A–D
   in the text.
   Which one
   does 'it' refer
   to?

5  Holmes suggests that his brother
   Mycroft is someone who
   A uses the railway to get to work.
   B is predictable in his routine.
   C spends most of his time
     outdoors.
   D is dedicated to his family.

   TIP: Read
   this part
   of the text
   carefully to
   work out the
   answer.

# THE BRUCE-PARTINGTON PLANS

Sir Arthur Conan Doyle

It was the third week of November and a thick yellow fog <u>had settled</u> over London. From the Monday to the Thursday it <u>had</u> rarely <u>been</u> possible from our windows in Baker Street to see even the houses across the street.
5 The first three of these days Holmes had been patiently studying a subject which had been his hobby for some time – the music of the Middle Ages. But when, for the fourth time, we pushed back our chairs from breakfast and saw the heavy brown mist outside the windows,
10 my friend's impatient and active nature could no longer take this dull existence. He <u>wandered</u> restlessly around our sitting-room; he <u>bit</u> his nails; he <u>tapped</u> the furniture nervously; and he complained about the inactivity.

'Nothing of interest in the paper, Watson?' he said.

15 I realised that by anything of interest, Holmes <u>was</u> <u>asking</u> about anything of *criminal* interest. There was the news of a revolution, of a possible war and of a likely change of government. However, these were of little interest to my companion. The only criminal reports I could
20 find were very ordinary. Holmes sighed impatiently and continued to wander around the room.

'The London criminal is certainly a dull person,' he said, sounding like a hunter who can find nothing to shoot. 'Look out of this window, Watson. See how people suddenly
25 appear, are briefly seen and then quickly disappear once more into the mist. On a day like this, a thief or a murderer could **stroll** round London like a tiger in the jungle. No one would see him until he made his move.'

'There have,' I said, 'been a large number of small
30 thefts.'

Holmes muttered something rude and then turned towards me.

'My abilities demand something far more worthy than that,' he said. 'It is fortunate for this community that I am
35 not a criminal.'

'It certainly is!' I agreed enthusiastically.

'Imagine that I had a good reason to want to kill someone,' continued Holmes. 'How easy it would be on a day like this! I could suggest a meeting, I could make
40 up an appointment and **it** would all be over. It is just as well they don't have days of fog in countries where murder is common.'

There was the sound of someone knocking.

'At last!' cried Holmes. 'Here comes something to
45 bring some excitement into our lives.'

He rushed over to open the door. It was the postman with a telegram. Holmes tore it open and before long burst out laughing.

'Well, well! I don't believe it!' he said. 'My brother
50 Mycroft is coming round.'

'And so …?' I asked.

'And so …?' said Holmes. 'It is like coming across a train in the middle of the road. Mycroft has his rails, like a train, and he stays on them. His home in Pall Mall, his
55 club, his office in Whitehall – that is where you find him. Once, and only once, has he been here. What disaster can have knocked him off his rails?'

'Doesn't he explain?' I asked.

Holmes handed me his brother's telegram.

60 'Must see you about Cadogan West. Coming at once. Mycroft.'

'Cadogan West?' I said. I had heard that name.

'It means nothing to me,' said Holmes. 'But it is extraordinary that Mycroft should do something so
65 uncharacteristic. The moon might as well stop going round the earth.'

from Cambridge Experience Readers,
*Holmes: Three adventures* adapted
by Richard MacAndrew

**Word profile** *patient*

Holmes had been patient studying a subject.

My friend's impatient and active nature could no longer take this dull existence.

**Talking points**

“ What makes a good story?

Why do you think some people prefer reading novels to watching films? ”

## GRAMMAR  Narrative tenses

**1** Look at the underlined verbs in the text on page 43. What tenses are they?

**2** Complete the rules with the correct verb forms.

> past continuous    past perfect    past simple

> We use narrative verb forms in stories to describe events and actions. We use the:
> **a** ............
> - to describe the main events of a story, in the order they happened.
> - to describe a short action that interrupts a longer action in the past continuous.
>
> **b** ............
> - to describe a longer or background action around a certain time.
> - to describe a longer action interrupted by a short action in the past simple.
>
> **c** ............
> - to describe a completed action that happened before another time in the past.
> - with sequencing expressions (*when*, *after*, *by the time*, *as soon as*) when one event happened before another event.

→ Grammar reference  **page 154**

**3** Read six sentences from later in the story about Sherlock Holmes. Choose the correct verb forms.

1 He *travelled / was travelling* back to Woolwich when he was killed and thrown out of the train.
2 Mycroft Holmes took off his overcoat and *sat / had sat* down heavily in an armchair.
3 At nine o'clock we *were all sitting / had all sat* in the study, waiting patiently for our man.
4 We *have just reached / had just reached* the dark shadows at the back of the house when we heard footsteps.
5 We were walking past his office when suddenly he *rushed / was rushing* off into the fog.
6 Lestrade and Mycroft met us outside Gloucester Road Station in the morning. We *left / had left* the back door of Oberstein's house open the night before.

**4** Read another sentence from later in the story, and notice the verb form. Complete the rules.

*Inspector Lestrade suddenly spoke. He **had been listening** to the conversation with some impatience.*

> **a** We use the past perfect continuous instead of the past perfect when we want to talk about a longer action that continued until another past action.
> **b** We form the past perfect continuous with ............ + ............ + *-ing*.

**5** Complete the sentences with the past perfect or past perfect continuous form of the verbs.

> call    cry    leave    play    rush    yell

1 The man ............ for almost an hour before anyone heard him.
2 By the time the game ended, we ............ for over three hours.
3 I could tell from her eyes that she ............ .
4 Sabrina was exhausted. She ............ around all morning.
5 The noises outside stopped a few minutes after we ............ the police.
6 I couldn't get into the concert because I ............ my ticket at home.

### ⊘ Corpus challenge

**Find and correct the mistake in the student's sentence.**

It is amazing to think all this had happened less than 30 years ago.

## VOCABULARY  Time phrases

**1** Complete the sentences with the words in the box.

> before    before    for    for    in    on

1 I only joined the school in March, but I made lots of new friends ............ **no time**.
2 He was disappointed not to do better because he'd been studying ............ **weeks on end**.
3 Holmes tore open the envelope and ............ **long**, he burst out laughing.
4 I smiled and waved to Bob because I hadn't seen him ............ **some time**.
5 I used to catch the bus to school, but **the week** ............ **last**, I got an amazing bike.
6 We waited there for hours ............ **end**.

**2** Complete the sentences about you. Compare your answers with a partner.

1 The year before last I …
2 I haven't ............ for some time.
3 Before long, I'd like to learn how to …
4 I often ............ for hours on end.
5 I could learn to ............ in no time.

## WRITING A story

**1** Read the task and look at the picture. What do you think will happen in the story?

> You have seen this announcement on your school website.
>
> ### Stories wanted
>
> We are looking for stories for our website. Your story **must** begin with this sentence:
> *Oliver wished he hadn't offered to look after Zoey while his cousin was on holiday.*
>
> Your story must include:
> bad weather
> a search
>
> Write your **story**.

**2** Read the story. Does it contain any of your ideas? Does the story include the ideas mentioned in the task?

**a** Oliver wished he hadn't offered to look after Zoey while his cousin was on holiday. It had been raining heavily all day, but the dog needed some exercise. Oliver sighed and gently stroked the animal's head.

**b** ¹............, the front door of the house burst open. Oliver's brother ran in and ran straight upstairs. Before Oliver could move, Zoey had disappeared out of the open front door. "Joe!" Oliver shouted. "Zoey's escaped!" In no time the brothers were chasing after her. She was heading towards the park. Oliver whistled loudly, but the dog ignored him. ²............, Zoey reached the park and disappeared.

**c** The brothers spent hours searching for the dog without success. When they finally got on the bus to go home, they were shaking with cold. ³............. ten minutes, Joe spoke. "Look. We're going past Sally's," he said. Oliver looked over at his cousin's house. Through the pouring rain, he could just see a dog on the doorstep. It was Zoey!

**d** ⁴............ that evening their cousin called and asked about her dog.
"Zoey's been fine," said Oliver happily.
"We took her out for a really long walk today!"

**3** Read the *Prepare* box, then read the story again. Match paragraphs a–d to the functions in the box.

> ending    background information
> opening events    developing story

### Prepare to write Stories

A good story should:
- include all the ideas mentioned in the task.
- be organised into paragraphs and have a clear beginning, middle and end.
- use suitable time expressions and different tenses to make it clear when actions happened in relation to other actions.
- use a range of vocabulary to make the story interesting or exciting.

**4** Complete the story with the time expressions.

> After    Before long    Just then    Later

**5** Explain why the writer uses these verb forms in the story.

> had been raining    had disappeared
> were shaking

**6** Replace the highlighted words in the story with the words in the box.

> cheerfully    glanced    make out    rushed
> vanished    yelled

**7** Read the task. Discuss what might happen in the story.

> You have seen this advertisement in a magazine.
>
> ### Stories wanted
>
> We are looking for stories for our magazine. Your story must begin with this sentence:
> *Hannah rushed over to Dan's house as soon as she heard the news.*
>
> Your story must include:
> a meal
> an accident
>
> Write your **story**.

**8** ● Write your story.
- Use the tips in the *Prepare* box.
- Check your grammar and spelling.
- Write 140–190 words.

## VOCABULARY  Community

**Your profile**

What do you like about the place where you live?
What would you like to change?

**1** Match the sentence halves. Are the adjectives used for people, places or both?

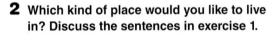

### where would you like to live?

**When I leave home, I'd like to live …**

1 somewhere quiet with a **relaxed**
2 somewhere busy and **urban**, with
3 in a place that's **remote** and **rural**,
4 in a community which is
5 somewhere friendly, with a **close**
6 near an **industrial**
7 in a city that's culturally **diverse**,

a in the middle of nowhere.
b **welcoming** and easygoing.
c atmosphere, like a **residential** suburb.
d estate or in an **inner city** neighbourhood.
e masses of entertainment and leisure facilities.
f with shops and restaurants from around the world.
g community, where everyone knows everyone else.

**2** Which kind of place would you like to live in? Discuss the sentences in exercise 1.

**3** ▶ 1.22  Listen to John, a British student, asking for advice about a place to study. Answer the questions.

1 What is he going to do next year? Where?
2 Which adjectives from exercise 1 describe his parents' town?
3 Which adjectives describe Bristol?
4 Which adjectives describe the kind of place where he'd like to study?

## READING

**1** Read five recommendations for John of places to study. Match two of them to the photos on page 47.

**2** Read the example question (0) in exercise 3. Follow the instructions.

1 Look at the underlined key words.
2 Find paragraphs that mention anything related to the underlined words.
3 Read these paragraphs and read the question again carefully. Then choose the correct answer.

**3** 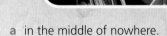 Read the recommendations again. For questions 1–10, choose from the people (A–E). The people may be chosen more than once.

**Which person**

0 recommends <u>studying</u> the local <u>language</u>?
1 recommends a winter sport?
2 complains about public transport?
3 mentions the quality of education?
4 mentions a family connection to the city?
5 describes some modern architecture?
6 mentions food from around the world?
7 says the city offers varied forms of musical entertainment?
8 recommends visiting some places of historical interest near the city?
9 says the students all get on well with each other?
10 describes a university set in a natural environment within a city?

**4** Find words or phrases in the recommendations with the following meanings:

1 university buildings and the land that surrounds them (A)
2 in, from or to other countries (C)
3 the outer area of a city or town (C)
4 place (C)
5 the way that you live (C)
6 the size or level of something (E)

## A DORUK – ISTANBUL

How about Turkey? I'm about to start at Koç University, 30 km from Istanbul city centre. It has a reputation for excellent teaching and international students are welcome. It would make a big difference if you learned some Turkish before coming, but don't worry about the classes – all of the university's undergraduate degrees are taught in English. When I visited, the campus seemed quite a close community and it's set in woods, so it feels as if you're in the middle of nowhere even though the city isn't far away. Istanbul itself is exciting because it's where the East meets the West and the old part of the city is a United Nations World Heritage Site.

## B NATALIA – BARCELONA

It sounds as if you'd love Barcelona. The main university dates from the 1450s and there's a huge student population in the city, making it very culturally diverse. The inner city neighbourhoods are full of fascinating old buildings and squares with cool cafés. The city isn't all old, though. There are Gaudí's crazy, nature-inspired houses in the suburbs and incredible contemporary buildings like The Forum on the outskirts. La Rambla is always busy with people walking up and down looking at the stalls, but my favourite spot is Parc Güell, on a hillside behind the city. There's always a performance or something going on. I go up there all the time – I think I'll go again this weekend, but the bus leaves at six in the morning!

## C SIMON – SYDNEY

It would make sense to go to an Australian university – they really cater for overseas students. I'm at Macquarie University and I love it. The campus is in the suburbs, surrounded by parkland, so it actually feels as if it's quite rural. There's a relaxed atmosphere and for me the only drawback is the location. I live 25 km away and my bus leaves once an hour, so if I miss it, I'm in trouble! There isn't much to do near the university, so most students meet up in Surry Hills. The city has a fantastic outdoors lifestyle and at the weekends you can check out the city's world-famous beaches. Sydney is wonderful – no wonder everyone here is so optimistic.

## D MARCO – MILAN

You should consider Milan. Lots of places offer undergraduate degrees in architecture, often in English. I don't live there, but I know Milan quite well because we visit relatives there every New Year. It's a lively university city, so you'll have a great social life. It's a major cultural centre too with everything from theatre and opera to festivals and pop concerts. After you've spent a few weeks there, you'll never want to leave. I've already decided I'm going to live there when I'm older. Milan is the centre of the Italian fashion industry, so it's great for window-shopping. You may find yourself sitting next to some very stylish classmates, but don't be put off – underneath, people are welcoming and down-to-earth.

## E CRISTINA – MÉXICO, D.F.

I study geography at the Tecnológico de Monterrey university, where all the classes are in English rather than Spanish. A friend on the architecture course says it's fascinating. Mexico City is a massive urban centre with millions of things to do – you'll certainly never be bored. There are restaurants from every continent and lots of surprises – you should definitely make use of the ski slopes on Popocatépetl, the nearby volcanic mountain. At the weekends, you can easily make your way out to the Aztec pyramids in the ancient city of Teotihuacan. If you're into archaeology, you'll definitely be impressed by the scale of the ruins. I'm a real fan and I'm going again next weekend.

### EP Word profile *make*

You should definitely make use of the ski slopes.

It would make sense to go to an Australian university.

You can easily make your way out to the Aztec pyramids.

page 134

### Talking points

" What makes a successful community?
What can young people gain from studying abroad? "

## GRAMMAR  Future (1): Review

**1** Read the examples then complete the rules with the correct verb forms.

1 *I'm about to start at Koç University …*

2 *It's a lively city, so you'll have a great social life.*

3 *I've already decided I'm going to live there when I'm older.*

4 *You may find yourself sitting next to some very stylish classmates.*

5 *I go up there all the time – I think I'll go again this weekend.*

6 *The bus leaves at six in the morning.*

7 *I'm a real fan and I'm going again next week.*

---

be about to     be going to     may
~~present continuous~~     present simple     will (x2)

---

We use:

a the ....*present continuous*.... for plans and arrangements.

b the ................. for regular, timetabled events.

c ................. for decisions you've just made.

d ................. for plans and intentions.

e *be going to* and ........... to make predictions.

f ................. / *might* / *could* for things that are possible in the future.

g ................. for events that are going to happen very soon.

---

→ Grammar reference **page 155**

**2** Read the examples and complete the rules. Do you use the same verb forms in your language?

1 *After you've spent a few weeks there, you'll never want to leave.*

2 *I'm going to live there when I'm older.*

---

After time conjunctions (e.g. *when*, *after*), we use the ........... simple or ........... perfect to talk about the future.

---

**3** Read the texts and choose the correct verb forms.

We've been talking about what we ¹ *do* / *'re going to do* after we ² *will leave* / *leave* school. I ³ *won't start* / *'m not going to start* university immediately because I've decided to have a year out, but I ⁴ *'ll definitely do* / *'m definitely going to do* a course the year after. I haven't chosen a subject yet. I'm fascinated by human behaviour, so I ⁵ *'m studying* / *might study* anthropology or social sciences, I'm not sure yet. I ⁶ *'m talking* / *'m about to talk* to a careers adviser. After I ⁷ *will talk* / *have talked* to her, I'll have a clearer idea.

I ⁸ *'ll meet* / *'m meeting* a friend at one o'clock. I can't get the next fast train because it ⁹ *doesn't leave* / *won't leave* until 12.30. I think I ¹⁰ *'m catching* / *'ll catch* the 11:45 even though the train stops at all the stations in the suburbs.

**4** Complete the sentences about you.

1 When I'm older …

2 This weekend I …

3 I … university.

4 After I've done my homework, I …

5 I'm about to …

---

---

## VOCABULARY  as if / as though

**1** Read the examples and choose the correct meaning for each sentence.

1 *It feels **as if** / **as though** it's going to rain.*

   a It's definitely going to rain.

   b I think it's going to rain.

2 *It sounds **as if** / **as though** we won't have enough money.*

   a I don't think we will have enough money.

   b We may have enough money.

3 *He was behaving **as if** / **as though** he'd received some bad news.*

   a He may have received some bad news.

   b He might receive some bad news.

4 *It looks **as if** / **as though** the train's going to be late.*

   a The train will probably be late.

   b The train might not be late.

**2** Make sentences about the people in the picture. Use *look* + *as if* / *as though*.

---

buy a paper     cross the road     get some crisps
like keeping fit     need a new umbrella
~~see something annoying~~     shout to a friend
walk into the bin

---

1 *She looks as though she has seen something annoying.*

## LISTENING

**1** You will hear a teenager called Andy Wood talking about a new skate park.
Read the sentences and predict what you might hear.

**A new skate park**

Andy says that the leader of the action group, Martin Ashton, is a (1) ............ who works locally.

Martin was able to help the group to apply for a (2) ............ .

Andy (3) ............ in order to raise money for the skate park.

After six months, the group had raised a total of (4) ............ .

A local resident called John Richardson worked on the (5) ............ stage of the project.

Andy mentions that the (6) ............ were the most impressive thing on Xcite's website.

At the community meeting, a (7) ............ took place to decide whether Xcite would design the skate park.

Andy says that (8) ............ is the main material used in the 'whale tail' for BMX riders.

When Ricky visited Andy's town from California, he brought some (9) ............ .

The skate park was built on land that was previously owned by (10) ............ in the town.

**2** ▶1.23 ● Listen. For questions 1–10, complete the sentences with a word or short phrase.

**3** ▶1.23 Compare your answers in pairs. Then listen again to check your answers.

## SPEAKING Comparing photographs

**1** You are going to compare two photographs. Look at the photographs. Then read points 1–3 and make notes. Think about:

1 similarities and differences between the two photographs
2 advantages and disadvantages of living in each village
3 how your home town differs from these villages

**2** ▶1.24 Listen to Ana and Ivan comparing the photographs in an exam. Answer the questions.

1 How many similarities and differences between the photographs does Ana mention?
2 How many comparisons does Ivan make between St Petersburg and the villages in the photographs?
3 How many of your ideas do they mention?

**3** ▶1.25 Read the *Prepare* box. Then listen to Ana and Ivan using the phrases.

**4** ● Compare the two photographs. Say what would be the advantages and disadvantages of living in each village. Use phrases from the *Prepare* box.

**5** Turn to page 130 and complete the task.

**Prepare to speak—Comparing and contrasting**

The main difference is …
Both of these places are …
Neither place looks as though …
It looks …, whereas the other village is …
While the village in the top photograph has …, the village in the second photograph has …
On the other hand, I assume that …

# Literature
## Poetry

**1** Read the text and four poems from the *Poetry in Motion* programme. Which poem do you like the most?

## *Poetry in Motion*

Trains and subways aren't places where people would typically learn about poetry, unless they live in New York City, of course. For several years, the Metropolitan Transportation Authority (MTA) has been running a cultural programme called *Poetry in Motion*. Every year, selected poems are displayed on posters in the city's train and subway systems, so passengers can read them while they travel. The programme has been very successful, and there has also been a similar programme called *Train of Thought*, with quotes from novels and other kinds of literature.

## A LEAF

A leaf, one of the last, parts from a maple branch: it is spinning in the transparent air of October, falls on a heap of others, stops, fades. No one admired its entrancing struggle with the wind, followed its flight, no one will distinguish it now as it lies among the other leaves, no one saw what I did. I am the only one.
*Bronislaw Maj (1953– )*

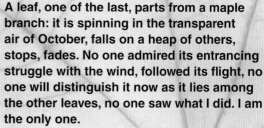

## Fireflies in the garden

Here come real stars to fill the upper skies,
And here on earth come emulating flies
That, though they never equal stars in size
(And they were never really stars at heart)
Achieve at times a very star-like start.
Only, of course, they can't sustain the part.
*Robert Frost (1874–1963)*

## GRAND CENTRAL

The city orbits around eight million
centers of the universe
and turns around the golden clock
at the still point of this place.
Lift up your eyes from the moving hive
and you will see time circling
under a vault of stars and know
Just when and where you are.

*Billy Collins (1941– )*

## Communication

I am talking to you about poetry
and you say
when do we eat.
The worst of it is
I'm hungry too.
*Alicia Partnoy (1955– )*

### Glossary

**hive** the place where bees live
**vault** a high, rounded ceiling
**emulating** trying to be similar
**sustain** continue, keep doing
**fades** loses colour and disappears
**entrancing** lovely or charming

**2** ▶ 1.26 **Listen to a student talking about the poem** *Grand Central*. **Then answer the questions.**

1  What is Grand Central? Where is it?
2  What are the 'eight million centers of the universe'?
3  Where is the golden clock located?
4  What does the phrase 'moving hive' describe?
5  Where is the 'vault of stars' in Grand Central?
6  What does the last line of the poem mean?

**3** **Work in groups. Choose one poem and discuss the following questions.**

*A leaf*
1  Find five verbs in the first sentence of the poem. Why are they important?
2  Why does the writer repeat 'no one' three times?
3  Why did Maj put the last three words on a new line?

*Fireflies in the garden*
4  Why do you think Frost compares fireflies to stars?
5  How does he say that fireflies are different from stars?
6  What does Frost mean by the phrase 'at heart'?

*Communication*
7  Why do you think the poem is called *Communication*?
8  What do you think Partnoy is hungry for?
9  Why do you think Partnoy uses five short lines for the poem?

**4** **Read the text about very short poems. What are 'shards'?**

**5** **Write your own haiku about the photo below. Use the correct number of syllables in each line. Don't forget to include a seasonal or natural reference.**

Line 1 ........................................................................
Line 2 ........................................................................
Line 3 ........................................................................

**6** **Share your haiku with the class. Then vote for the best haiku in different categories, such as:**

- the most beautiful
- the funniest
- the most unusual

# Very short poems

Some poems, like *Communication* on page 50, express a lot of ideas in just a few lines. In fact, some are even shorter, such as this poem by Vera Pavlova:

> **If there is something to desire**
> I broke your heart.
> Now barefoot I tread
> on shards.

In this very short poem, Pavlova transmits several ideas. She says that she has broken someone's heart and that she treads – or walks – on shards, which are usually pieces of broken glass. However, in this poem, the shards could be the pieces of someone's heart. When the writer says that she is walking barefoot on the shards, without any shoes, she suggests that she is also in pain about the situation.

Short, powerful poems are very typical in Japanese literature. They are called *haiku*, and they commonly have three lines. There are usually five syllables in the first and third lines, but seven syllables in the second line. There is also a break in the middle of the poem, often shown with a full stop or a comma.

> reference to nature
> Summer sun shining —— 5 syllables
> On my shoulders as I swim. —— 7 syllables
> Wet and cool they burn. —— 5 syllables

Traditional haiku include references to the seasons and the natural world, but modern poets may decide to break this rule. Many people now write haiku in other languages as well.

**Project**

Find a poem that you would like to share with your class. Print the poem, or copy it onto a piece of paper, and add a suitable photo or drawing.

Write a description of the poem using the questions below.

1  What does the poem seem to be about?
2  What message is the writer trying to get across?
3  What do you know about the poet who wrote it?
4  What do you like about this poem?

# Review 2
## Units 5-8

## VOCABULARY

**1 Match the words to the meanings.**

> ancestor   decade   inhabitant
> kingdom   myth   tribe

1 a group of people who have a traditional way of life
2 a period of ten years
3 someone who lives in a particular place
4 an ancient story that may explain an event in history
5 a country that is ruled by a royal family
6 a relative who lived a long time ago

**2 Complete the sentences by adding an adverb from the box in the correct place.**

> constantly   eventually   quickly

1 They can't understand him when he speaks.
2 He's so careless! He's breaking things.
3 He got round to apologising to me ten days later.

> alternatively   outside   definitely

4 She's been ill for weeks now, so she needs to see a doctor.
5 It's lovely and sunny – why don't we have lunch?
6 You may use the computers in the library. You can use the laptops in room 23.

**3 Match the sentence halves.**

1 I don't get anxious     a of heights.
2 I'm so fed up            b with this awful weather!
3 I'm petrified            c about exam results.

4 He's furious            d with second best.
5 I was a bit irritated   e about what you said.
6 I'm never content       f by all their questions.

**4 Complete the conversation with suitable adjectives.**

**Adrian:** Has your family always lived in Moscow?
**Anna:** No. In fact, my grandparents grew up in a really ⁰ r..*emote*.. area – Altai.
**Adrian:** That's in the middle of nowhere!
**Anna:** Yes, but they loved it. The ¹ r........... way of life at that time was much more ² r........... than the motorways and ³ i........... estates of modern ⁴ u........... life. It's a beautiful area and their village was a ⁵ c........... community where everyone knew everyone else. The people were much more friendly and ⁶ w........... than in a city.

## 5 Complete the text using the past simple or past continuous forms of the verbs.

> kneel   lean   rush   stroll   tap
> whisper   whistle   yell

Detective Inspector Digby waited on the bridge in silence. Soon, she could see someone through the darkness. The man ¹ ........... along the road – it certainly didn't look as if he was in a hurry. Inspector Digby put her hand on the side of the bridge and ² ........... forward slightly to get a better view, but the figure was too far away to recognise. He ³ ........... a tune and suddenly the detective was sure he was the man they were looking for. 'It's him,' she ⁴ ........... quietly into her police radio. As the figure walked past, D.I. Digby ⁵ ........... out of the shadows and grabbed hold of the man's shoulder. 'Argh!' he ⁶ ........... with surprise, and dropped his bag. A dozen mobile phones fell out of the bag, all over the pavement. While the man ⁷ ........... on the ground trying to pick them up, someone ⁸ ........... D.I. Digby gently on the shoulder.

## GRAMMAR

**6 Complete the sentences using the correct forms for present and past habits.**

1 When I was younger I ........... into trouble. (constantly / get)
2 We ........... in the sea every day as children. (swim)
3 You ........... reasons not to visit these days! (always / find)
4 I'm lucky because I ........... my friends most weekends. (see)
5 Nowadays, he ........... at 6:45, even at weekends. (get up)
6 My cousin and I ........... games for hours when we were children. (play)

**7** Complete the sentences with the correct future forms.

1 Once you ............ (finish) your exams, you'll be able to relax.

2 'Have you chosen a university course yet?' 'Yes, I ............ (study) Italian.'

3 The bus ............ (leave) in 20 minutes.

4 I'd like to own a car when I ............ (be) older.

5 Jed's still here, but he ............ (leave), so you'll have to be quick if you want to talk to him.

6 I'm stuck in traffic, so I ............ (arrive) a bit late. I'm not sure what time yet.

7 The food all looks lovely. I think I ............ (have) a piece of that cake.

8 I ............ (meet) Jen on Saturday morning. Why don't you come too?

**8** Complete the sentences with the correct form of *be/get used to.*

1 I had never driven a car before, but I ............ it quite quickly once I started.

2 I ............ washing up. I do it all the time.

3 The course was hard because I ............ studying for eight hours a day.

4 When we were living in Madrid, I ............ watching films in Spanish.

**9** Complete the text with the correct narrative tenses.

Karen Miller [1] ............ (enjoy) the sunshine on the front steps of the house when the post arrived. Along with the usual adverts and bills for her landlord, there [2] ............ (be) a letter in a plain brown envelope. The sender [3] ............ (type) her name and address on it in capital letters, but there were no stamps or postmarks. The envelope [4] ............ (look) a bit dirty, as if someone [5] ............ (step) on it by accident. Karen [6] ............ (open) the envelope and [7] ............ (take) out a photograph. Her face went white as soon as she saw it. It was of her, taken while she [8] ............ (study) law in Paris 15 years previously. Karen had a completely different job now. She [9] ............ (work) in Bristol on a temporary contract and no one [10] ............ (know) she was in the city, not even her family. 'Who [11] ............ (send) this letter?' she wondered. 'And how [12] ............ (they / find) me?'

**10** Tick the two sentences without mistakes. Correct the mistakes in the other sentences.

1 Every night we were going to the cinema and it was fantastic.

2 My mother told me that the old lady who was telling us stories died.

3 Also, I will be more independent from my parents, who are used to taking me everywhere.

4 I've been disappointed many times in my life, so I have used it.

5 Laura and her five friends were playing in the forest for three hours and Laura had said she didn't want to continue.

6 He saw a woman he never met before.

7 I think that we're going to have a wonderful weekend.

8 Try to read a book and you are going to see the difference.

**11** Read the text below and decide which answer (A, B, C or D) best fits each gap. There is an example at the beginning (0).

Amanda Wright, aged 17, has surprised everyone she knows by writing for weeks on (**0**) ....C.... to produce a full-length science-fiction novel. She frequently worked right through the night to complete the 375-page story, *Parallel Decades*.

Amanda's teachers and family began to get (**1**) ............ about her when she stopped being her usual cheerful self. She was (**2**) ............ falling asleep during classes and she would wander around (**3**) ............ quietly to herself about imaginary characters and faraway civilisations. No one had a clue what was going on, until a teacher asked her to talk about the most important thing she'd (**4**) ............ in her life. 'I've written a novel,' she said. The class fell silent with astonishment. Back at home, her parents were immensely proud as soon as they found out. When it (**5**) ............ out that this was the reason for her moods, they (**6**) ............ with relief. Finally, Amanda's odd behaviour made (**7**) ............ .

Will there be more? 'Yes, I'll write another, but I won't (**8**) ............ up every night writing it,' she promises.

| 0 | **A** time | **B** weeks | **C** end | **D** finish |
|---|---|---|---|---|
| 1 | **A** optimistic | **B** concerned | **C** furious | **D** irritated |
| 2 | **A** absolutely | **B** readily | **C** rarely | **D** constantly |
| 3 | **A** muttering | **B** whistling | **C** yelling | **D** shaking |
| 4 | **A** made | **B** been | **C** achieved | **D** compared |
| 5 | **A** went | **B** worked | **C** made | **D** turned |
| 6 | **A** sighed | **B** charged | **C** bounced | **D** mumbled |
| 7 | **A** impression | **B** use | **C** sense | **D** understanding |
| 8 | **A** back | **B** give | **C** wake | **D** stay |

## VOCABULARY Collocations

**1** Complete the quiz with the verbs in the box.

| achieve | go | have (x2) | looks | make (x2) |
|---|---|---|---|---|
| making | put | see | take | |

**Your profile**

Do you feel positive or negative about the future? Are you generally optimistic or pessimistic?

### Optimistic? Pessimistic? Realistic?

Are you an optimist, pessimist or realist? Read the statements and decide on your scores from 1 (= strongly disagree) to 5 (= strongly agree).

**1** I'm good at ........... **the best of** a bad situation.

**2** I think the future of mankind ........... **bright**. For instance, one day, science will ........... **an end to** major diseases.

**3** I'm always willing to ........... **a go** at something new. I always ........... **opportunities** that come my way and I ........... **the most of** them.

**4** I rarely consider myself to be at fault when things ........... **wrong**.

**5** I ........... more **strengths** than **weaknesses**.

**6** I'd really like to ........... **a difference** to the world and I believe that I can achieve this.

**7** I expect I will ........... all my **goals** in life.

**8** I often ........... **the best** in people, rather than **the worst**.

OPTIMISM

REALISM

PESSIMISM

**2** Match the verbs and **phrases** in exercise 1 to the meanings.

a make something stop happening *put an end to*
b attempt to do something
c try to be positive about a bad situation
d improve a situation
e appreciate the best/worst qualities
f be full of hope
g succeed in your aims
h use an occasion to do or say something
i have good/bad qualities
j develop problems
k take full advantage of something because it may not last long

**3** ▶ 2.02 Listen to the conversation. Write Dan's scores for each quiz question.

**4** Read the quiz again and decide on your scores. Work in pairs and give reasons for your answers.

**5** Add up your scores for each question, then turn to page 130. What does the quiz say about Dan and you / your partner? Do you agree?

## READING

**1** Read the text quickly and answer the questions.

1 What are the messages about?
2 Which people are optimistic/pessimistic?
3 Which person is writing about someone else?

**2** Read the text again. Write the correct names: **Ruby, Glen, Hannah, Adam. Who …**

1 is concerned about the future but it doesn't make them unhappy?
2 knows someone who is good at staying positive?
3 has made a difference to their life by taking new opportunities?
4 can't see themselves changing their feelings about the future?

**3** Answer the questions.

1 What did Ruby do to change the way she thought about her future?
2 What problems does Glen think he will have in the future?
3 What does Hannah do to help her stay optimistic?
4 What does Adam's dad try to avoid?

**4** In pairs, discuss who you would give the prize to. Give reasons. Then vote as a class.

# Your future looks bright
## ... or does it?

A few weeks back on this forum, someone posted these two pictures showing very different visions of the future (see right and bottom). So far over 12,000 of you have pressed the 'like' button.

What do *you* think the future will be like? Will the world really have become polluted and miserable? Or do you believe the optimistic picture is right?

We'd like to hear your feelings on *your* future and whether you're optimistic about it so we're running a competition.

As a bit of encouragement, we've managed to get hold of a special prize for the best entry. We aren't going to tell you what it is yet, but let's just say, if your future looks *too* bright, you'll appreciate a pair of these!

**How we used to think of the future**

03-March 12.46 pm   #1

**Rubyred**
Name: Ruby

I used to think my future looked really unsure. I've never been particularly good at school and I often failed exams. I started to feel that nothing would ever go right for me and that I'd never get anywhere in life. However, last year I made a serious effort to change this. Talking to my teachers and friends was really effective and I even read a book for practical advice. Some of the advice included developing lots of interests. So I've taken up the guitar and formed a group with a few friends. By next month, I'll have been learning Spanish for a year – and have an exam I'm actually looking forward to! Then in August, I'll be going to Spain to do some volunteering at a farm, so my Spanish will be really valuable. Things are looking up!

03-March 2.13 pm   #2

**Ziggs**
Name: Glen

No matter how hard I try, I just can't imagine a future that's happier than now. I have very few responsibilities at the moment. In a few years, I'll be at university. And looking at my brother, I get the impression that university is a lot tougher than school. What's more, he's had to borrow a fortune to go there! I can't see it getting any cheaper. So in five years, I'll be working – assuming I can find a job! I'll have taken out a few loans by then too, which means I'll be back living at home for a while. I hope that by my late twenties, I'll have moved out of my parents' house. But at the moment I'm concentrating on making the most of being young!

03-March 2.56 pm   #3

**Musicfan**
Name: Hannah

I've always been an optimistic person and I probably always will be. I genuinely look forward to each day when I wake up. Something that helps me is knowing what I enjoy in life. Everyone needs a passion – mine is surfing. As long as I get to do that regularly, I can deal with most things. Whenever I'm down about something, I just think: I'll be standing on a surfboard at the weekend and I'll have forgotten all about this by then. And if that doesn't work, I distract myself with my favourite music or a good comedy show. It's difficult to feel fed up when you're laughing.

03-March 4.12 pm   #4

**Citizen**
Name: Adam

My dad must hold the world record for being optimistic. He's constantly cheerful about life. He's always saying that the way to avoid pessimistic thoughts is to get rid of the negative things in your life. The news, for example, gets him down so he doesn't watch it. And the same applies to people and friendships. Whenever I mention how someone's negative attitude is getting on my nerves, he has this saying he always uses : 'If you want to fly with the eagles, stop hanging out with the ducks!'

**EP Word profile** *hold*

My dad must **hold** the world record for being optimistic.

We've managed to **get hold of** a special prize.

**Hold on!** That's not true!

page 135

**Talking points**

> Do you think in general it's better to be pessimistic, realistic or optimistic?

**How we think of the future now**

Being positive   55

## GRAMMAR   Future (2): Continuous and perfect

**1** Read the examples. How do we form the future continuous, future perfect and future perfect continuous?

1 *In August, I'll be going to Spain to do some volunteering.*
2 *In five years, I'll be working.*
3 *By my late twenties, I'll have moved out of my parents' house.*
4 *By next month, I'll have been learning Spanish for a year.*

**2** Complete the rules with *continuous, perfect* or *perfect continuous*.

> We use the:
> **a** future ........... for an action that will be in progress in the future or an action that is planned for the future.
> **b** future ........... for an action that will be complete at a future time.
> **c** future ........... to say how long an action has been in progress at a future time.

→ Grammar reference **page 156**

**3** Complete the predictions about life in 50 years using the future continuous or future perfect. Which predictions do you agree with?

> 1 Technology ........... (put) an end to our energy problems and mankind ........... (generate) most of its electricity from the sun.

> 2 We still ........... (not find) life on other planets by then, but some of us ........... (live) on them.

> 3 I definitely ........... (not work) because I ........... (earn) enough money to retire!

> 4 People ........... regularly ........... (live) until they are over 150, as scientists ........... (discover) a cure for all known diseases.

**4** Write sentences about your future in three years. Use the ideas below and your own ideas. Use the future continuous, future perfect or future perfect continuous.

1 study at university – Yes/No?
2 travel abroad without your parents – Yes/No?
3 learn English – How long?
4 live with your parents – Yes/No?
5 learn to drive – Yes/No?
6 do an interesting job – Yes/No?

### Corpus challenge

Find and correct the mistake in the student's sentence.

I would like to go on holiday in July because I don't know if I will work or not in September.

## VOCABULARY   Adjective and noun suffixes

**1** We use suffixes to form adjectives and nouns. Complete the examples. Then check your answers in the text on page 55.

1 *value* (noun) ⟶ ........... (adjective)
2 *effect* (noun) ⟶ ........... (adjective)
3 *practice* (noun) ⟶ ........... (adjective)
4 *compete* (verb) ⟶ ........... (noun)
5 *encourage* (verb) ⟶ ........... (noun)
6 *responsible* (adjective) ⟶ ........... (noun)
7 *friend* (noun) ⟶ ........... (noun)

**2** Read the text and decide which kinds of words are needed in each gap. How do you know?

### Happiness and health

Scientists have often linked (0) ...*emotional*... problems, such as depression, to illness, but, until recently, there has been little research into how happiness can be (1) ........... to your health. However, a recent study has shown a close (2) ........... between both. Conversely, a lack of (3) ........... of daily activities and a pessimistic (4) ........... are closely associated with illness. The link between happiness and health is good news for teenagers, as a second report has found that 16 to 17-year-olds express higher levels of (5) ........... with their lives than any other age group.
Furthermore, the (6) ........... of teenagers also say they are optimistic about the future. It seems that the happiest and healthiest of us all are Dutch teenagers.
Despite being among the least (7) ........... of the teenagers studied, watching too much television and doing too little exercise, a (8) ........... 95% of them said they were content with their lives.

| EMOTION |
| BENEFIT |
| RELATION |
| ENJOY |
| PERSONAL |
| SATISFY |
| MAJOR |
| ACT |
| REMARK |

**3** Complete the text in exercise 2. Use the word given in capitals to form a word that fits in each gap.

# WRITING  An essay (2)

**1**  **Look at the two photos. Discuss the questions.**

  1  When do you think these pictures were taken?

  2  How are the lives of the young people in each photo different?

**2**  **Read the task. Add more information and your own idea to the notes.**

**Life is better for young people now than it was 50 years ago. Do you agree?**

**Notes**

Write about:

1  friendships and family — *easier to stay in touch now*

2  hobbies

3  ................. (your own idea)

**3**  **Read the essay and answer the questions.**

  1  Did the writer mention any of your ideas from exercise 2?

  2  What subjects other than friendships and families or hobbies did the writer mention?

It is common to hear adults talk about how things were different when they were young. Some believe life has improved dramatically for young people, whereas others feel life was simpler in their day.

On the one hand, life was more straightforward half a century ago. While young people today are obsessed with their computers and phones, these things didn't exist then. Furthermore, unlike now, parents weren't constantly anxious about their children's safety. As a result, young people would spend more time playing sport outside, or being sociable with their friends.

On the other hand, in comparison with 50 years ago, teenagers' lives are full of opportunities. Technology has made it easy for us to learn about anything and make friends with people who share similar interests. Moreover, we can easily stay in touch with friends and family, wherever they are in the world.

In my view, compared to now, life was definitely less complicated for young people 50 years ago. On balance, however, I believe life today is far more interesting and enjoyable, as long as we make the most of our lives and the opportunities we receive.

**4**  **The highlighted words in the essay are used to organise ideas. Write the words next to the functions.**

  1  Adding a new point ............, ...........

  2  Introducing a personal opinion ...........

  3  Showing a logical consequence ............

  4  Summing up ............

**5**  **Read the *Prepare* box and find the expressions in the essay. Then choose the correct words below.**

## Prepare to write — Comparing and contrasting

These expressions are used to compare and contrast ideas:

*in comparison with/to*

*compared to/with*

*unlike*

*while/whereas*

*on the one hand / on the other hand*

  1  *While / Unlike* my brother, I'm an optimist.

  2  *In comparison with / Compared* my friends I get to go out a lot.

  3  My best friend wants to leave school after the exams *whereas / compared to* I want to do a degree.

  4  *Compared to / On the one hand* many young people, my life is easy.

  5  In ten years, I'll have my own place which will be great, but *whereas / on the other hand* I'll be paying for everything myself!

**6**  **Read the task. Add some information and your own idea to the notes.**

**Young people's lives will be harder in 25 years than they are now. Do you agree?**

**Notes**

Write about:

1  home life

2  education

3  ................. (your own idea)

**7**  ⬤  **Write an essay. Use all the notes and give reasons for your point of view.**

- Organise your essay into paragraphs.
- Use phrases from the *Prepare* box to compare and contrast the present and the future.
- Use expressions from exercise 4 to organise your ideas.
- Check your grammar and spelling.
- Write 140–190 words.

# 10 Surprise!

## VOCABULARY  Phrases with *in, out of, at, by*

**Your profile**

Do you like surprises? Why?
What's the biggest surprise you've ever had?

**1** ▶2.03 Listen and match the speakers (1–5) to the topics. There is one extra topic.

a an unexpected extra
b a surprise win
c an unexpected visit
d a surprise party
e a surprise wedding
f a shock result

**2** ▶2.03 Complete the sentences with the words in the box. Listen again and check.

> at fault     at risk     by accident     by chance
> in advance     in all     in detail     in secret
> out of character     out of nowhere

0 It was only ...by chance... that I glanced through the door.
1 The whole concert lasted for three hours ............ .
2 Unfortunately, he found out about it ............ .
3 I'd left an email open ............ .
4 He burst into my room ............ .
5 It's not exactly ............ for my brother to turn up like that.
6 United are now ............ of finishing the season without any trophies.
7 The goalkeeper was partly ............ for the goal.
8 She refused to speak ............ about the ceremony, but said it had taken place ............ a few months ago.

**3** Match the phrases in exercise 2 to their meanings.

a before a particular time
b including all the information about something
c altogether
d without telling other people
e unusual in terms of someone's personality
f suddenly and unexpectedly
g without intending to do something, not on purpose
h when something happens because of luck
i responsible for something bad that has happened
j in a situation where something bad is likely to happen

**4** Check the meaning of the bold phrases. Discuss the questions.

1 What time of day are you **at your best**?
2 What kinds of things do you **learn by heart**?
3 How do you **keep in touch** with your friends?
4 Do you get rid of clothes when they go **out of fashion**?
5 Which of your friends do you **have** the most **in common with**?
6 How do you feel when you speak **in public**?

## READING

**1** Read the article quickly and choose the best title.

a Why we should ban flash mobs
b The world's best flash mobs
c The different sides to flash mobs

**2** Read six sentences that have been removed from the article. Notice the underlined words.

A As a result of incidents such as this, some cities have banned flash mobs.
B Flash mobs began occurring all over the world, often organised through social media and text messaging.
C Despite this, the police kept a close eye on the participants.
D Over the next three months, he organised seven successful flash mobs in shops, hotels, parks and stations all around New York.
E Companies have realised the potential of promoting their products by creating unexpected events in public.
F Recently, over a million people took part in one, at different times on the same day, in over 25 cities around the world.
G One afternoon, he emailed 60 friends, inviting them to meet at a small local shop at exactly 7.24 pm.

**3** ⬤ Choose from the sentences A–G the one which fits best each gap (1–6). There is one extra sentence which you do not need to use. Use the underlined words in the text to help you decide.

**4** Replace the bold phrases with the correct form of the highlighted phrasal verbs in the article.

1 I've got used to Sam **arriving** late.
2 They're **doing** tests to see if the building is safe.
3 Jem **'s thought of** an idea for the end-of-term party.
4 When we got back, Nate **had already tidied everything away**.
5 I didn't enjoy that book, but don't let that **discourage you**.

# FLASH MOB FUN?

Imagine, it's Saturday at a busy shopping centre. People are doing all the things you'd normally expect – chatting on phones, looking in shop windows and so on. Then suddenly, the people in front of you stop moving. They're completely still, frozen in the middle of whatever they were doing. You look around you. There are more of these people – perhaps a hundred or so. Other shoppers look just as confused as you are. Several minutes go by and the frozen shoppers remain in exactly the same positions. Then, as suddenly as they stopped, they begin moving again, as if nothing had happened. You've just experienced a flash mob!

The definition of a flash mob is 'a group of people who meet suddenly in a public place, perform an unusual act for a brief time, then quickly leave'. An American, Bill Wasik, came up with the idea. **1** [ ] They shouldn't say anything to the assistants or each other. They didn't need to buy anything. They just had to browse for precisely seven minutes and then leave. It would have been the world's first flash mob. However, someone had warned the police and when Bill and his friends arrived, they were waiting.

Bill wasn't put off by this failure and started planning the next event. **2** [ ] Each time, Bill's friends received their invitations by email. They met at an exact time, carried out their instructions, such as forming a queue or just clapping, and then they left.

Before long, stories and videos of these funny and often bizarre events appeared online. Wasik's idea instantly captured the attention of creative types everywhere. **3** [ ] The flash mob had become part of modern urban culture and the phrase was even added to the Oxford English Dictionary.

One of the most popular events has been the annual international flash mob pillow fight. **4** [ ] However, one pillow fight left a park in San Francisco covered in thousands of feathers! It was estimated that it would cost thousands of dollars to clear up the mess. The organisers posted a message online. 'We shouldn't have left such a mess,' they wrote. 'We're sorry.'

Flash mobs are not only potentially costly, though. There is also a danger that they can get out of control. Someone called Eve advertised a 'silent disco' at a London station. The instructions were to bring music, wear headphones and dance. Before the event, Eve wondered if anyone would come. 'I remember thinking that I should have sent the invitation to more people,' she said. She needn't have worried. Twelve thousand people turned up. After 45 minutes the station was closed, trains were delayed and thousands of normal passengers were furious. **5** [ ]

Since the early days of flash mobs, the events have developed into commercial opportunities. **6** [ ] In one advertisement for a mobile phone, a crowd of 500 singers and dancers flooded into Heathrow Airport arrivals to greet people who had just got off flights. The performers had rehearsed for months in secret before the day and the company were terrified it would go wrong. However, the resulting advert more than lived up to everyone's expectations and has been seen by millions.

## Talking points

" Do you think most people find flash mobs fun or annoying? Why?

Are flash mobs just entertaining, or can they have a more serious purpose? "

## GRAMMAR Modals (2): Modals in the past

**1** Read the examples. What type of word follows *would have*, *should(n't) have* and *needn't have*?

1 It **would have been** the world's first flash mob.
2 We **shouldn't have left** such a mess.
3 I **should have sent** the invitation to more people.
4 She **needn't have worried**.
5 They **didn't need to buy anything**.

**2** Complete the rules with some of the modal verbs from exercise 1.

> We use:
>
> **a** *would have* + past participle to imagine something in the past that didn't happen.
>
> **b** ............ or *shouldn't have* + past participle to criticise or express a regret about the past.
>
> **c** ............ + past participle to talk about something which happened but wasn't necessary.
>
> **d** ............ + infinitive to talk about something which didn't happen because it wasn't necessary.

→ Grammar reference **page 157**

**3** Choose the correct words.

1 He *wouldn't / shouldn't* have driven when he was so tired. He put all our lives at risk.
2 You *needn't / wouldn't* have bought me a present. But thank you!
3 We left at eight because we *didn't need to be / needn't have been* there until nine.
4 I'm glad I didn't see that spider. I *should / would* have been petrified.
5 I *needn't / shouldn't* have watched that film. I'm going to have difficulty sleeping tonight.
6 You *should / would* have told us you were going to be late. We were really concerned.

**4** ⬤ Complete the second sentence so that it has a similar meaning to the first, using the word given. Do not change this word.

1 It was wrong of you to use my mobile without my permission. SHOULD
You ........................ before you used my mobile.
2 It wasn't necessary for you to panic. HAVE
You ........................ in a panic.
3 It was careless of him to go without checking the times in advance. SHOULD
Before going out, ........................ the times.
4 It was a bad idea for me to speak. KEPT
I ........................ shut.
5 Why didn't you tell me you were going out? SHOULD
You ........................ me know you were going out.

### ⊙ Corpus challenge

**Find and correct the mistake in the student's sentence.**

*I don't know what I had done without your help because I didn't know where to go.*

**5** Complete the sentences about you. Work in pairs and compare your answers. Ask more questions to find out details.

1 Yesterday I would have ............ , but …
2 Last weekend I shouldn't have …
3 This morning I didn't need to …
4 Last week I needn't have …
5 Last year I should have …

## VOCABULARY Extended meanings of words

**1** Read the examples. What do *frozen* and *flooded* mean here? What is their literal meaning?

1 *They were completely still, **frozen** in the middle of whatever they were doing.*
2 *A flash mob of 500 singers and dancers **flooded** into Heathrow Airport arrivals.*

**2** Complete the sentences with the correct form of the words in the box.

> boil    bright    flood    freeze    hit    weigh

1 You're an excellent student with a ............ future.
2 The students have been ............ by the news that their teacher is leaving.
3 Mind if I leave the door open? It's ............ in here.
4 Having ............ up the pros and cons, he's decided to go to university.
5 She ............ when she saw the spider.
6 I opened the curtains and light ............ into the room.

**3** What do you think the bold words mean in these sentences?

1 Simon is hardly an **angel**.
2 My memory is **foggy**.
3 The police **grilled** the suspect.
4 The good news **lifted** everyone's mood.
5 Josie **sailed through** her exams.
6 Ruby and Isabel have a **stormy** relationship.

## LISTENING

**1** ▶2.04 Listen to part of a radio interview. What do you think happened to Rachel at the weekend?

**2** Read the question carefully.

1 Why didn't Rachel suspect her friends were organising something on Saturday?
   A They often went to a café before seeing a film.
   B She had arranged to go to the cinema.
   C Saturday wasn't actually her birthday.

**3** ▶2.04 Think about these questions. Then listen again and choose the best answer in exercise 2.

- Was it normal for Rachel and her friend to go to this café?
- Was the trip to the cinema a reason why Rachel didn't suspect anything?
- What does Rachel say about her actual birthday?

**4** ▶2.05 ● You will now hear the complete radio interview. For questions 2–6, choose the best answer (A, B or C).

2 When Rachel's uncle saw her,
   A he felt uncomfortable.
   B he realised that he was late to meet a friend.
   C he said that he preferred to sit by himself.

3 What did Rachel think about Lucy's suggestion to go downstairs?
   A It was strange because they weren't going to eat.
   B It wasn't worth moving because they had to leave soon.
   C It was a good idea because it might be quieter there.

4 When Rachel first saw the party she
   A was surprised about some of the people there.
   B was uncomfortable because it was being filmed.
   C became emotional and couldn't stop crying.

5 What does Rachel say about her parents?
   A They stayed too long at her party.
   B Her dad sang her a special song.
   C Her mum's speech made her a bit uncomfortable.

6 What did Rachel's parents think about the idea of a surprise party?
   A They were concerned about the cost.
   B They didn't think Rachel would enjoy it.
   C They were worried it would be too much work.

### EP Word profile *expect*

I hope no one expected me to make a speech.

Companies create unexpected events in public.

United were expected to beat City easily.

page 135

## SPEAKING   Surprising news

**1** ▶2.06 Listen to the conversation. What is Ahmed surprised about?

**2** ▶2.06 Listen again and complete the extracts

1 Did she? That's ............ !
2 I'd never have ............ Sally was a good writer.

**3** ▶2.07 Listen to another conversation. What were both Dan and Ahmed surprised about?

**4** ▶2.07 Read the *Prepare* box. Then listen to Dan and Ahmed again. Which expressions do you hear?

### Prepare to speak — Expressing surprise

I'd never have guessed.
It was the last thing I expected.
You're kidding!
That's amazing!
No way!
Really?
Was he? Did she? (echo questions)

**5** Prepare three pieces of surprising news about yourself. Use the ideas in the box or your own ideas.

| | |
|---|---|
| a birthday present | moving house |
| someone you met | an accident |
| something you bought | something you read online |

**6** Work in groups.

- Tell each other your news and react.
- Use phrases from the *Prepare* box.

A: *I got a scooter for my birthday!*
B: *Did you? You're so lucky!*

# Culture
## World music

**1** ▶ **2.08** Listen to eight samples of World Music. Match them with the countries below.

 Australia  Brazil  China  India  Ireland  Morocco

**2** ▶ **2.08** Listen again. Use the following adjectives and your own ideas to describe the music.

 Russia  the US

| cheerful | dramatic | fast | fun | happy | lively | peaceful |
|---|---|---|---|---|---|---|
| relaxing | rhythmic | sad | slow | smooth | | |

**3** Read the text. Who invented the term 'World Music'?

# THE INVENTION OF 'WORLD MUSIC'

**DO YOU ENJOY DISCOVERING NEW TYPES OF MUSIC ON THE INTERNET?**
If you do, then you know there are many terms to describe musical styles, like pop, rock, dance or hip hop, to name only a few. When we hear those names, we usually know what type of music to expect. However, in the case of World Music, it's difficult to be sure, since the term is used to describe a wide variety of styles and sounds.

## WHEN DID 'WORLD MUSIC' BECOME POPULAR?

In the late 1980s, British recording companies started using 'World Music' as a marketing label to describe music from countries outside Western Europe and North America. It was intended as a general category which could include everything from Andean folk songs to Zambian dance rhythms. This new term helped recording companies promote alternative sounds and consequently sell more music. It was also more convenient for music shops to have a specific World Music section where customers could look for foreign artists or browse for international trends. However, some musicians weren't entirely convinced by the term, which seemed to mean 'anything except typical Western music'. For this reason, some musicians felt that 'World Music' was a negative term that labelled their work as foreign and exotic, but not popular or successful.

### What does the term mean today?

Since the 1980s, World Music has become so diverse that it's difficult to give a simple definition. Now it can refer to traditional music from anywhere in the world, including Irish folk songs, Spanish flamenco or Cajun ballads from the United States. People's definitions of what qualifies as World Music will depend on their own cultural views. So modern pop music from countries like France or Italy might be considered World Music by people in distant countries, like China or Japan, where it may sound unusual to local ears. In this way, people's definitions of what qualifies as World Music will depend largely on their own cultural perspective.

New styles of music have also appeared, such as Latin Jazz, Indian Techno and Afro-Celt Music, which blend sounds from different cultures. These mixed styles, often called World Beat or Global Fusion, have been popularised by pop singers, like Sting and Shakira, and famous DJs like David Guetta. In addition, the rise of the internet and downloadable music now makes it easier for anyone to explore new trends at the touch of a mouse or a finger. If that's true, then World Music may soon become the music of the world.

## EARLY YEARS

**1980 The World of Music**, Arts and Dance Organisation (WOMAD) was created and two years later, the first WOMAD Festival took place in the UK. Since then, there have been more than 160 WOMAD festivals around the world.

**1983 Charlie Gillett**, a BBC radio host, created a new musical programme called 'A Foreign Affair'. He introduced British listeners to many international musicians, such as Youssou N'Dour from Senegal in West Africa.

**1986 Paul Simon**, an American pop musician, recorded the album *Graceland* with a South African vocal group called Ladysmith Black Mambazo. The album sold over 16 million copies, creating new global interest in African music.

**1987 The expression** 'World Music' was chosen as a marketing term by a group of record companies during a meeting in London. However, the name was invented in 1960 by Robert E. Brown, a music professor and ethnomusicologist from New York, in the United States.

**1989 The British pop** musician Peter Gabriel, one of the founders of WOMAD, established a new company called Real World Records to record and promote World Music singers and groups.

**4** Read the text again and find the names of

a a type of music from Spain.

b a DJ who has helped to make World Music more popular.

c the principle World Music Festival.

d an African musician.

e a top-selling album.

**5** Do you agree with the following sentences? Why? / Why not? Discuss your answers in pairs.

1 World Music is such a general term that it doesn't really mean anything.

2 The term World Music means different things to people in different countries.

3 If a band's music is labelled as World Music, it probably won't be successful.

4 The term World Music makes it easier to discover new musical trends on the internet.

5 International music festivals are a good way to promote music from other countries.

**6** ▶2.09 Listen to a podcast about WOMAD festivals. Then answer the following questions.

1 How many people attended the first festival in 1982?

2 What problem did WOMAD have with that first festival?

3 How many days do WOMAD festivals usually last?

4 Which countries have national WOMAD organisations?

5 Besides concerts, what activities do WOMAD festivals offer?

**7** ▶2.10 Listen to Alicia and Janice giving a presentation about the singer Shakira. As you listen, complete the notes below with the words in the box.

| Beyoncé | Brazilian | Colombia | Italian | Latin |
| Lebanese | Middle-Eastern | 1996 | | |

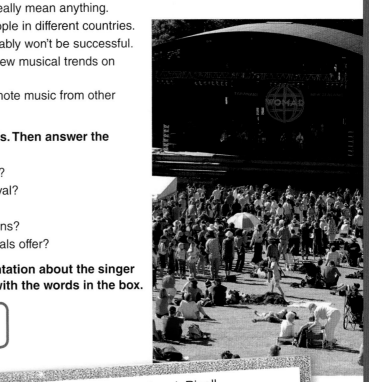

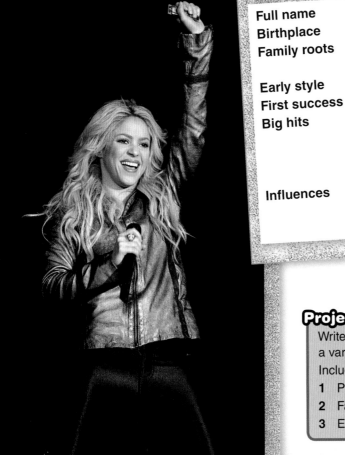

| **Full name** | Shakira Isabel Mebarak Ripoll |
| **Birthplace** | Barranquilla, (**1**) ..........., 1977 |
| **Family roots** | Mother: Colombian, Spanish and (**2**) ........... |
| | Father: (**3**) ........... -American |
| **Early style** | (**4**) ........... pop and rock |
| **First success** | The album *Pies Descalzos* (**5**) (...........) |
| **Big hits** | *Whenever, Wherever* (2001), *Hips Don't Lie* (2006), *Beautiful Liar* with (**6**) ........... (2007), *Waka Waka* (2010), *Can't Remember to Forget You* with Rihanna (2014) |
| **Influences** | Andean folk music, (**7**) ........... and Indian music, Spanish Flamenco, and (**8**) ........... Bossa Nova |

**Project**

Write a fact-file about another singer that is influenced by a variety of musical styles.

Include information for the following categories.

1 Place of birth 4 First success

2 Family roots 5 Big hits

3 Early musical styles 6 Influences

## VOCABULARY Phrasal verbs: relationships

Who do you get on best with in your family? Why?
How do family relationships differ from friendships?

**1 Match the sentence halves.**

1 Sarah really **looks up to** her father.
2 My eldest sister **looks down on** me.
3 Luke **takes after** his father.
4 My family always **sticks together**.
5 I don't want to **fall out** with you.
6 My brother's **gone off** his girlfriend.
7 Lisa has just **finished with** her boyfriend.
8 I didn't **hit it off** with Jake.
9 I can always **count on** my parents.
10 Anna won't **let** you **down**.

a He's 1.92 m tall, the same as his dad.
b She makes me feel completely unimportant.
c I found him very difficult to talk to.
d I think they're going to split up.
e We never fall out and we're very close.
f I hate arguments.
g They'll always help me if I need them to.
h He's a very good role model for her.
i She's single again now.
j If she says she'll help, she will help.

**2** ▶ 2.11 **Listen to each conversation and answer the questions on the recording.**

**3 Ask and answer the questions about your family or friends.**

1 Have you ever met someone and hit it off with them immediately?
2 Have you ever let anyone down? How?
3 Who can you really count on?
4 Who do you look up to? Why?
5 Who do you take after?

## READING

**1 Look at the example (0) in the first paragraph of the text. What type of word is missing in the gap?**

**2 Discuss what specific words could fit in the gap.**

**3**  **Read the first paragraph of the text. For questions 1–8, think of the word which best fits each gap. Use only one word in each gap.**

**4 Read the rest of the text. Match the sub-headings to sections A–C in the text. Two sub-headings are not needed.**

1 Citizens of the world
2 Opposites attract
3 Family nightmares
4 Wrong number
5 Staying local

**5 Answer the questions.**

1 What 'mistake' did Attis make?
2 Why did the Palestino fans take pity on Nobu?
3 Why does Lucinda feel like she isn't 'from' anywhere?
4 What nationalities and countries are mentioned in the texts?

# WHO DO YOU THINK YOU ARE?

No one says (0) ............ part of a family is always easy, but families do generally provide you with love, comfort and security. No two families are alike: some are small and close to one (1) ............ , while with others it is hard to keep track of who is who. (2) ............ some families have lived in (3) ............ same region for centuries, increasingly factors such (4) ............ work opportunities and even romance have caused significant population movements. When families move abroad, they often lose (5) ............ mother tongue and adopt the language and customs of the new country – even the spelling (6) ............ surnames can change. This can make it hard to trace family histories and work out (7) ............ your family have lived in a particular area for generations or are relatively recent immigrants. Perhaps all we *can* say with any certainty is that families are full of surprises and (8) ............ some cases, coincidences and complications create amazing tales.

## B

### Pancho Yamamoto
#### Talcahuano, Chile

*Pancho Yamamoto's parents didn't exactly hit it off the first time they met.* The Yamamotos moved from Japan to Chile to work in the mines around 1915. Pancho's father, Nobu, was a big fan of Huachipato, a football team from his home town of Talcahuano. Nobu took pride in going to every Huachipato match and one winter, he travelled 500 km to Santiago de Chile, where Huachipato was going to play against Palestino. At the match, he was surprised to find that he was the only Huachipato fan in the stadium. The Palestino fans laughed and whistled at lonely Nobu throughout the game. Then, when the game ended, some of them took pity on him, invited him for dinner and they soon forgot all about their teams' rivalry. One Palestino fan, Carolina Fernández, had been laughing at Nobu all along, like the others. But she knew it was wrong, so she made an effort to get to know him during dinner. They began a long-distance relationship and wrote around 200 letters in all before Carolina became Mrs Yamamoto.

## A

### Markos Fafoutakis
#### Athens, Greece

*It was love at first sight for Markos's grandparents, despite the fact that they had fallen out before they met face to face.* It all started when his grandfather, Attis Fafoutakis, called a friend. Marie Wouters, who had just moved to Greece from Belgium, answered the phone. When she explained that she didn't know his friend, Attis argued with her. But when she repeated her number slowly, Attis realised his mistake. He was in a hurry, so he simply hung up. Later, Attis couldn't stop thinking about the woman he had spoken to. There was something in her voice which had really appealed to him and so he decided to start all over again. Attis re-dialled the number that he had called by accident and used all his charms to apologise to Marie. She forgave him and they ended up chatting for ages. In fact, they got on so well that they arranged to meet and the rest is history.

## C

### Lucinda Shah
#### Marrakesh, Morocco

*Lucinda Shah doesn't feel like she's 'from' anywhere.* To her Moroccan friends, Lucinda is British and although she does have a British passport, her roots are all over the place.

Lucinda's mother, Rachana, who is Indian, grew up in Mumbai and worked as a designer in New York. Lucinda's father, Amir, a film producer whose work is mainly in the UK, was born in India to an Afghan father and a Scottish mother. Amir Shah met Rachana in 1999. They got on really well and were married the same year in Paris. When their daughter, Lucinda, was just five, Amir Shah announced, 'We're moving to Marrakesh!' For him, it was a magical place he'd always wanted to take his family to. They moved from London to Marrakesh, where Lucinda speaks Arabic and is studying at the American school. But now, all of a sudden, Rachana Shah is talking about moving to Thailand. All in all, Lucinda knows that her family's adventures aren't over yet.

---

**EP Word profile *all***

He decided to start all over again.

All in all, Lucinda knows that her family's adventures aren't over.

Her roots are all over the place.

Carolina Fernández had been laughing at Nobu all along.

page 135

**Talking points**

❝ Do you think it is important to know about your family history?
What makes a happy family? ❞

## GRAMMAR Relative clauses

**1 Read the examples and underline the relative clauses. Are they defining or non-defining?**

1 *Marie Wouters, who had just moved to Greece, answered the phone.*
2 *Attis couldn't stop thinking about the woman he had spoken **to**.*
3 *Attis re-dialled the number that he had called by accident.*
4 *There was something in her voice which had really appealed to him.*
5 *Lucinda's father, whose work is mainly in the UK, was born in India.*
6 *Nobu travelled to Santiago, where Huachipato was going to play against Palestino.*

**2 Read the rules and check your answers.**

> **a** A defining relative clause gives essential information about a noun. We:
> - can leave out the relative pronoun if it is the object of the clause.
> - cannot leave out the relative pronoun if it is the subject of the clause.
>
> **b** A non-defining relative clause adds extra information about a noun. We:
> - cannot leave out the relative pronoun.
> - do not use *that* for people or things.
> - always use commas before and after the relative clause.

→ Grammar reference **page 158**

**3 Look at the examples in exercise 1 again. Where is the bold preposition in example 2?**

**4 Read the text and add a relative pronoun or adverb (*where, when*) before each relative clause. Put the relative pronoun in brackets if you can leave it out.**

*I'll never forget the time (when) we had a family holiday in Greece.*

I'll never forget the time we had a family holiday in Greece. We went to the island of Rhodes, my ancestors used to live. It's an area has a fascinating history and my parents wanted to find the village they used to live. We couldn't find any records could help us, but eventually we found a village just like the one in the old photos we had been given. We asked in a café and we were introduced to an old man great-grandparents had lived next to our old family home. The house had been knocked down, but it was nice to make a connection with someone knew a bit about our family history.

**5 Rewrite the pairs of sentences using relative clauses.**

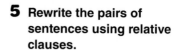

0 I have a cousin the same age as me. She is really good fun.

*I have a cousin the same age as me, who is really good fun.*

1 This is our family home. Four generations have grown up here.
2 Our apartment has views across the whole city. It was built five years ago.
3 My uncle is now a teacher at our school. He always played with us as children.
4 Last year we visited Poland. My grandparents came from there.
5 This is a photo of my grandparents. They got married in 1967.

### ⊙ Corpus challenge

**Find and correct the mistake in the student's sentence.**

I've got the information, who you need about the new art class.

## VOCABULARY Compound adjectives

**1 Complete the compound adjectives. Use the past participle form of the words in the box.**

> age   balance   behave   ~~build~~   organise   pay

0 Sam is 1.88 m and 95 kg. He's fairly well- *built* .
1 The holiday was well-..........., thanks to my mum.
2 My dad's 45, so I guess he's middle-........... .
3 I try to eat a well-........... diet.
4 My aunt has a very well-........... job.
5 I can't stand badly-........... children!

**2 Complete the sentences. Combine one word from each box to form compound adjectives.**

> grown   high   last   ~~long~~   self   short

> confident   ~~distance~~   minute   tech   term   up

0 We make a lot of *long - distance* phone calls.
1 Mark is ...........-........... . He knows what his strengths are.
2 My uncle's living with us at the moment, but it's only a ...........-........... arrangement.
3 I've got two ...........-........... cousins. One is 25 and the other is 28.
4 There's always a lot of ...........-........... equipment here because my mum's a software developer.
5 We didn't book the football tickets until the day before the match. It was a ...........-........... decision.

## WRITING  An article (2)

**1** Read the article. In what way has Dan's brother influenced him?

### Someone I admire

Can you think of someone who you really look up to? Is there anyone who you can rely on, no matter what? For me that person is my older brother, Louis.

When I was 13, he had a big impact on my life. I was having problems with a gang at school who used to bully me all the time. Talking to my parents didn't help because they don't understand teenage stuff, but I did talk to my brother about it. Discussing the issues with him made a huge difference to me. The thing I admired most about him was his patience. I must have talked about the same problem 100 times, yet he always listened as if it was the first time. I think that's pretty amazing!

Louis has been a really important influence on me ever since. What I've learned more than anything is the importance of being thoughtful. Instead of sounding sympathetic and then forgetting all about friends' problems, I listen properly now.

What about you? Who has been a big influence in your life?

by Dan

**2** Read the task, then read Dan's article again. Discuss the questions.

> You see this notice on your school noticeboard.
>
> **Articles needed!**
> * Which family member or friend do you most admire? Why?
> * How has this person influenced you?
>   Write an article for the school magazine answering these questions. Include a title. The best article will be published in our magazine next month.
>
> Write your **article**.

1 Can you think of a more interesting title for Dan's article?
2 Does Dan answer the three questions in the task?
3 How does he organise his answers?
4 How does Dan get the reader's attention?

**3** Read the *Prepare* box. Match the sentence structures in the *Prepare* box to the highlighted parts of the article.

**Prepare to write – Varying sentence structure**

You can make your writing more interesting by varying your sentence structure. Try using:
* questions.
* *-ing* forms as subjects.
* structures which add emphasis.

**4** Complete the second sentence so it has a similar meaning to the first. Use ideas from the *Prepare* box to help you.

1 I met Adam and that changed my life.
............ Adam changed my life.
2 I admire her kindness the most.
What I ............ is her kindness.
3 I love my uncle, especially his sense of humour.
The thing ............ about my uncle is his sense of humour.
4 I spent time with my aunt and that helped me become more confident.
............ with my aunt helped me become more confident.
5 I find his determination really amazing.
What ............ amazing is his determination.
6 I really like his positive attitude to life.
The thing ............ his positive attitude to life.

**5** Read the task in exercise 2 again and plan your own article.
* Think of a family member or friend.
* Make notes. Think of examples and develop your ideas.
* Put your ideas in order.
* Think of a topic sentence to begin each paragraph.
* Think of an interesting title.

**6** ● Write your article.
* Try to vary your sentence structure.
* Remember to address your reader to get their attention.
* Check your grammar and spelling.
* Write 140–190 words.

## VOCABULARY Communication and effect

**Your profile**

Which of the photos below do you like best? Why?
How can these things make a difference to people?

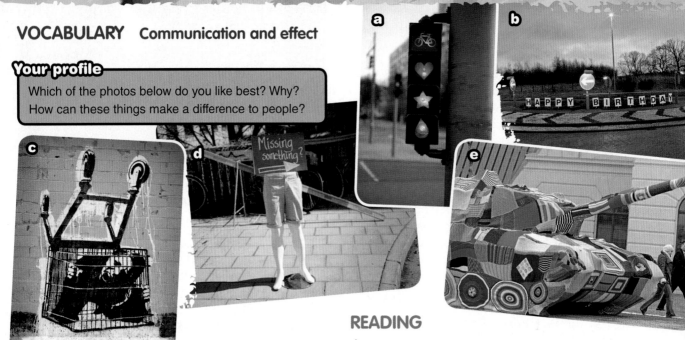

**1 How many of the photos can you match with each sentence?**

1 This was done to **cheer** people **up**.
2 This is probably intended to **amuse** people.
3 This is intended to **persuade** people to do something.
4 This is to **congratulate** someone on a special occasion.
5 I think this is there to **stimulate** people to think.
6 Whoever did this wanted to **express** their opinion about an issue.
7 Things like this **inspire** people to be optimistic.
8 I think it is there to **promote** a business.

**2 ▶2.12 Listen to Dan and Sara discussing photos a–d. Which two verbs do they associate with each photo?**

**3 ▶2.12 Listen again. Who expresses these opinions? S (Sara) or D (Dan)?**

1 ............ says things like the heart on the traffic light improve your day.
2 ............ thinks personal messages by the side of the road are a nuisance.
3 ............ suggests that the street art is trying to get across a certain message.
4 ............ thinks the legs could be an advert for a second-hand clothes shop.

**4 Discuss three things that …**

• cheer you up.
• inspire you.
• you'd like to express your opinions about.

## READING

**1 Read the text quickly. What is a random act of kindness? Give two examples.**

**2 Read the text more carefully. Are the statements true or false?**

1 Andrew's response to the driver's offer was immediate and decisive.
2 For Ali, the most enjoyable thing about a 'random act of kindness' is observing how people respond.
3 Ali was upset because the old lady refused to tell him what was going on.
4 The campaign in Sydney has had a great deal of influence worldwide.
5 Andrew found the customer's request in the café difficult to hear.
6 Andrew feels pleased because he believes the idea of 'caffè sospeso' shows the good side of human behaviour.

**3 Complete the sentences with the highlighted words in the text.**

1 I'm going to work as a ............ while I'm at university.
2 My ............ is, 'Live and let live'.
3 You always ask the most ............ questions!
4 There's a ............ van parked at the end of the road.
5 I've posted a video on YouTube, I really hope it goes ............ .
6 Her friends take advantage of her ............ .

**4 Discuss the questions**

1 Which of the random acts of kindness appeals to you the most? Why?
2 How do you think you would react if someone offered you a random act of kindness? Why?
3 Would you leave a *caffè sospeso* for someone? Why? / Why not?

# RANDOM ACTS OF KINDNESS

By Andrew Longman

Have you experienced a Random Act of Kindness yet? Imagine the scene: it's late and you've spent the whole day shopping with a friend. It has started to rain. You've both got heavy shopping bags to carry and neither of you has any energy left. You're dreaming of the sofa when, all of a sudden, a voice says, 'Can I give you a lift?' – What would you say? After all, we all know the dangers of accepting lifts from strangers.

As a matter of fact, when this happened to me, I was very suspicious. As far as I know, I don't look as if I need to have my bags carried! 'It's just a random act of kindness,' the guy said. I glanced at my friend and raised my eyebrows. The man seemed trustworthy, so I mumbled our thanks and accepted the lift.

As we were driving over Sydney Harbour Bridge, the driver introduced himself as Ali and gave us a small, well-used card. It explained that a random act of kindness is doing a favour for someone you have never met before, and for no special reason. The whole idea is simply to cheer strangers up. 'Take the card, pass it on,' he said. I asked whether he did this all the time. 'I like to do a few random acts every once in a while. It makes me feel good about myself,' explained Ali. 'It could be any number of things, from picking up litter in a stranger's garden to swapping places with the person behind you in a queue. As far as I'm concerned, by far the best part is watching people's reactions. Some people are comfortable with it immediately, others are doubtful initially, but a few don't actually want to be helped.'

Ali's interest began when he was hugged by a complete stranger at a bus stop on a trip to the United States. An old lady was standing there with a sign that said *Free Hugs*. When Ali asked her what it meant, the woman didn't say anything – she just hugged Ali. 'It made a real difference to my day,' he said. While Ali was waiting, the woman hugged several other people – young and old, men and women. A few days later, Ali came across the video for *All the Same* by Sick Puppies, which shows the first Free Hugs group hugging shoppers in Sydney. It went viral really quickly and it has now had 74 million hits! As a result of this, the idea spread quickly online and there are now Free Hugs campaigns in most countries. Millions of people have been inspired by the idea, which has gone beyond mere hugs to include other random acts of kindness, like the one we experienced.

A few weeks later, I went into a café to get a takeaway coffee. While I was being served, a man walked in behind me and asked, 'Are there any free coffees?' I could hardly believe my ears, especially when the barista said, 'Yes'. The customer got her to give him a coffee – for nothing. Then she crossed off a mark on the blackboard. When he had left, I asked her what was going on. '*Caffè sospeso*', she explained. 'It's an old tradition from Naples, in Italy. It means "suspended coffee" in Italian, and it's when someone who's had good luck or who is feeling generous orders two coffees, one to drink and one a *sospeso*, for a future customer who needs a coffee but can't afford one. We take the payment and add a mark here on the board. Then people can come in and ask if we have any *sospesos* – any free coffees. We don't promote it, but our regulars know we do it.' In such a competitive world, I felt glad to witness such generosity of the human spirit. Wondering whether charity and kindness could become the philosophy of the modern age, I ordered a *cappuccino* 'to go' – and one *caffè sospeso*.

## EP Word profile *as*

As a matter of fact, when this happened to me, I was a bit suspicious.

As far as I know, I don't look as if I need to have my bags carried!

As far as I'm concerned, by far the best part is watching people's reactions.

As a result of this, the idea spread quickly online.

page 136

## Talking points

" What makes people do random acts of kindness?

Why might you sometimes not accept a random act of kindness?

Do you think people should do more to help each other? "

## GRAMMAR The passive (1): Review

**1** Read the passive examples. What tenses are they?

1 She **was hugged** by a complete stranger.
2 Millions of people **have been inspired** by the idea.
3 While I **was being served**, a man walked in behind me and asked …

**2** Read the rules. Why is the passive used in each sentence in exercise 1?

We use the passive:

**a** when who or what does something is unknown, unimportant or obvious.

**b** if we don't want to say who does something, or if we want to avoid blame.

**c** to emphasise the person who receives an action, rather than the person who does the action.

We use by if it is important to add who or what does something.

→ Grammar reference **page 159**

**3** Complete the text with the passive form of the verbs.

# Free hugs stop the city

**M**embers of the Free Hugs Campaign
⁰ ....*have been asked*.... (ask) to go home
early after their annual meeting caused chaos
this evening. Although thousands of members ¹ ............
(invite), organisers only expected a few hundred to
turn up. They were wrong and huge numbers of people
turned up. Roads around the city centre ² ............ (block)
by the huge crowds for three hours earlier today and
even now drivers ³ ............ (advise) to avoid the area
until midnight. Police are warning that public transport
⁴ ............ (might / affect) until later tonight as well.
'Throughout the day, we ⁵ ............ (impress) by the
organisers,' said a police spokesperson. 'I ⁶ ............
(never / hug) by so many people in one day!'

## Causative

**4** Read the examples and answer the questions.

1 I didn't need to **have** my bags **carried**.
Who did the writer think should carry his bags?

2 I was pleased to **get** my shopping **delivered**.
Who was delivering the writer's shopping?

3 The customer **got** her **to give** him a coffee – for nothing.
Who gave the customer a coffee? Did the customer pay?

**5** What could be done in the following situations? Use the verbs in the box and the causative.

| cut | redeliver | repair | ~~replace~~ | wash |
|---|---|---|---|---|

**0** Your dad's watch stops.
He could have/get the batteries replaced.

**1** Your sister's hair is too long.

**2** Your mum's car is dirty.

**3** The screen on your phone cracks.

**4** There's a note to say a parcel was delivered while you were out.

## VOCABULARY both, either, neither

**1** Read the examples, then match the words to the meanings.

You've **both** got heavy shopping bags to carry.
**Both (of my)** bags are full of shopping.
Is **either of** you tired?
I'll carry **either** this bag **or** that one.
**Neither of** you has any energy left.
**Neither** you **nor** your friend has any energy left.

| 1 both | **a** one or the other |
|---|---|
| 2 either … or | **b** one and the other |
| 3 neither … nor | **c** not one or the other |

**2** Choose the correct verbs.

1 Both of them is / are mine.
2 Either George or Sam is / are lying.
3 Neither Sam nor Jo was / were willing to help.

**3** Complete the sentences using 1–3 words in each gap.

1 I couldn't go along ............................ Park Street or Market Street because ............................ roads were blocked.

2 A police officer and a taxi driver were offered hugs, but ............................ them accepted.

3 Two students asked me if I'd like a free hug, so I had hugs from ............................ them!

## LISTENING

**1** ▶2.13 You will hear a woman called Amy Linton talking about hearing a violinist playing in an underground station. What was surprising about the performance?

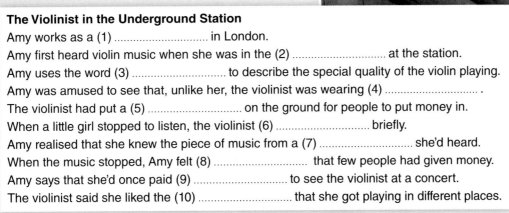

**2** ▶2.13 ⬤ Read the sentences below carefully. Try to work out what kinds of answer are needed. Then listen again and for questions 1–10, complete the sentences with a word or short phrase.

### The Violinist in the Underground Station

Amy works as a (1) ............................. in London.

Amy first heard violin music when she was in the (2) ............................. at the station.

Amy uses the word (3) ............................. to describe the special quality of the violin playing.

Amy was amused to see that, unlike her, the violinist was wearing (4) ............................. .

The violinist had put a (5) ............................. on the ground for people to put money in.

When a little girl stopped to listen, the violinist (6) ............................. briefly.

Amy realised that she knew the piece of music from a (7) ............................. she'd heard.

When the music stopped, Amy felt (8) ............................. that few people had given money.

Amy says that she'd once paid (9) ............................. to see the violinist at a concert.

The violinist said she liked the (10) ............................. that she got playing in different places.

## SPEAKING  Discussing options

**1** ▶2.14 Listen to Elena and Hans talking as part of a speaking exam. They are talking about giving help to disabled children in the local community.

1 Tick the five things that they talk about.

2 What do they both agree they would help with?

> access to school    computer gaming
> going shopping    going out at the weekend
> homework    reading and writing    sports    tidying up

**2** ▶2.15 Read the *Prepare* box. Then listen to part of the conversation again. Which expressions do you hear?

### Prepare to speak – Keeping talking

**Starting to talk**
Let's start with …

**Asking for clarification**
What exactly do you mean?
Are you referring to … ?

**Keeping talking**
Again, as with …, we could …
What else? / Anything else?
I was just going to say that …
Do you want to add anything?

**3** ▶2.16 ⬤ Listen to the instruction and look at the task for one minute. Then complete the task. Use phrases from the *Prepare* box.

> household jobs          computer assistance
>
> **What services could students offer to help elderly people in the local community?**          shopping
>
> transport          someone to talk to

**1** Read the text. What are Wikipedia, Memrise and Goldcorp?

# CROWDSOURCING
## THE POWER OF COLLABORATION

**Crowdsourcing** is an interesting new **application** of the saying 'many hands make light work'. In the same way that classmates might work together on an assignment, now **dozens**, **hundreds** or **thousands** of people can collaborate on projects that would be too large or complex for a **small group** of co-workers. At the same time, crowdsourcing follows the old saying that 'two heads are better than one'. When many people collaborate, they not only **work faster**, but they also **work better**, by combining their **intelligence** and **experience**.

**Perhaps one** of the most famous examples of crowdsourcing is Wikipedia – an online encyclopedia that is written, edited and managed by people all over the world. The writers are volunteers who offer their time and work for free. And thanks to them, Wikipedia now offers more than 4 million free articles in English, and millions more in almost 300 other languages. That's an amazing achievement for a project that only started in 2001.

**Other crowdsourcing** projects operate in the same way as Wikipedia. For example, there is a community learning website called Memrise, which offers more than 6,000 free educational courses in all types of subjects. The courses, which are created by volunteers, include photos, videos, games and quizzes to help people learn quickly and have fun at the same time.

**Traditional institutions**, such as London's Tate Museum, have also used crowdsourcing for projects. In 2010, the museum started the Tate Movie Project website, where children learned how animated films are made. The children also wrote stories, drew their own characters and sent them to the website. After that, professional animators worked with the children to make a collaborative film called *The Itch of the Golden Nit*. The film was shown on BBC television.

**Finally, crowdsourcing** can also be a way for people and companies to make money. Some businesses organise crowdsourcing websites to get suggestions for new products, services or advertising campaigns. They may also offer prizes for the best ideas. For example, the Goldcorp mining company offered a prize for a list of good locations for discovering gold. The best list won $575,000 and the company found $3 billion dollars of gold.

## "What do you think?
Is CROWDSOURCING the way of the future?"

**2** **Choose the best definition for crowdsourcing.**

1 offering a prize for suggestions about products, services or advertising campaigns

2 asking many people to help with a project, often using the internet to find volunteers

3 using a website to collect information that many people around the world can use

**3** **Answer the following questions with information from the text.**

1 How can Wikipedia offer so many different articles for free?

2 Why are Memrise courses fun?

3 What did children learn from the Tate Movie Project?

4 Why do you think the Goldcorp company offered such a big prize?

**4** **Share your opinions about these questions in pairs or groups.**

1 Do you agree with the saying that 'many hands make light work'?

2 What problems may people have when they work together on a big project?

3 Why do you think people volunteer for projects like Wikipedia or Memrise?

4 Can you think of more projects that use crowdsourcing?

**5** **Read the web post. What kind of help does the school want?**

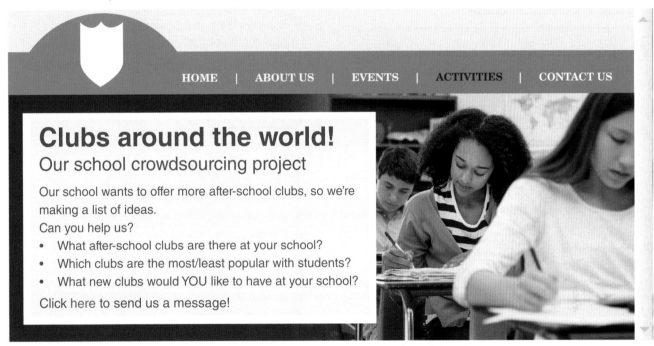

HOME | ABOUT US | EVENTS | ACTIVITIES | CONTACT US

# Clubs around the world!
## Our school crowdsourcing project

Our school wants to offer more after-school clubs, so we're making a list of ideas.
Can you help us?

- What after-school clubs are there at your school?
- Which clubs are the most/least popular with students?
- What new clubs would YOU like to have at your school?

Click here to send us a message!

**6** ▶ 2.17 **Listen to the first meeting of the 'Clubs around the world' committee (Tina and John) with the headmaster, Mr Prentice. Put the project tasks in order.**

a have a meeting with the headmaster after the vote

b make a shortlist of the most popular suggestions

c write a webpost with three different survey questions (1) Tina

d check the emails and make a list of the club ideas

e ask for volunteers to collect the votes in class

f post the survey questions on social media sites

## Project

Design your own crowdsourcing project. Use the following questions to help you.

1 What type of project could you create at school, at home or with your friends?

2 What would you need to do in order to set up the project?

3 Which members of your team would do which tasks?

4 Design a web post to get volunteers for your project.

# Review 3
## Units 9–12

## VOCABULARY

**1 Match the two parts of the phrases.**

1 make the      **a** goals
2 put an      **b** best of something
3 take every      **c** go at something
4 have a      **d** best in people
5 achieve your      **e** opportunity
6 see the      **f** end to something

**2 Complete the meanings with a preposition from A and a word from B.**

**A** | at   by   in (x2)   out of

**B** | common   fashion   fault   favour   heart

1 When you learn something like a poem so you can remember it all, you learn it ............ .
2 When people don't wear a particular style any more, it's gone ............ .
3 When you share interests with someone, you have something ............ .
4 When you're responsible for something that's going wrong, you're ............ .
5 When you agree with a plan or an idea, you're ............ of it.

**3 Complete the conversations with a compound adjective that means the opposite of the underlined words. Use a word from A and a word from B.**

**A** | short   last   well   badly   self

**B** | -confident   -minute   -built   -behaved   -term

1 **A** Is Martin the tall <u>slim</u> boy?
   **B** No, he's the ............ one.
2 **A** Did you plan your holiday well <u>in advance</u>?
   **B** No, it was a ............ decision.
3 **A** Were the students <u>good</u>?
   **B** There were a few ............ boys, but nothing serious.
4 **A** Is your brother's job abroad <u>permanent</u>?
   **B** No, it's only a ............ contract.
5 **A** Is Louise still as <u>shy</u> as she used to be?
   **B** No, she's much more ............ now.

**4 Rewrite the underlined phrases using the phrasal verbs in the box. Make any other changes necessary.**

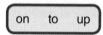

fall out   stick together   take after
look down on   go off   let down

1 I feel terrible about <u>disappointing Tom</u>, but I'm just too tired to go out tonight.
2 We always <u>support each other</u> in my family.
3 My brother <u>is a lot like</u> our dad.
4 I've <u>stopped enjoying</u> chocolate.
5 My sister and I are constantly <u>having arguments,</u> but we always make friends again.
6 It always feels as if Susanna is <u>thinking that I'm less important than her</u>.

**5 Match the sentence halves. Add a word from the box if necessary.**

on   to   up

1 Olivia's drama teacher inspired her
2 I expressed my opinion
3 I tried to cheer Frank
4 Everyone congratulated Mike
5 They've been promoting that phone
6 I've persuaded my brother

**a** his excellent exam results.
**b** all over the place recently.
**c** several times, but no one listened to me!
**d** become an actress.
**e** but he's really down.
**f** lend me some money.

## GRAMMAR

**6 Complete the second sentence so that it has a similar meaning to the first.**

1 Everyone has been given a certificate.
   Certificates ........................................................
2 This computer was given to me by my brother.
   I was ........................................................
3 Our house was painted while we were away.
   We had ........................................................
4 Your teacher should have told you what to do.
   You should ........................................................
5 I persuaded the company to replace my phone for free.
   I got my ........................................................
6 Is Simon persuading you not to go?
   Are you being ........................................................

**7 Choose the correct sentence or ending.**

1 By the end of the year, …
   a we'll be finishing this book.
   b we'll have finished this book.

2 Maybe we could borrow my dad's car.
   a He won't have used it today.
   b He won't be using it today.

3 I might be tired on Saturday evening as …
   a I'll have been revising all day.
   b I'll have revised all day.

4 I will have been learning Spanish …
   a by the time I go to Madrid.
   b for a year soon.

5 I can give Mike the key.
   a I'll be seeing him later.
   b I'll have seen him later.

6 Emily's going to university when
   a she's finished school.
   b she'll have finished school.

7 I wish you hadn't cleared up.
   a I needn't have done it.
   b I would have done it.

8 Sally made all the arrangements in advance, so …
   a we needn't have done anything.
   b we didn't need to do anything.

9 John was depending on you for help yesterday.
   a You shouldn't have let him down.
   b You wouldn't have let him down.

10 I'm glad I didn't wear my jacket.
   a I should have been boiling.
   b I wouldn't have been comfortable.

11 Josie would have loved that film.
   a I should have persuaded her to come.
   b I shouldn't have persuaded her to come.

12 It was an easy test. I spent ages learning dates, but …
   a I needn't have.
   b I didn't need to.

**8 Complete the sentences with *who, that, which, whose, where, when* or *why*. Write the word in brackets if you can leave it out.**

1 This is the hospital ............ Sam's dad works.

2 We waited for Marcus, ............ eventually turned up 30 minutes late.

3 My brother is someone ............ I really look up to.

4 My brother, ............ is never normally so well-organised, has done everything.

5 Sam's the girl ............ mum you met.

6 Can I borrow the book ............ you were reading?

7 Do you know the date ............ we have to hand in our essay?

8 I don't know the reason ............ he left.

**Corpus challenge**

**9 Tick the two sentences without mistakes. Correct the mistakes in the other sentences.**

1 Finally, in your letter you mentioned that you have to leave by 4.50 pm. There is no problem about that, because we will have been finished by then.

2 You do not have to worry about it because all the activities will have finished by 4 o'clock.

3 The time that the show should start was 19:30 but it started forty-five minutes later.

4 It had been better to stay in bed.

5 Your group has been booked into the Palace Hotel, which address you will find in the leaflet.

6 That time we spent together was great because I made some good new friends which are some of my closest.

7 It was a beautiful big house and I loved it – maybe because I had been raised there.

8 The hotel been built in the town centre, so we did not have to walk miles to get where we intended.

**10 ●● For questions 1–8, read the text below. Use the word given in capitals at the end of some of the lines to form a word that fits in the gap in the same line. There is an example at the beginning (0).**

| | |
|---|---|
| 'I had great (0) ....*admiration*.... for my grandfather,' said 17-year-old Josie Taylor. 'He was such a kind | **ADMIRE** |
| and (1) ........... person that I felt I needed to do something when he died.' After some (2) ........... , Josie | **SENSE** |
| came up with an (3) ........... idea: | **CONSIDER** |
| she decided to perform 90 random acts of kindness for strangers – one for each year of her grandfather's life. So far she's done 24, from picking up litter to buying a stranger's coffee. Josie says most people have reacted | **ORIGIN** |
| with (4) ........... and simply thanked | **ASTONISH** |
| her for her (5) ........... . Others have looked at her as if she was mad. | **GENEROUS** |
| 'I have to use my (6) ........... carefully when I choose people I'll help,' she says. One of her most | **JUDGE** |
| (7) ........... acts has been when she baked a cake for a lonely | **MEMORY** |
| elderly neighbour. By an (8) ........... coincidence it was his birthday that day and he was absolutely thrilled. | **BELIEF** |

## VOCABULARY   Leadership and achievement

**Your profile**

What do you think are the qualities of a good leader?
Which of these qualities do you think you have?

**1** Read the quiz. Check the meaning of the words and phrases.

## Team player?   Team leader?

| | |
|---|---|
| **1** | I rarely **doubt** my ability as I'm a confident and **motivated** person. |
| **2** | I include everyone in activities and treat people **fairly**. |
| **3** | I am more **adventurous** than **cautious**. |
| **4** | I prefer spending time with friends, but I'm happy in **my own company**. |
| **5** | People think of me as a **sympathetic** person who is always ready to listen. |
| **6** | I show **appreciation** for the kind things my friends do for me. |
| **7** | I react positively to **criticism** even though I may not agree with it. |
| **8** | I have a lot of **influence** on people and they often look up to me. |
| **9** | I set myself **targets** and I'm **strict** with myself about achieving them. |
| **10** | I'm willing to be different and **stand out** from the crowd. |

**2** Read the quiz. Give yourself a score from 1–3.
1 = not true for me, 2 = sometimes true for me,
3 = always true for me.

**3** Add up your scores for the quiz and then turn
to page 131. What does the quiz say about you?
Do you agree?

**4** ▶2.18 Complete the table. Use the sentences in
the quiz to help you. Then listen and check.

| Noun | Adjective | Verb |
|---|---|---|
| 1 | 2 | sympathise |
| 3 | appreciative | 4 |
| 5 | 6 | criticise |
| 7 | 8 / | motivate |
| doubt | 9 | 10 |

**5** ▶2.19 Listen to four people. Which of them do
you think would make good leaders? Why?

**6** ▶2.19 Listen again. Complete the sentences with
the correct names: *Phoebe, Mo, Nathan* or *Ruby*.

1 ............ is doubtful he will ever be a leader.
2 ............ appreciates what his teacher did for him.
3 ............ hasn't got much sympathy with people who
make excuses. She thinks they lack motivation.
4 ............ is sometimes too critical of other people.

## READING

**1** ▶2.20 Listen to someone talking about the *Three
Dot Dash* challenge. What do all the teenagers'
ideas have in common?

**2** Read the profiles of four teenagers taking part
in *Three Dot Dash*. In pairs, decide which basic
needs each teenager is addressing.

**3** ● Read the profiles again. For questions 1–9,
choose from the people (A–D). The people may
be chosen more than once.

**Which person**
1 has been recognised for their project in their
own country?
2 has improved the lives of a very large number
of people through their idea ?
3 is working locally on their project at the moment
but wishes to expand it to other locations?
4 has worked with the kinds of people involved in
their project for a long time?
5 has involved their relatives closely in their project?
6 was motivated when they suffered from a
personal experience?
7 is aiming their project at primary school age
children to begin with?
8 did some research to find out the extent of a
problem?
9 has helped individuals to get back in contact
with each other?

## A

### Hector Ferronato

has always wanted to make a difference in the world. So for his project he combined two of his favourite interests: computer programming and the environment. Hector knew that in general young children and teenagers appreciate being involved in their learning. So he and two friends created 'The World of Piatã', a website about the adventures of a young Brazilian girl. Visitors are taught about environmental issues through fun and motivating games. The initial target of the project is 7–11 year olds, but Hector wants to expand it to older children and start a revolution in environmental education.

## B

### Yash Gupta's project

was inspired by breaking his glasses! While he was waiting for a new pair, Yash had to go to school for a week without them. Unable to see clearly, Yash soon found keeping up in class difficult. Yash went online to find out more about poor sight and discovered that around 130 million people worldwide depend on their glasses every day. Furthermore, he learned that an astonishing 300 million need glasses but can't afford them. In developing countries, around 10% of children at primary school, between 6 and 11, have poor vision and often struggle in class as a result. So Yash set up *Sight Learning*, which distributes unwanted glasses to eye clinics to give children their vision back. The first clinic to be started was in Mexico and has already given thousands of young children the glasses they need. This initial success has led to further clinics in India, Honduras and Haiti. Yash has insisted on being involved in each of the clinics and has visited them all. 'To see first hand that the work you are doing is helping someone is a great feeling and I'm glad we've been able to make an impact.'

## C

### For Natasha Suric

it all began when her older sister got a part-time job at a bakery. One evening, Natasha's sister turned up at home with a huge bag of bread and cakes that the bakery had been planning to throw away. Natasha was shocked at the amount of wasted food in a country where one in six people don't get enough to eat every day. She started thinking about how this food could be distributed to people who need it. With the help of friends and family, Natasha began collecting food from two local bakeries and delivering it to homeless shelters and retirement homes. This led to the website *FoodSync*. Natasha had this built for her to give live reports on the availability of leftover food and those in need of it. In just a few months she has delivered 500 kg of food that would have gone in rubbish bins. Natasha set up FoodSync in New York, but really wants her project to be adopted all over the country.

## D

### Anoop Virk has always

been passionate about helping people and started volunteering at homeless shelters at a young age. Having been brought up by a single mother, Anoop is aware of both the importance of family and friends in our lives. She knew that there were many organisations providing essentials to the homeless, but wanted to do something different. Project HELLO (Helping Everyone Locate Loved Ones) was founded when Anoop was 16. It aims to put homeless residents in Vancouver, Canada, in touch with lost family and friends. In three years, Project HELLO has reconnected 300 people with their friends and family through letters, phone calls and even face-to-face meetings. In addition to her invitation to Three Dot Dash, Anoop was recently included in the '20 under 20' list, which celebrates Canada's future leaders.

---

**EP Word profile *lead***

I think I lead more than I follow.

This initial success has led to further clinics.

Celebrities find it hard to lead a normal life.

→ page 126

**Talking points**

" Why do you think some people are motivated to try and help others?

What qualities do you think young people need to take on the *Three Dot Dash* challenge? "

## GRAMMAR The passive (2): Other structures

**1** Read the examples and complete the rules with *be*, *to be* or *being*.

1 *Natasha* **wants** *her idea* **to be adopted** *all over the country.*

2 *The first clinic* **to be started** *was in Mexico.*

3 *Yash has* **insisted on being involved** *in each of the clinics.*

4 *She started thinking about how this food* **could be distributed** *to people who need it.*

5 *Hector knew that in general young children and teenagers* **appreciate being involved** *in their learning.*

> There are some special structures for the passive. We use:
>
> a ............ + past participle after some verbs (*enjoy*, *feel like*, etc.).
>
> b ............ + past participle after some verbs (*want*, *hope*, etc.).
>
> c ............ + past participle after prepositions.
>
> d ............ + past participle after *the first/second/ last* + noun.
>
> e ............ + past participle after modal verbs.

→ Grammar reference **page 160**

**2** Complete the second sentence so it has the same meaning as the first sentence. Use a passive form.

0 They invited her first.
She was the first ............... *to be invited.* ...............

1 He hates it when people criticise him.
He hates ....................................................................

2 They blame me all the time and I am fed up with it.
I am fed up with ....................................................

3 Everyone would appreciate it if you were on time.
It would ..................................................................

4 We must treat everyone fairly.
Everyone must .......................................................

5 I hope they make me captain of the team soon.
I hope .....................................................................

6 They told me last.
I was the last .........................................................

**3** Write the sentences in the passive form.

0 I hate / tell / what to do.
*I hate being told what to do.*

1 Everyone expects / criticise / from time to time.

2 He insisted on / put / in charge.

3 The first student / award / a prize was from my class.

4 You will / give / the results of your exam this week.

5 The singer would like / take / seriously as an actress.

**4** Complete the sentences with a passive verb and your own ideas. Compare your answers in pairs.

1 I can't stand being …

2 I prefer being … to being …

3 In a few years I hope to be …

4 I dream of being …

## VOCABULARY Phrasal verbs with *up*

**1** Complete the sentences with the correct form of the phrasal verbs in the box. Check your answers in the profiles on page 77.

> keep up    set up    turn up

1 One evening, Natasha's sister ............ at home with a huge bag of bread and cakes.

2 Natasha ............ FoodSync in New York.

3 Unable to see clearly, Yash soon found ............ in class difficult.

**2** Match the phrasal verbs in exercise 1 to the meanings.

a start a company or organisation

b arrive

c go as quickly as someone else

**3** Match the phrasal verbs to the meanings.

1 If you want to be heard, you'll need to **speak up**.

2 I **made up** an excuse about being busy because I couldn't be bothered to go.

3 I was waiting outside the station when a young man **came up** to me.

4 The film didn't quite live up to my expectations.

a invent something

b approach someone

c speak louder

d be as good as expected

**4** Ask and answer the questions.

1 Which of your friends always turns up last when you meet?

2 Do you find it easy to keep up with schoolwork?

3 Have you ever been to an event that didn't live up to your expectations?

4 Are you good at making up stories?

5 Have you ever set up a club or something similar yourself?

# WRITING   A review (1)

**1** Read the task and answer questions 1–3.

> You see this notice on a school noticeboard.
>
> > **Reviews wanted!**
> > Is there a TV show that you never miss? Or one that you can't stand watching?
> > Write a review for the school website. Explain what the show is about and why you do or don't enjoy it.
>
> Write your **review**.

1 What do you have to write about?
2 Who will read the review?
3 What information do you need to include in your review?

**2** In pairs, tell your partner about the best and worst TV shows you have seen recently.

**3** Read the review and answer the questions.

1 Does the writer enjoy the show or not?
2 What words and expressions help you decide?
3 Would you like to watch this show? Why? / Why not?

## The Teenage Boss

a I'm a massive fan of reality TV shows and I watch them a lot. My absolute favourite is 'The Teenage Boss'.

b In this show, twelve teenagers compete to win a prize of £20,000. In each episode, they're divided into two teams and set a surprisingly challenging task. For instance, once they had just three days to come up with an original concept for a video game, make an advert and present it to a group of experts! The winning team is rewarded with a cool experience, such as a helicopter ride. However, the leader of the losing team must decide on the people who were most at fault for failing to win. Finally, the celebrity judges 'fire' one person, which means they are out of the competition.

c The contestants live together for the whole series and they are clearly under a lot of pressure. They can be extremely critical of each other, especially if they think they might be in danger of being fired. This, along with some difficult and even arrogant personalities, makes the show brilliantly entertaining and I'm totally addicted to it.

d This really is a fantastic show. I thoroughly recommend it to anyone of my age.

**4** Read the *Prepare* box. Match the paragraphs in the review to the functions.

> description of show    introduction
> recommendation    strengths/weaknesses

### Prepare to write – Features of a review

A review should:
- have a title.
- be well organised into paragraphs.
- clearly express the opinion of the reviewer.
- have a range of vocabulary related to what is being reviewed.
- use descriptive vocabulary to make it interesting.
- make a recommendation.

**5** Read the review again. Answer the questions.

1 What vocabulary related to TV shows does it contain?
2 What descriptive vocabulary does it contain?
3 What expression does the writer use to make a recommendation?

**6** Are the descriptive expressions positive or negative? Add them to the table. Can you think of any more?

> rather dull    brilliantly entertaining
> extremely amusing    absolutely gripping
> not very exciting    rather predictable

| Positive | |
| --- | --- |
| Negative | |

**7** ● Read the task in exercise 1 again. Write your review of a TV show for the website.
- Use the tips in the *Prepare* box.
- Check your spelling and grammar.
- Write 140–190 words.

## VOCABULARY  Phrasal verbs

**1** **Read the sentences and match them to the pictures (a–l).**

1 We were **held up** because there was an accident further down the road.
2 We **broke down** in traffic.
3 We had to wait for the car to **cool down**.
4 I put my foot on the brake and the car **slowed down**.
5 The train **pulled into** the station exactly on time.
6 As I got to the platform, the train was **pulling out** of the station.
7 The car **pulled up** quickly outside the bank.
8 The car indicated and **pulled over** to the side of the road.
9 I found it really hard to **keep up with** him.
10 I **ran over** some glass and got a puncture.
11 The bus **drove off** without waiting.
12 I could just **make out** the red lights of a car in front.

**2** ▶ **2.21 Listen to eight situations and decide what is happening. Use the phrasal verbs in exercise 1.**

*1 Sophie's dad has driven off without her.*

## READING

**1** **Look at the types of holiday below. Which types of holiday have you been on? Which would you like to go on?**

A Camping
B Language learning trips
C Independent travelling
D Volunteer holidays
E Package holidays

**2** **Read the article quickly. Match paragraphs 1–5 with holidays A–E in exercise 1.**

**3** **Read the article again. Answer the questions in your own words.**

1 Which type of holiday do you think the writer enjoys the most?
2 What is it important to find out before you fly to a country?
3 What did Mark's trip offer him that it would be difficult to get on another holiday?
4 What significant advantage of a camping holiday does the article mention?
5 What advantages of a package holiday are mentioned?
6 What does the writer advise you should look for in a volunteer holiday?
7 Why can volunteer holidays get quite expensive?
8 What advantages does independent travelling offer over package holidays?

**Your profile**
Describe the longest journey you've ever made.
Describe the best or worst journey you've ever been on.

# YOUNG, INDEPENDENT AND ON HOLIDAY!

## A GUIDE TO YOUR FIRST HOLIDAY – *WITHOUT* YOUR PARENTS

The end of the year is in sight and it's time to start planning some holidays! For thousands this year will be a bit different – a first holiday without parents. Ethan Kay has put together some suggestions and advice.

## SOME PRACTICAL STUFF

No one wants to break the law, so it's worth checking out how old you have to be to travel in countries without an adult. Some countries insist on travellers being at least 18, while others simply require young people to have written permission from a parent. Similarly, if you're going to be flying, check airline rules. Click here for more 'before you go' tips.

**1** ............

**Tina Frey**, who runs teenage-holidays.com, says the best holidays can be those arranged through friends and family overseas. She recommends looking up long-lost relatives and friends abroad and getting in touch.

Mark Price, 17, spent last summer with the family of a business friend of his mother's in Argentina. He said the plan had been for him to practise his Spanish before starting his degree in languages. 'And it worked. I'm loads more confident at speaking now. What's more, I got to experience everyday life in an Argentine family. That was the best part.'

**2** ............

**Many sites** have a policy of over 18s only and are particularly cautious about all-male groups, Tina points out. So always check beforehand. Otherwise, no holiday offers greater freedom at this price. The initial costs of buying necessary equipment can be shared among you and your mates, or you may be able to borrow stuff. If you're not sure open-air living is for you, try a weekend music festival – you can even rent tents at most of them and you'll have no trouble feeding yourself.

**3** ............

**If you want** the simplest of holidays abroad, with a guide in your hotel who speaks your language, then look no further. Flights and accommodation are organised for you and often some meals are included which will save you money. There are downsides, though. Resorts are often some distance from local towns and cultural attractions – the expectation is that you'll be spending much of your time in the pool or throwing yourself into the hotel entertainment programme. Of course, this may be *exactly* what you *are* planning!

**4** ............

**Although** there are no official figures, Ed Snow of inspiredholidays.org estimates that over 150,000 British teenagers will be travelling abroad this summer aiming to 'make a difference'. It's the chance to work in a totally different environment to your home and meet people from all over the world while doing something beneficial. Even the strictest parents are bound to give their permission!

Research is key. What are you passionate about? Can you find something relevant to that? Although you're offering your time, you'll be expected to cover major travel expenses and almost certainly need to contribute towards the training you will receive. Prices can get quite high. As Ed points out, 'Few people arrive with any experience of the job they are about to start. This holiday is as much about learning as it is about helping.'

**5** ............

**OK, so** persuading your parents to let you go 'flights only' might prove difficult. But if the idea of planning your own travel schedule appeals to you, then have a go! It's by far the most adventurous of holidays, with numerous opportunities to meet interesting people, practise another language and get a genuine taste of a different culture. Internet facilities are now so good that you need never break that promise of staying in regular contact with your parents.

### Talking points

"At what age should teenagers be allowed to go on holiday without their parents? Why?

Which types of holiday do you think are most suitable for young people? Why?"

## GRAMMAR Reported speech

**1** Read the direct and reported speech. Why do you think the tenses sometimes don't change? Read the rules and check.

'The best holidays **can** be those arranged through friends and family.'

'The plan **was** for me to practise my speaking skills.'

'About 150,000 British teenagers **will** be travelling abroad this summer.'

**1** Tina **says** some of the best holidays **can** be those arranged through friends and family.

**2** Mark **said** the plan **had been** for him to practise his speaking skills.

**3** Ed **estimates** that over 150,000 British teenagers **will** be travelling abroad this summer.

> **a** When we report sentences we usually change the tense, e.g. past simple ⟶ past perfect.
>
> **b** We <u>don't</u> usually change the tense when we are talking about:
>   • general truths and opinions.
>   • an event which is not in the past.
>
> **c** In these cases, we often use a reporting verb in the present simple or present perfect, e.g. *says, agrees, has said,* etc.

→ Grammar reference **page 161**

**2** Choose the correct words.

**1** 'I'm sorry I haven't been able to call.'
Joe told me he was sorry he *hasn't / hadn't* been able to call.

**2** 'It's far quicker to go by bus.'
Tom says *it's / it was* far quicker to go by bus.

**3** 'You should learn to drive.'
He said I should *learn / have learned* to drive.

**4** 'You must carry your passport with you at all times.'
The law says you *had to / must* carry your passport with you at all times.

**5** 'The holiday will be my first without my parents.'
Sarah admits that the holiday *will / would* be her first without her parents.

**6** 'We're going there on Wednesday.'
Dad told me last week that *they were / they're* going there last Wednesday.

### ⊘ Corpus challenge

Find and correct the mistakes in the student's sentence.

*Last week he said me that you are working very hard.*

**3** Complete the reported speech sentences.

**1** 'The hotel won't take guests under 18.'
The travel agent says ...............................................

**2** 'I want to take a year off before university.'
My sister told my parents ...............................................

**3** 'My mum's a better driver than my brother.'
Amy reckons ...............................................

**4** 'I've been travelling through Europe in the holidays.'
Dylan said ...............................................

**5** 'We've been waiting for over an hour!'
Amy claims ...............................................

## VOCABULARY Reporting verbs

**1** Read the sentences and underline the reporting verbs.

**a** My sister agreed to slow down.

**b** My grandparents insisted that I went home early.

**c** Tom persuaded his friend to overtake the car in front.

**d** The instructor criticised me for braking too often.

**e** The woman enquired if the trains were on time.

**f** The policeman pointed out that his driver's licence wasn't valid.

**g** She recommended travelling after the rush hour.

**h** He confessed to driving above the speed limit.

**2** ▶ 2.22 Listen and match the speakers to the sentences in exercise 1.

**3** ● Complete the second sentence so that it has a similar meaning to the first sentence, using the word given. Use between two and five words.

**1** 'It's best to leave your passports in the hotel safe,' the receptionist told them.
**RECOMMENDED**
The .................................... passports in the hotel safe.

**2** 'You never remember my birthday, David,' Jen said. **CRITICISED**
Jen .................................... her birthday.

**3** 'It was me who lost the tickets,' Jo said.
**CONFESSED**
Jo .................................... the tickets.

**4** 'OK. I'll give you a lift,' Dad told Sally. **AGREED**
Sally's .................................... a lift.

**5** 'I definitely remember locking the door,' Sam said. **INSISTED**
Sam .................................... the door.

**6** 'Do you accept people under 18?,' Karen asked the campsite. **ENQUIRED**
Karen .................................... people under 18.

**7** 'You know, going camping would be the best idea,' Mr Thomas told Kurt. **PERSUADED**
Mr Thomas .................................... camping.

**8** 'Sharing a room will be cheaper,' the travel agent told us. **POINTED**
The travel agent .................................... a room would be cheaper.

## LISTENING

**1** Look at the photos. Can you explain the travel problem in each photo? Have you experienced any of these problems yourself?

**2** ▶2.23 Listen to five people talking about bad travel experiences. Match the people to the photos. Which person's story doesn't match a photo?

**3** ▶2.23 ● Listen again. For questions 1–5, choose from the list A–H what each speaker says. Use the letters only once. There are three extra letters which you do not need to use.

**A** I was too young to understand what the problem was.
**B** What started as a joke, ended in disaster.
**C** The problem I had was my own fault.
**D** Illness prevented me from enjoying myself.
**E** An accident spoiled the trip for everyone.
**F** An unexpected event delayed our arrival.
**G** I blame someone else for what happened.
**H** Nobody could have predicted what happened to us.

Speaker 1 ☐ **1**
Speaker 2 ☐ **2**
Speaker 3 ☐ **3**
Speaker 4 ☐ **4**
Speaker 5 ☐ **5**

## SPEAKING  Making decisions

**1** ▶2.24 Ahmed and Dan are going camping together. Listen to their conversation. How do they decide to travel?

**2** ▶2.24 Read the *Prepare* box. Listen again and number the phrases in the order you hear them.

### Prepare to speak – Making decisions

**Presenting an argument**
It makes sense if we …
What about this for an idea?

**Giving a counter argument**
That's true, but …
The trouble with … is …

**Asking somebody's opinion**
What do you reckon about … ?
Do you think it's best to … ?

**Making a decision**
Are we agreed?
What we've decided is …

**3** Imagine you are planning a day trip to celebrate the end of exams. What would be the good and bad points about going to these places?

> a big shopping mall   a city
> a theme park   the beach

**4** Work in pairs. Discuss the different places and make a decision about where to go. Use phrases from the *Prepare* box.

### EP Word profile *break*

My mum says it still breaks her heart when she thinks about how upset I was.

You need never break that promise.

No one wants to break the law, so it's worth checking out how old you have to be.

page 136

# Culture
## Cultural highways

**1** Look at the map. The red line shows the Silk Road, an important trade route for over 1,500 years. Before you read the text, answer the questions below. Then read Part A of the text and check your answers.

   **1** How long do you think the Silk Road is?

   **2** What was it used for?

**2** Read Part B of the text. Why has the importance of the Silk Road declined over the past 500 years?

# Much more than just silk

**A**    In ancient and medieval times, the Silk Road was a vast network of trade routes that extended from the Mediterranean Sea, across Central and Eastern Asia, to the Pacific coast of China – a total distance of more than 6,400 km. The Silk Road also had branches that ran south to cities on the Arabian Sea and the Bay of Bengal.

   As its name suggests, the Silk Road was famous as a route for traders bringing Chinese silk to European markets. However, other luxury products were also transported along this ancient highway, such as gold, amber, precious stones, glass bottles, fine porcelain and paper. In addition, there was an increase in demand for exotic food products from other countries, such as spices, oranges, apples, olive oil and wine.

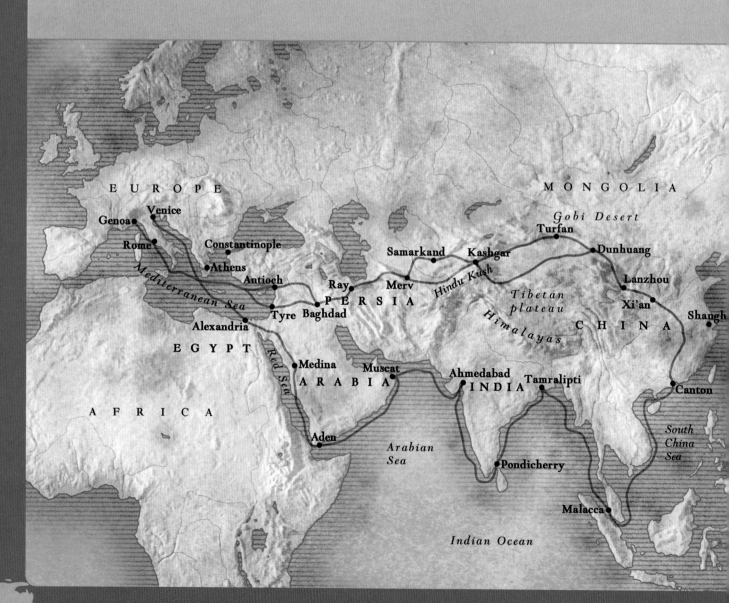

B    In many areas along the Silk Road, there were, in fact, no roads at all, especially where the terrain was too rocky or sandy. As a result, merchants usually travelled by horse or camel, with extra pack animals to carry their goods. Unfortunately, there were often thieves who attacked and robbed them, so merchants often travelled in large groups, called caravans. As a result of all this traffic along the Silk Road, many towns and large cities were established to provide food, water and shelter for travellers, as well as market-places where people could buy and sell goods that came from all directions.

Although trade was the original purpose of the Silk Road, it also served as an important cultural highway, transmitting new ideas from country to country, as people moved backwards and forwards. In this way, people learned about new styles of art, music, literature, fashion and even leisure activities. Technological advances also spread from one area to another. For example, the irrigation water-wheel was invented in the Middle East, but it soon appeared in agricultural areas all along the Silk Road. Similar innovations in metal-working, textiles and pottery were also transmitted this way.

The Silk Road remained the most important East-West trade route until the early 1500s, when merchants started using newly-discovered sea routes around the southern tip of Africa. Transporting goods by ship was faster and easier, and it allowed Europeans to trade directly with merchants in East Asia. As a result, the Silk Road's importance declined slowly over the years. Nevertheless, some of the old trade routes are still open today for international transport, as well as new forms of tourism. For long-distance cyclists and other adventure tourists, the Silk Road offers thousands of kilometres of excitement, as well as an important source of income for local economies that can no longer depend on trade.

**3** **Are these sentences about the Silk Road true or false, according to the text?**

1 The Silk Road was a single route from the Mediterranean to the Pacific.
2 The Silk Road was only used by silk traders.
3 Merchants only transported goods from East to West along the Silk Road.
4 Travelling on the Silk Road was sometimes dangerous.
5 The Silk Road is as busy and important now as it was in medieval times.

**4** **Think about your answers to the questions. Then discuss them in pairs or groups.**

1 Nowadays, what forms of transport do traders use to transport their goods?
2 In addition to travelling, how do people today exchange new ideas and customs?
3 How do you and your friends learn about new fashion, music and other trends?
4 Would you like to travel the old Silk Route by bicycle as an adventure tourist?

**5** ▶ 2.25 **Listen to two people talking about exciting routes they have travelled. Complete the chart.**

|  | Route 1 (Jenny) | Route 2 (Michael) |
|---|---|---|
| **Starting point** |  |  |
| **Finishing point** |  |  |
| **Distance travelled** |  |  |
| **Length of time** |  |  |
| **Form(s) of transport** |  |  |
| **Types of landscape** |  |  |
| **Highlights** |  |  |

**Project**

Design a cultural route for visitors to your country or another country that you choose. Use the questions below to plan your route.
1 Where will the tour start and finish? What major stops will you make?
2 What time of year will it happen? How many days or weeks will it take?
3 What transport will people use? What landscapes will they see?
4 What festivals and other events will people experience?
5 What other interesting experiences will they have?

## VOCABULARY  Global issues: nouns and verbs

**Your profile**

What national or global issues do you feel concerned about? Why?

**1** Match the sentence halves. Check the meaning of the verbs.

1 Aid agencies are **cooperating**
2 We've **collected**
3 Cars should be **banned**
4 The local council has been **criticised**
5 You seem to think I don't **support**
6 It's great that Ann's been **elected**

a for not dealing with litter in the city.
b your views on animal rights.
c £100 for an anti-poverty charity.
d with the state government.
e as the student representative.
f from busy city streets.

**2** ▶ 2.26 Listen to six people and check your answers to exercise 1.

**3** ▶ 2.26 Complete the sentences with the noun forms of the verbs in exercise 1. Listen again and check.

> ban   collection   cooperation
> criticism   election   supporter

1 Unfortunately, ............ between the two organisations has been made more difficult.
2 Sometimes we organise a food ............ for a local homeless hostel.
3 A ............ on private cars would make a huge difference in the city centre.
4 There has been further ............ of the local council.
5 I'm a great ............ of animal rights.
6 The ............ was for student representatives from the other years too.

## READING

**1** Look at the title, the photo and the two grey quotes in the text. Answer the questions below. Then read the interview quickly and check your answers.

1 What do you think the interview will be about?
2 What do you think 'MYP' and 'UKYP' could mean?
3 Do you think this young person enjoyed her experience of youth politics?

**2** Read three summaries of the interview. Choose the best one.

1 Charity talks about her personal experiences and gives a few examples of specific projects she has worked on.
2 Charity mentions some of the things she achieved as an MYP and gives advice to readers who may wish to be elected as MYPs.
3 Charity describes the range of people you are likely to meet as an MYP and how to handle them.

**3** Complete the sentences with the highlighted expressions in the introduction.

1 Every ............ of our daily life is influenced by technology.
2 Are you interested in taking part in ............ about future education policy?
3 Please ............ that your name is at the top of the form.
4 Let's ............ a meeting between the teachers and students.
5 I don't want to be in a ............ of responsibility.
6 Do the students ............ this website themselves?
7 Do you ever have to make ............ in front of loads of people?

**4** Find these underlined sentences in the interview. Explain what you think Charity means.

1 It's all about getting a good work–life balance.
2 If you put in the work, you will get loads back in return.
3 My year was when history was made.
4 Communication is key if you want to get something done.
5 You just need to take the opportunities that come your way.
6 It will all be worth it in the end.

# MYPs @ UKYP

The UK Youth Parliament is a youth organisation in the United Kingdom, consisting of elected members aged between 11 and 18. There are currently hundreds of MYPs who meet with MPs and local politicians, organise events, run campaigns, make speeches, hold debates and ensure the views of young people are listened to by decision makers. A key aspect of any MYP's job is to make sure they represent the views of the young people in their area. We talked to Charity Mhende about her recent position as an MYP.

*Charity, your year as a Member of the Youth Parliament must have been a really interesting experience. Did it live up to your expectations?*

It was absolutely amazing! I have grown so much and have been given so many incredible opportunities. I really believe now that you have to make the most of every opportunity that comes along, as it could be something that has an impact on your life forever.

> **‘ You have to make the most of every opportunity that comes along. ’**

*It can't have been easy though, doing this on top of your schoolwork and everything else that a normal 15-year-old likes to do! Did anything suffer?*

For some people, being involved in the UKYP means they end up giving up their social lives, but it shouldn't be like that. It's all about getting a good work–life balance. At the same time, you always have to remember that you only get what you give. If you put in the work, you will get loads back in return.

**EP Word profile *key***

A key aspect of any MYP's job is to make sure they represent the views of the young people in their area.

Communication is key if you want to get something done.

▶ page 137

**Talking points**

❝
- Do you think young people should have a role in government? Why? / Why not?
- In what other ways can young people help to improve their society?
❞

*And what did you focus on as an MYP?*

I was elected as one of the Media Representatives for the West Midlands, where I live, so I was heavily involved in media work. And my year was when history was made – we were the first non-Members of Parliament to be allowed to debate in the House of Commons like real politicians. It was my role to make sure the press knew about it and that our work got recognised. My biggest achievement was being on the national TV news and on the radio.

*You must be very proud of that. It sounds like the experience might have changed your approach to life. Has it?*

Yes, I have definitely grown in confidence and I have learned the art of socialising and negotiating, because communication is key if you want to get something done. In this role you can make links with decision-makers and people that could help you a great deal in the future. You just need to take the opportunities that come your way.

> **‘ Don't be afraid to ask questions! ’**

*Some situations must have been quite scary, in that they were completely new for you. What advice would you give other teenagers in that position?*

Well, it's true that you might be put into unexpected situations, but you just need to be brave and do the best you can. And don't be afraid to ask questions! Youth workers, staff and other MYPs will all be happy to help you. You will meet so many people and have loads of new challenges, but it will all be worth it in the end.

## GRAMMAR  Modals (3): Deduction

**1** Read the examples. Is each sentence about the past, the present or the future?

1 You **must** be very proud of that.

2 It **could** be something that has an impact on your life forever.

3 The experience **might have** changed your approach to life.

4 Some situations **must have** been quite scary.

5 It **can't have** been easy.

**2** Complete the rules with the correct modal verbs.

> can't    could    couldn't    may    may not
> might    might not    must

> We use modal verb + infinitive to make guesses about the present and future.
> We use modal verb + *have* + past participle to make guesses about the past.
> We use:
>
> a ............ for things we are certain about.
>
> b ............ or ............ for things we are certain are not true.
>
> c ............ , ............ or ............ for things that are likely.
>
> d ............ or ............ for things that are unlikely.

→ Grammar reference  **page 162**

**3** Choose the correct modal verbs.

1 Clare *could stick / must have stuck* that poster here. She's trying to advertise her charity event.

2 There's someone at the door. It *must be / can't be* Jon; he's not around today.

3 Simon often collects money for this group, so he *must / couldn't* support our ideas.

4 We're waiting for an important document. There was a postal strike last week, so that *must delay / might have delayed* it.

5 Kids from that school *couldn't damage / couldn't have damaged* the car. The damage happened while the kids were still in classes.

6 I think their representative is sick, so they *mustn't have / might not have* anyone to talk to.

7 My brother usually keeps in touch, but we haven't heard from him for ages. I'm not sure, but there *can't / may* be some sort of problem.

8 Anna has sent a few text messages of support, so she *could lose / can't have lost* her phone.

**4** Look at the photos. In pairs, make guesses about the situations.

### Corpus challenge

Find and correct the mistakes in the student's sentence.

The show should started at half past seven, but nothing happened.

## VOCABULARY  Phrases with *in*

**1** Charity used the phrase *in return*, meaning 'in exchange for'. Match these phrases to the meanings.

1 in all          a happening or being done now
2 in general      b one after another
3 in progress     c considering the whole of
4 in public          something
5 in secret       d without telling other people
6 in turn         e as a total amount
                  f where everyone can see or hear

**2** Complete the sentences with the phrases from exercise 1.

1 The politician had said the wrong thing ............ and was forced to apologise.

2 Josh and Liam met ............ to discuss their plans to split up the band.

3 There were over forty student representatives ............ at the regional meeting.

4 Let's speak to everyone ............ and then report their views back to the class.

5 Building work is ............ , so the library will remain closed until Friday.

6 Apart from your studies, how are things going for you ............ ?

# WRITING An essay (3)

**1** Look at the diagram about employment. Choose two more topics and create a diagram for each.

1 education      3 health
2 travel         4 the environment

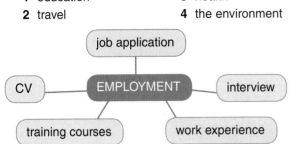

**2** Read the essay. Is it about employment, education or both?

This is a complex question and conditions vary greatly around the world. In my own country, there are no job opportunities, or very few. Once teenagers leave school aged 16–18, they often find it very hard to get work. Youth unemployment is 50% higher than it was ten years ago. Employers these days are happy to employ young people, provided they already have some experience, but it can be difficult for young people to get experience. That's why many young people accept unpaid jobs, just to learn more about the world of work.

On the other hand, the opportunities to learn are much greater than they used to be. It is possible to study a wider range of subjects today and it is much easier to get into university. My grandfather never had the chance to attend university, whereas a large percentage of today's generation will do so. They say that travel broadens the mind. Young people today have a lot more opportunity to travel now that there are lots of low-cost airlines and you can plan trips online. It has never been easier to gain experience of other cultures.

In conclusion, considering the job market is difficult at the moment, today's young people still have more opportunities than their parents and grandparents did.

**3** Choose the question that matches the essay in exercise 2.

1 How has access to education and work changed over the past two generations?
2 What life skills can young people acquire today that their grandparents couldn't?
3 Does society offer more or fewer opportunities for young people today?

**4** Read the *Prepare* box. Then find examples of linking words in the essay.

## Prepare to write – Linking words (1)

We use linking words to join short sentences together, to make complex sentences:
*I've got a car. I can visit you more often.*
→ *I can visit you more often **now** I've got a car.*
You can use these linking words to join sentences:
*considering, now, once, or, provided*

**5** Complete the sentences with the correct linking words.

> considering    now    once    or    provided

1 The situation at school has been improving, ............ that's what we've been told.
2 Are you sure you want to leave? Remember that you can't criticise the group ............ you've left.
3 She's enjoying the position ............ that she's got more responsibility.
4 I'll lend you my camera, ............ you look after it properly.
5 She did really well, ............ how little experience she had had.

**6** Read the task. Add some information and your own idea to the notes.

> **Many environmental problems could get worse in the future. Do you agree?**
>
> **Notes**
> Write about:
> 1 population growth
> 2 pollution
> 3 ................. (your own idea)

**7** ⬤ Write your essay.
- Write about all the ideas in the notes.
- Use linking words to make complex sentences.
- Check your grammar and spelling.
- Write 140–190 words.

## VOCABULARY   Advertising: nouns and verbs

**Your profile**

Which current TV adverts do you love and hate? Why? What do you think makes a good advert?

**1** ▶3.02 **Look at the pictures of adverts. Listen to Dan and Emma talking and answer the questions.**

1 Which ad don't they talk about?
2 Who prefers each ad? Why?
3 Who do you think the products are aimed at? Why?
4 How does Dan's attitude to advertising change during the conversation?

**2** ▶3.02 **Complete the sentences. Listen again and check.**

| aimed at | commercial breaks | consumer |
|---|---|---|
| launching | logo | on offer | sample | sponsored |

1 Emma enjoys the ............ on TV.
2 The shampoo advert isn't ........... people like Dan.
3 Emma has a ............ of the advertised product.
4 Emma likes to know what products are ............ .
5 A car manufacturer is ........... a new model.
6 Emma says Dan is a ............ like everyone else.
7 Dan's football team is ............ by a bank.
8 A ............ on a football shirt is very good publicity for sponsors.

**3** **Discuss the questions.**

1 What do you think of the commercial breaks on TV?
2 Who sponsors your favourite team?
3 Do you wait until things are on offer before you buy them?
4 What kinds of free samples do you like receiving in magazines?
5 Which well-known logos can you describe?

## READING

**1** **Read the text quickly. What is the main idea?**

1 Most advertisers have started to use guerrilla marketing.
2 Guerrilla marketing involves several new and clever methods.
3 Viral marketing is the latest trend in online advertising.
4 Guerrilla marketing will take over from traditional advertising.

**2** ⬤ **Read the first paragraph and think of the word which best fits each gap. Use only one word in each gap.**

**3** **Match the highlighted words in the text to their meanings.**

1 a hole or opening
2 against the law
3 easily noticed
4 easy to remember for a long time
5 a short video, often on a website
6 the amount of money available to be spent
7 a group of people who like a particular type of product
8 advanced, working in a clever way

**4** **Answer the questions.**

1 Why is viral marketing relatively cheap?
2 Why isn't viral marketing guaranteed to succeed?
3 Why isn't reverse graffiti against the law?
4 Why is body advertising an uncommon sight?
5 Why do actors doing undercover marketing have to be unknown?
6 What is the risk associated with undercover marketing?

# Guerrilla Marketing

Wherever you are in the world, (0) ...if/when... you switch on the TV or open a magazine, you'll probably see an advert. Love it or hate it, publicity is a fact of modern life. For the keen consumer, ads are entertaining (1) ............ well as informative. Attractive logos, witty slogans and beautifully designed ads are a welcome addition to their day. According (2) ............ others, we live in an increasingly crowded, noisy world in (3) ............ adverts are just a nuisance. Their creation is a waste (4) ............ resources and their appearance is no less than visual pollution. No matter what your feelings are, ads (5) ............ getting more sophisticated every day. Adverts (6) ............ developed hand in hand with technological advances, appearing first as simple printed messages, then (7) ............ the radio and in TV commercials, on email and as pop-up windows online. Now, in the digital age, 'guerrilla' marketing (8) ............ using innovative techniques – always imaginative, sometimes irritating – to get ads seen.

## Viral marketing

Imagine that you're a computer games developer and you're trying to launch a new BMX racing game on a limited budget. You need to promote the game cheaply if you have little money for publicity, so you commission a short film with talented but unknown BMX riders. The film is dramatic and fast-moving, following a crazy ride around an inner-city neighbourhood to a soundtrack of heavy rock music. The clip shows the riders arriving home exhausted, lying on the sofa and playing your game. It ends with your logo and a link to your website. A BMX magazine uploads the video to YouTube and you're very lucky: viewers love it. If the clip is shared and 'liked' on social media, you'll end up with millions of hits. If the same clip had appeared as a TV commercial, it would have cost millions to broadcast it. How many viral videos like this have you watched and how many products have you helped to promote for free?

## Reverse graffiti

If you sprayed an image onto a wall, you'd probably get arrested – graffiti is illegal. But reverse graffiti is clever, as there's no need to break the law. To create reverse graffiti, you cut words and shapes into a sheet of plastic. Then lay the plastic against a flat surface and spray water and cleaning products into each gap. The result is a clean, bright image surrounded by a dirty bit of wall or pavement. It is cheap and there are no laws against cleaning, which means it is popular with street artists who want to create beautiful images in unloved urban locations. The process is often used just for local advertising, but photos of the best reverse graffiti ads can be seen by millions globally if they go viral.

## Body advertising

How would you like an advert painted on your body? It would have to be somewhere visible such as your forehead or even your eyelids! Body advertising looks striking, some might say offensive, but the ads can usually be washed off after a couple of days. Still, it's no wonder you don't see it very often. It is either used to advertise to a specific, local audience, or photos of the ads are intended to go viral.

## Undercover marketing

Actors are sometimes paid to raise awareness of products secretly. For example, a phone company might place an actor with their latest mobile in a city centre location. The actor approaches passing strangers, the type of person the phone is aimed at and asks, 'Would you mind taking a photo of me on my phone?' While their photo is being taken, the actor chats with the potential customer about what an amazing phone it is. It's no good using well-known actors: undercover marketing only works if the actors' identities and motives remain secret. It would damage a company's reputation if consumers realised it was marketing. Undercover marketing is expensive, but effective, because an interaction with a real person is much more believable and memorable than any other kind of advertising.

> **EP Word profile *no***
>
> There's no need to break the law.
>
> It's no wonder you don't see it very often.
>
> It's no good using well-known actors.
>
> **page 137**

**Talking points**

" Which guerrilla marketing techniques do you think are most likely to be effective? Why?

Do you think that guerrilla marketing will ever replace TV advertising? Why? / Why not? "

## GRAMMAR  Conditionals (1): Review

**1** Read the examples and answer the questions.

1 *If you* **switch** *on the TV or open a magazine, you'll probably* **see** *an advert.*
  Is it certain or possible you will see an ad?

2 *If the same clip* **had appeared** *as a TV commercial, it* **would have cost** *millions.*
  Did the commercial appear on TV? Did it cost millions?

3 *You* **need** *to promote the game cheaply* **if** *you* **have** *little money for publicity.*
  Is this a possibility or a true statement?

4 *It* **would damage** *the company's reputation* **if** *consumers* **realised** *it was marketing.*
  Was the company's reputation damaged?

**2** Read the examples again and complete the rules.

> future    general    past    present

> We use the:
> a  zero conditional to talk about ............ truths.
> b  first conditional for possible or probable events in the ............ .
> c  second conditional for impossible situations in the ............, or unlikely situations in the future.
> d  third conditional for imaginary results of ............ situations that never happened.

→ Grammar reference  **page 163**

**3** Match the sentence halves.

1 If you take LongLife vitamins,
2 You wouldn't have been late
3 If I wasn't using my laptop,
4 If it's raining later,
5 This door makes a loud noise

a she'll probably get the bus.
b of course I'd lend it to you.
c you'll be healthy forever.
d unless you open it carefully.
e if you'd left home on time.

**4** Complete the conditional questions. Then ask and answer the questions.

1 If you ............ your phone, what would you do? (lose)
2 What ............ yesterday if your classes had been cancelled? (you / do)
3 What ............ when the weather is hot? (you / wear)
4 If you ............ your exams, will you go to university? (pass)
5 Where ............ if you had £1 million? (you / go)

### ⊙ Corpus challenge

**Find and correct the mistake in the student's sentence.**

*We would win if I hadn't made a mistake.*

## VOCABULARY  Adverb + adjective collocations

**1** Complete the sentences with the correct adverbs.

> incredibly    ecologically    scientifically    well
> financially    globally    constantly    environmentally

**①** It's fast, it's cheap, it's ............ friendly. Travel by Metro!

**②** Take VitX every day – ............ **proven** to give you extra energy. Remember – always take vitamins as part of a ............ -**balanced** diet.

**③** Buy the app now, it is ............ **updated**, so you'll never be out-of-date.

**④** This ............ **recognised** brand is a bestseller on every continent.

**⑤** Don't you want to be ............ **independent**? Work part-time from home and earn extra cash now!

**⑥** Our printers use ............ **sound** inks and they're ............ **economical** to run.

**2** Complete the second sentence using the correct form of the bold words.

0 The head teacher always **welcomes** parents very **warmly**.
  Parents are always ...warmly welcomed... .
1 Your brother always **dresses** in **nice** clothes.
  Your brother is always ............ .
2 The program **generates** a new password **automatically** every day.
  A new password is ............ every day.
3 I am **involved** in their project quite **actively**.
  I am ............ in their project.
4 The railway is **located** at a **convenient** distance from the college.
  There's a ............ railway station near the college.
5 My dad has a **natural talent** for telling jokes.
  My dad is a ............ comedian.
6 The recipe says you have to **chop** the onions **finely**.
  The recipe requires ............ onions.

# LISTENING

**1** You will hear a girl called Anita Lloyd talking about the subject of advertising. Underline key words in sentences 1–10 and predict what you might hear.

**3** Discuss the questions.

1 What do you think of undercover advertising?
2 What would you do if you were Anita?
3 How would you feel if an ad agency wanted you to work with them?

**2** ▶3.03 ● Listen and for questions 1–10, complete the sentences with a word or short phrase. Listen again and check.

## Advertising

Anita recently took up the official role called (1) .............................. in her school.

Anita originally thought that the parcel she received must be from a (2) .............................. .

Anita's favourite item in the box was a personalised (3) .............................. .

The band called The Emissary aims to appeal to girls in the (4) .............................. age group.

Advertisers believe that (5) .............................. is the best form of advertising for Anita's age group.

Anita uses the word (6) .............................. to describe the advertisers' clever tactics.

Anita was given tickets for a concert held in a local (7) .............................. .

Anita was invited to London by a (8) .............................. .

Anita was asked to take part in something known as (9) .............................. advertising.

Anita was excited to meet some well-known (10) .............................. at an event in London.

# SPEAKING  Opinions

**1** ● Look at the photographs. Complete the task.

> **The photographs show two advertisements.**
> **Student A:** Compare the photographs and say which advert you think is the most effective and why.
> **Student B:** Talk briefly about which shoes you would prefer to wear.

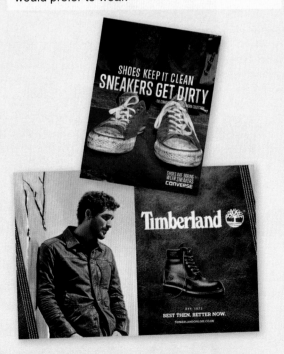

**2** Turn to page 131 and complete the task.

**3** ▶3.04 Look at the task below and listen to the conversation. What form of advertising do Emma and Dan agree is the best value for companies?

street posters    guerilla marketing    viral ads

**Why might companies choose these different forms of advertising?**

magazine ads

TV commercials    online pop-up ads

**4** ▶3.05 Read the *Prepare* box. Then listen to Emma and Dan using the phrases. Which expressions do you hear?

> **Prepare to speak — Expressing opinions**
>
> **Expressing opinions**
> I assume/imagine/reckon (that) …
> I get the feeling/impression that …
> The good/bad thing about … is …
> As I see it, …
>
> **Justifying opinions**
> It seems to me that …
> On the one hand, … on the other hand, …
> From the point of view of …
> If you think about it, …

**5** ● Work in pairs. Answer the question in the task in exercise 3. Use phrases from the *Prepare* box.

# Geography
## Tourism

**1** Read the website article. Is the author in favour of mass tourism or against it?

| 🏠 HOME | 📄 NEWS | 📑 ARTICLES | ❓ ABOUT US |

# MASS TOURISM
## *A victim of its own success?*

Sandy beaches, snow-capped mountains, lush rainforests and exotic wildlife. For countries that want to attract visitors, these natural wonders can be an enormous advantage. With proper care, they can bring in millions of tourist dollars to stimulate the economy and create new jobs. However, this sort of tourism can be a victim of its own success if appropriate measures aren't taken to protect the natural environment.

**LANDSCAPE CHANGES:** Mass tourism requires the development of new infrastructure, such as roads, bridges and airports, as well as other facilities, like hotels and shopping centres. As a result, large areas of land may be cleared for new construction. Unfortunately, this destroys plant life, which can lead to erosion. In some cases, rivers are diverted to fill swimming pools, or keep gardens and golf courses green. These changes have a terrible effect on the same natural areas that attract tourists.

**INCREASED POLLUTION:** As a rule, the more visitors there are, the more pollution there will be. Some examples include:

- air and noise pollution from traffic
- litter that people may drop on the ground
- rubbish from hotels and shops
- light pollution from too many street lamps
- visual pollution, such as large, ugly buildings

**DISRUPTION OF ECOSYSTEMS:** Physical changes to the natural environment can destroy entire ecosystems. For example, when forests are cut down, many animals lose their natural homes. Similarly, when tourists use too much water, there may not be enough for wildlife. Some animals might also change their habits, for instance, by eating food waste from rubbish bins. Other animals move away from the area because of excessive noise or too much artificial light at night. At the same time, people often introduce new plants and animals that compete with native species.

> **Talk back! Is mass tourism its own worst enemy? Send us your comments.**

### COMMENTS

**envirokid@** This is so true! I live near a natural park and lots of campers visit at weekends. They always leave litter and they make a lot of noise at night.

**tanya18@** I think the worst thing about mass tourism in my country is how ugly hotels ruin the views of our beaches. It's such a shame!

**2** Read the text again. Then match the sentence halves.

1 A country's tourist industry could suffer if it
2 New infrastructure may be necessary when
3 There could be problems with erosion
4 When there is too much artificial light,
5 An increase in road traffic may result in
6 If a country protects its natural areas,

a if forested areas are cleared for buildings.
b the tourist industry will benefit.
c problems with air and noise pollution.
d doesn't protect the environment.
e some animals may leave the area.
f more tourists start visiting an area.

**3** Discuss these questions with a partner or in a group.

1 How does tourism stimulate an area's economy?
2 Why does mass tourism require more infrastructure?
3 What problems can golf courses cause?
4 Why should tourist areas try to stop visual pollution?
5 Why shouldn't tourists give food to wild animals?

**4** Look at the advert for a national park. What do you think people can see and do here?

**5** ▶ 3.06 Listen to a podcast about the park. Answer the questions.

1 When were Loch Lomond and the Trossachs declared a national park?
2 How much of the park's land area is covered in forest and woodland?
3 How many rivers are there inside the park's borders?
4 Approximately how many people visit the national park every year?
5 What will happen if the four goals are met?

**6** ▶ 3.07 Listen to the first part of the podcast again. What do these numbers refer to?

| 22 | 55 | 71 | 1,865 | 15,000 |

**7** ▶ 3.08 Listen to the second part of the podcast again. Complete the park's four goals.

communities  conserve  cultural  enjoyment
natural  public  responsible  social

1 'To ............ and promote the park's natural and ............ heritage'
2 'To promote ............, sustainable use of the area's ............ resources'
3 'To promote ............ understanding and ............ of the park'
4 'To promote the ............ and economic development of local ............'

**Project**

Write a class presentation about a national park in your country.

1 Where is the park? How big is it?
2 When was the park established?
3 What types of landscape does it have?
4 Is there any typical plant or animal life?
5 What activities can visitors do there?
6 How is tourism affecting the park?
7 What should people do to protect it?

# Review 4
## Units 13-16

## VOCABULARY

**1** Complete the words with the correct noun, adjective or verb endings.

1 Mike seems nice but he isn't very sympath............ .
2 Thanks for all your help, we really apprec............ it.
3 Do you think this is a valid critic............ of your work?
4 I'm not feeling very motivat............ at the moment.
5 It's doub............ that anyone will actually listen to us!
6 Cooperat............ is vital if we want to get finished on time.

**2** Complete the sentences with the correct form of phrasal verbs. Use a word from A and a word from B.

Ⓐ break    cool    keep    live    pull    speak

Ⓑ down x2    out    up    up to    up with

1 My scooter ............ all the time, it's really unreliable.
2 Can you ............ a bit? I can't hear you very well.
3 I got to the platform as the train was ............ .
4 Did the party ............ your expectations?
5 It's hard to ............ her because she walks so fast.
6 This breeze is really ............ me ............ .

**3** Complete the sentences with the correct form of the pairs of verbs. Add another word if necessary.

agree / help    confess / break    criticise / make
persuade / get    point out / plan    recommend / get

0 Fabio said: 'It's quicker and safer to get the bus.'
  Fabio ..persuaded.. his friends ..to get.. the bus.
1 Nick says: 'You should get a new phone.'
  Nick ............ a new phone.
2 Sara said: 'It was me who broke your headphones.'
  Sara ............ my headphones.
3 Jules said: 'I wish you wouldn't make a mess.'
  Jules ............ me ............ a mess.
4 Lydia said: 'Yes, I'll help you to fill in this questionnaire.'
  Lydia ............ me fill in the questionnaire.
5 Danny said: 'Planning ahead will make a big difference.'
  Danny ............ ahead would make a big difference.

**4** The underlined words in the text are in the wrong places. Write the correct words.

*0 brand*

The world's leading phone ⁰ <u>products</u> has just ¹ <u>sample</u> a budget handset for the first time. It is ² <u>brand</u> at ³ <u>publicity</u> who can't afford the £500+ ⁴ <u>launched</u> that have made the brand so successful. There has been a huge amount of ⁵ <u>aimed</u> surrounding the new handset and it has been hard for shops to get even a ⁶ <u>offer</u>, never mind actual stock of the phone. The phone is expected to be on special ⁷ <u>consumers</u> for about a month before being sold at around £150.

**5** Match the sentence halves.

1 Our website is constantly          a friendly car.
2 It's an environmentally             b generated, so ignore it.
3 I eat a fairly well-                c proven benefits.
4 The email was automatically         d updated with new data.
5 There are no scientifically         e recognised brand.
6 It's a globally                     f balanced diet.

## GRAMMAR

**6** Look at the picture and read the sentences. Tick the two true sentences. Rewrite the six false sentences using another modal verb form.

1 Person C **must be** on holiday.
2 Person B **can't have stolen** the bag.
3 Person A **might have chased** Person B.
4 Person B **couldn't notice** the ladder.
5 Person C **might fall off** the ladder.
6 Person A **might not have wanted** to talk to Person B.
7 Person B **may not have paid** his bill in the café.
8 Person A **can't have been** angry with Person B.

**7** Complete the sentences using the correct passive forms.

1 I love ........... for dinner. (take out)
2 You won't be the last person ........... this question. (ask)
3 Were you pleased ........... a prize? (award)
4 Who else should ........... to the party next week? (invite)
5 Why does he always insist on ........... first? (serve)
6 No one likes ........... at. (laugh)
7 They're hoping their product ........... the best new brand. (name)
8 The problem arose from ........... the wrong forms. (give)

**8** Write or complete the conditional sentences using the underlined words.

1 It's a pity you missed the party last week. <u>you / love / it / if / you / go</u>
2 Alex will be here in a few minutes. We've met him before, so I'm sure <u>we / recognise / him / when / he / arrive</u>
3 This kind of food is very rich, so I don't eat it very often. <u>if / I / eat / it / regularly, / I / put on / weight</u>
4 Imagine winning a £1,000 holiday! <u>if / you / win / one / who / you / take?</u>
5 I know you didn't go to university, but <u>what / you / study / if / you / go?</u>
6 You know about science, don't you? <u>if / you / heat / copper / what temperature / it / melt / at?</u>

**9** Complete the reported sentences.

0 Rob: 'I don't think Chelsea will win tonight.'
   Rob says he ...*doesn't think*... Chelsea will win tonight.
1 Jane: 'I've always loved cycling.'
   Jane says she ........... cycling.
2 Clare: 'I haven't seen the new Tintin film yet.'
   Clare told me she ........... the new Tintin film.
3 Evan: 'They speak Portuguese in Brazil.'
   Evan says they ........... Portuguese in Brazil.
4 Carl: 'I'll collect you at 18:45.'
   Carl has promised he ........... collect us at 18:45.
5 Jo: 'I read this book last year.'
   Jo said she ........... that book the previous year.
6 Anna: 'I might not be able to go to your party.'
   Anna has said she ........... to go to our party.

**10** Tick the two sentences without mistakes. Correct the mistakes in the other sentences.

1 Firstly the salary of course! How much do you expect to be pay?
2 These programmes must not watched by children.
3 The officer told that David had forgotten to turn his camera off.
4 John said he had some good news to tell me.
5 Now I can write the letters with the computer I needn't to get annoyed about my typewriter.
6 I needn't buy a new computer right now.
7 I died if the men that were fishing had not called the police.
8 I will offer you a 10% discount if you booked for 18 months.

**11** ⬤ Read the text and think of the word which best fits each gap. Use only one word in each gap. There is an example at the beginning (0).

**The new public transport**

As populations rise and congestion gets worse, new ways of keeping citizens moving need to (0) ..*be*.. found. In cities, increasing numbers of people are being persuaded (1) ........... cycle because it's quick and cheap. (2) ........... you cycle, you'll often arrive before a car, bus or underground train. A number (3) ........... urban cyclists use public bicycle-hire systems. Using a credit card or their mobile, customers can release a bike locked at a 'docking station' and ride it for (4) ........... long as they like. Most hire systems allow you to use the bike for free for 30 minutes, with (5) ........... small fee for subsequent periods. (6) ........... first large-scale system was the 'Vélib' in Paris (2007), (7) ........... 20,000 bicycles are now ridden by 100,000 people aged 14 or over every day. Without the Vélib's success, London, New York, Barcelona, Mexico City – over 600 cities globally – might not (8) ........... funded their own bicycle-hire systems.

# 17 Making headlines

## VOCABULARY   The media

**1** Read the quiz. Match the phrases in the quiz to the meanings a–i below.

### What's the media there for?

*The media is there to …*

1  help me **keep up to date** with the sports results  ☐
2  **celebrate achievements** such as discoveries and firsts  ☐
3  **gossip about** celebrities  ☐
4  **review performances**, like films, live gigs, TV shows  ☐
5  **make fun of** public figures  ☐
6  **comment on current events**  ☐
7  **keep** me **amused**  ☐
8  **highlight the need for** change  ☐
9  help me to **chill out**  ☐

a  give positive information about successes
b  help someone feel interested and happy
c  give opinions about the news
d  make people think about things that should be improved
e  allow someone to relax
f  talk about famous people's private lives
g  give opinions about plays, concerts, etc.
h  make unkind jokes about well-known people
i  give the latest information about football, tennis, etc.

**2** ▶ 3.09 Listen to four short recordings. What is happening in each one? Use the phrases from exercise 1 in your answers.

**3** Read the quiz again and tick the statements you agree with. Compare your answers in pairs.

**4** Think about recent news stories. Which statements do they match?

## READING

**1** Look at the photos and read the whole text quickly. Choose the best description of the text.
  1  A complaint about modern trends in journalism.
  2  An example of someone following a particular style of journalism.
  3  An essay about the development of journalism.
  4  A recommendation for a new branch of journalism.

**2** Look at the example answer (0) in the first paragraph of the text. What type of word is it? Why does this type of word fit the gap?

**3** ⬤ Read the first paragraph. For questions 1–8, think about what type of word is missing. Use the word given in capitals to form a word that fits in the gap.

**4** Read the text again and answer the questions.
  1  How did Yoro Touray feel when he realised that the most recent web page on Gambian music was ten years out of date?
  2  How will Yoro being a citizen journalist 'turn a disappointment into an opportunity' (column 2)?
  3  How do you think Yoro Touray felt while he was in The Gambia?
  4  How do you think Yoro's audience would have reacted to his presentation?
  5  How did the trip to The Gambia change Yoro Touray's life?

**5** Match the highlighted words in the text to the meanings.
  1  difficult to deal with or do
  2  full of ideas, energy and enthusiasm
  3  in or to other countries
  4  thinking about something all the time
  5  when a show is seen or heard as it is performed
  6  whole or complete, with nothing missing

# COULD YOU BE A *Citizen Journalist?*

If you wanted news, reviews or (0) ...entertainment... (ENTERTAIN) 25 years ago, you had to buy a newspaper or turn on the radio or TV. Nowadays, on the other hand, we expect (1) ............ (CONTINUE) online news coverage. Before the digital revolution, there was no alternative to the mass media news (2) ............ (ORGANISE). Their reporters were (3) ............ (PROFESSION) trained and supported by editors and researchers. To some (4) ............ (EXTEND) they created trends and kept them alive. However, these days, any individual with a computer can publish their own material and the number of 'citizen journalists' online is (5) ............ (BELIEVE) high and growing. In an emergency, such as an earthquake, these bloggers play a vital role, reporting on the local (6) ............ (SITUATE) in real time. They offer an important alternative to the mass media and provide a wider (7) ............ (VARY) of news stories. It can be said with a fair degree of (8) ............ (CERTAIN) that someone, somewhere is blogging about a topic that interests you.

Of course, citizen journalism isn't all about dramatic news events, as is shown by the story of Yoro Touray. The son of a couple from The Gambia, a tiny country in West Africa, Yoro was born and raised in the United States and as a 16 year old in Miami, he developed an interest in the music of The Gambia. His parents recalled a dynamic music scene, with men playing tall 'sabar' drums and musicians visiting from neighbouring Senegal. However, when Yoro looked up the Gambian music scene online, all the information was completely out of date. He had expected to find at least a handful of reviews of recent gigs or albums, but the few articles he did find dated back at least ten years.

Yoro was extremely disappointed to find so little information and decided to do something about it. As a young boy, he had been obsessed with keeping up to date with current affairs and so he had chosen media studies at high school. In class, the topic of citizen journalism had fascinated him and it gave him the idea of doing some real-life citizen journalism on the forgotten Gambian music scene.

This seemed not only the perfect homework project for his media studies class, but it also turned a disappointment into an opportunity.

At the start of the winter vacation he flew to The Gambia and travelled on to Serekunda, where his parents came from. Yoro only speaks English and although this is The Gambia's national language, most of the people he met were more comfortable speaking the local Mandinka language. Luckily, Yoro's parents still have good friends in Serekunda – if it weren't for their friendship, his trip could have been very tricky. During his 10-day visit, they accompanied Yoro to a dozen live gigs and toured markets buying recordings of Gambian singers dating from the 1980s right up to the present day. They also acted as interpreters during the many interviews that Yoro conducted with musicians and audiences and after his trip, they provided the subtitles for the Gambian speakers recorded by Yoro on video.

On his return to Miami, it took Yoro weeks to transcribe his notes and edit the first of his videocasts. His 'homework' was late, but when it was ready, he gave a presentation to the entire high school. The talk, in which he reviewed the Gambian music scene and showed music videos, was unlike anything a student had prepared before. Yoro also wrote a number of pieces commenting more generally on life and culture in The Gambia, which he published on his blog, finally giving Gambian culture the overseas attention and digital presence it deserved. Two years later, Yoro is close to the end of his journalism studies in New York, and is currently 'Young Journalist of the Year', a title he wouldn't hold now if he hadn't made those first bold steps into the world of citizen journalism.

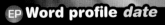

## EP **Word profile** *date*

All the information was completely out of date.

The articles dated back at least ten years.

As a young boy he had been obsessed with keeping up to date with current affairs.

▶ page 137

## Talking points

" What do you think are the advantages and disadvantages of citizen journalism?

Do you think citizen journalism could ever replace professional journalism? Why? / Why not? "

# GRAMMAR  Conditionals (2): Mixed

**1 Read the examples and answer the questions.**

1 *If it **weren't** for their friendship, his trip **could have been** very tricky.*

Was Yoro's trip tricky?

Do Yoro's parents still have friends in Serekunda?

2 *He **wouldn't hold** the title now if he **hadn't made** those first bold steps into the world of citizen journalism.*

Did Yoro make 'those first bold steps' into citizen journalism?

Does he hold the title of 'Young Journalist of the Year'?

**2 Match the examples in exercise 1 to the rules.**

> Mixed conditionals combine elements of the second and third conditional. We use them:
>
> **a** to talk about an imaginary situation in the present that is affected by a past action:
> *if* + past perfect, *would/might/could* + infinitive.
>
> **b** to talk about an imaginary situation in the past that is affected by a present situation:
> *if* + past simple, *would/might/could* + *have* + past participle.

→ Grammar reference **page 164**

**3 Complete the mixed conditional sentences.**

0 We haven't got the internet because our server went down last night.

We ...*would have*... the internet if the server ...*hadn't gone*... down last night.

1 We speak English, so we understood the report.
We ........... the report if we ........... English.

2 This is a safe area, so I didn't lock the house.
If this ........... a safe area, I ........... the house.

3 You're wet because you didn't bring an umbrella.
If you ........... an umbrella, you ........... wet.

4 You are a hard worker, so you passed your exams.
You ........... your exams if you ........... a hard worker.

5 David missed the bus. That's why he isn't at home now.
David ........... at home now if he ........... the bus.

**4 Write questions using mixed conditionals.**

0 Today's a weekday, but what (you / do / this morning / if / Saturday)

*... but what would you have done this morning if it was a Saturday?*

1 The internet was launched in the 1980s, but (if / they / not invent / it / how / life / be / different)

2 You aren't a millionaire, but (where / you / go / on holiday / last summer / if / be / millionaire)

3 You haven't left school yet, but (if / you / already / leave / where / live)

4 Mobile phones became popular in the 1990s, but / how / you / communicate / with your friends / if / they / not become popular

**5 Ask and answer the questions in exercise 4.**

A: *What would you have done this morning if it was a Saturday?*

B: *If it was a Saturday, I'd have had a late breakfast.*

## ⊙ Corpus challenge

**Find and correct the mistake in the student's sentence.**

*The book's OK, but if you seen it on television you would like it much more.*

# VOCABULARY  Phrasal verbs

**1 Match the sentence halves.**

1 I managed to **get** the point **across**
2 He **followed up** his TV interview
3 The news item **brought up** an
4 I got out my tablet and **caught up on**
5 These points were **left out**
6 His family **backed** him **up**
7 We need to **clear up**
8 The programme **looked into**

a with a Twitter conversation for fans.
b to the audience.
c of the article about guerrilla marketing.
d the issue of fees for higher education.
e interesting point about equality.
f after he confessed he was lying.
g a few problems before we can move on.
h all the latest gossip on social media.

**2 Replace the underlined words and phrases in the email with a phrasal verb from exercise 1 with a similar meaning.**

> Dear Jonas
>
> While I'm [1] <u>learning about</u> how everyone's getting on, I just want to confirm your responsibilities as the newsletter editor. Your main role is checking the content of the blogs. I [2] <u>mentioned</u> the issue of sources when I spoke to some of the writers a while back, so do make sure you [3] <u>emphasise</u> to them the importance of using accurate sources. They mustn't [4] <u>forget to include</u> their references either. It's the webmaster's job to learn about and [5] <u>solve</u> problems, such as photos that don't upload, so don't worry about those. Let me know if you want me to [6] <u>check</u> the accuracy of any sources and references! I'm here to [7] <u>support you</u>, as you know. If you want me to [8] <u>do more</u> on ideas for the next newsletter, just let me know.
>
> See you soon,
>
> Clare

**3 In pairs, make sentences using the phrasal verbs in exercise 1.**

# WRITING  A review (2)

**1** **Read the first paragraph of a magazine review.**

1 Who do you think the review is aimed at?

2 Do you think the style is lively or serious? Which words and phrases tell you this?

**Think Ink** magazine

**How to get published**

Are you into writing and art, but tired of the same boring old magazines? Then you should check out 'Think Ink'. It's a new magazine specially for teenagers who are into writing, art and photography. It's full of interesting articles and original stories. The photos are amazing too.

**2** **Read two options for the rest of the review and answer the questions.**

1 Which has a similar style to the first paragraph?

2 Which option do you think is more appropriate for a review? Why?

**A** It seems to be the case that magazines for teenagers tend to concentrate on celebrities and fashion, but arguably, publishers fail to understand their market if they see celebrity culture as a teenager's chief concern. However, 'Think Ink' is not in this category, because its readers are treated like adults. What's more, the content is totally created by its readers, which makes it unique and genuinely attractive to a teenage audience.

Nevertheless, it has to be said that the poetry section is rather disappointing. If the poems didn't seem so childish, they would be a little more appealing. On the other hand, the articles feature many original topics and the fiction is generally excellent. While 'Think Ink' isn't perfect, it is a thoroughly good read and highly recommended.

**B** As we know, most magazines for teenagers are stuffed full of articles about celebrities and fashion. Do publishers really think we only want to read trivial gossip? Teenage magazines get very boring after a while, but 'Think Ink' is refreshingly different. For a start, it treats its readers like adults. That makes a nice change and I know you'll really love its style! And the best thing is that we, the readers, write everything that's in it, giving us the opportunity to get across ideas that a teenage audience will relate to.

I do feel that the poetry section lets the magazine down a bit. Who wants to read poems aimed at children? But then again, the creative fiction really stands out and the articles are excellent as well. 'Think Ink' is definitely worth a read, so look out for it!

**3** **Read the *Prepare* box. Then read review B again and underline examples of a–d.**

a informal phrases

b direct questions

c phrasal verbs

d a friendly tone

## Prepare to write – Language for reviews

Reviews written for teenagers will generally:

- have a friendly tone rather than a formal one.
- contain informal phrases, such as *really cool* and *stuff like that*.
- use direct questions, which address the reader personally.
- include phrasal verbs, such as *get across* and *stand out*.

**4** **Read the task and plan your review.**

You have seen a notice on an international students' forum asking for reviews of websites.

### Submit a review!

We are looking for reviews of new websites. Write us a review of a website you know well, telling us:

- what it is called and what it is about
- who it is aimed at
- what kind of articles and stories it includes
- whether you would recommend the website.

Write your **review**.

**5** ⬤ **Write your review.**

- Use the tips in the *Prepare* box.
- Remember to give your review a title and organise it into paragraphs.
- Remember to express your opinion and make a recommendation.
- Check your grammar and spelling.
- Write 140–190 words.

# 18 Start-up

## VOCABULARY  The world of work

### Your profile

Have you ever worked during school holidays?
Would you like to have a holiday job? Why? / Why not?
What do you think 'work experience' is?

**1** Jobs have different qualities. Can you think of a job for each of the qualities below?

a  doing something creative

b  having opportunities for foreign travel

c  being able to take lots of time off

d  doing something that is personally rewarding

e  having flexible working hours

f  being very well-paid

g  being your own boss

h  working shifts

i  working in a professional job

j  doing manual work

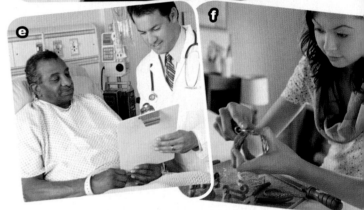

**2** Look at the pictures. Which qualities in exercise 1 apply to these jobs?

**3** ▶3.10 Listen to Sara, Dan and Emma. Make notes on their future career plans. Which area of work would be most appropriate for each? Why?

**4** ▶3.10 Listen again. What aspects of work does each person mention?

Sara: being her own boss

**5** Which person is most like you? What will be important to you in your future job?

## READING

**1** ● Read the blog. For questions 1–6, choose the answer (A, B, C or D) which you think fits best according to the blog.

1  From the first paragraph we understand that Thelma …
   A  believes she still has a chance of becoming famous.
   B  is worried about how much she'll earn in the future.
   C  has little idea about her future plans.
   D  thinks most teenagers want to become famous.

2  In line 16, 'making it' means …
   A  becoming successful in a chosen field.
   B  being discovered at a very young age.
   C  deciding to follow up on a hidden talent.
   D  having the chance to earn some money.

3  What does Thelma think of investment banking?
   A  The work might be too difficult for her.
   B  The hours would be too physically demanding for her.
   C  The job wouldn't be an appropriate one for her.
   D  The career is morally unacceptable to her.

4  What do Thelma's parents agree is important to her career choice?
   A  that she seeks further qualifications
   B  that they continue to support her financially
   C  that she avoids the mistakes they both made
   D  that she finds something she is enthusiastic about

5  Thelma feels that law and medicine …
   A  are careers she can't take seriously.
   B  require too much studying.
   C  are professions she wouldn't understand.
   D  have a predictable career path.

6  What steps has Thelma taken toward planning the future?
   A  She's arranged some work experience.
   B  She's shown her blog to some local newspapers.
   C  She's started saving some money for a course.
   D  She's applied for a course in journalism.

# THE BIG DECISION

**With just over a year of school to go, sooner or later I'll be making some decisions about my future. Do I want to spend another three or four years studying at college or university? What would I choose? Am I ready for the world of work? What work? The only thing that's clear to me is that my vague dreams of making films, singing in a band, competing in the Olympics or generally earning a fortune while socialising with (other) celebrities are becoming more and more unlikely. It's probably nothing unusual, but I've just come to the realisation that, although I'm good at lots of things, I'm not *brilliant* at anything.**

I'm not upset by this. Research about teenagers' career ambitions reveals that those prioritising fame and fortune above other ambitions are likely to earn 20% less in adult life than teenagers who have realised their futures may be less glamorous. And even if I did have a genuine talent, the statistics aren't encouraging. In baseball, for example, by far the largest sport in the US, only the top 250 amateur players out of every 300,000 will be selected for the professional leagues. For musicians, there's
line 16 even less chance of **making it**. Unless you are discovered before your twenties, which is incredibly unlikely, you'll probably struggle to make a living from your talent.

At school recently, we did an online questionnaire about our academic strengths, interests and career priorities. The aim was to give us all some ideas for the future. OK, so economics and maths are my best subjects. But while 'investment banking' might be good for my bank balance, is it really 'personally rewarding' and 'able to offer flexible working hours', two things I consider important in a job? And besides, don't investment bankers have to get up really early in the morning? I can do that, but really, *every* morning?

My parents, trying desperately not to influence my choice, have so far offered limited guidance. My dad, who went into construction straight from school and doesn't regret a thing, talks about being passionate about whatever you do. My mum, a teacher, holds the same view. However, on balance, she feels that qualifications gave her more options when she was ready to decide. However, now and then I get the feeling she'd rather have done something different.

Most of my friends seem to be in the same position as me. One or two have decided on degrees in medicine or law. Six months ago we might have laughed at them. Saving someone's life in an operating theatre or giving speeches in a court seemed so grown up! Now I'm actually jealous of their plans. Forgetting about the hard work for the moment, or even if I'd be capable, their futures are more or less decided: a degree, training and then work. In ten years, they'll all have respectable careers.

But what about me? Well, I've been writing this blog for a year now and some of you seem to enjoy reading my posts. Perhaps journalism is my 'thing'. I've already applied to several local newspapers for some work experience and I was able to use this website as useful proof that journalism isn't just a sudden idea I've had. No replies, as yet, but I'm hopeful. It's a competitive industry, I know, so I'd have to do some more study first. I've been researching relevant courses – both short and longer degrees – though the thought of borrowing thousands to pay for a full degree is depressing. However, a realistic approach to my future is good progress, I feel. Naturally, I'll keep you updated here, so come back soon!

## Talking points

66 How do you think schools and parents can help young people plan for their futures?

How do you think young people can help themselves when planning a career? 99

**EP Word profile *balance***

I want a balance between work and my social life.

… while 'investment banking' might be good for my bank balance, is it really 'personally rewarding'?

On balance, she feels that qualifications gave her more options when she was ready to decide.

page 138

 **Video extra**    **Start-up    103**

## GRAMMAR  Uses of verb + -ing

**1** Match the examples to the rules.

1 *Some of you seem to enjoy **reading** my posts.*
2 *Do I want to spend another three years **studying**?*
3 ***Giving** speeches in a court seemed so grown up!*
4 *My dreams of **making** films are pretty unlikely.*
5 *I've been **researching** relevant courses.*
6 *My parents, **trying** desperately not to influence my choice, have so far offered limited guidance.*

> We use verb + -ing:
> **a** as part of continuous verb forms.
> **b** after prepositions.
> **c** after certain verbs, e.g. *like, admit, keep*.
> **d** as the subject, or part of the subject, of a verb.
> **e** after certain phrases, e.g. *spend time*.
> **f** in participle clauses, to give more information about a noun.

→ Grammar reference **page 165**

**2** Complete the first part of the story with the *-ing* forms of the verbs in the box.

> be    cook    ~~do~~    create    change    try    work

> A 15-year-old boy has inspired a supermarket's next best-selling ready meal. Matthew Lilley was ⁰ ..*doing*.. work experience in the product development department of a leading supermarket when he suggested ¹ ............ some of the ingredients in a new recipe they were ² ............ . ³ ............ is not normally one of Matthew's strengths, but after ⁴ ............ the new sample, experienced tasters ⁵ ............ with Matthew admitted ⁶ ............ very impressed.

**3** Read the second part of the story. Find and correct nine more mistakes. Use *-ing* forms.

> *developing*
> Matthew spent two weeks ~~develop~~ and test his creation – a beef, tomato and potato dish. After receive positive feedback from tasters, the supermarket decided to start sell Matthew's dish. Before do the work experience, Matthew had few career plans. However, see how food products are taken from be just an idea to the finished product has inspired Matthew. He's now hope to follow a career in food product development and the supermarket has been given him advice on the qualifications he'll need to succeed in the industry.
>
> To show their appreciation for his work, Matthew recently received a present from the supermarket: a box contained 50 of the dishes he created!

**4** Complete the sentences about you. Use the *-ing* form of a verb.

1 I can't stand …
2 I spend a lot of time …
3 I don't think it's worth …
4 I'm thinking of …. one day.

### ⊙ Corpus challenge

**Find and correct the mistake in the student's sentence.**

*I would strongly recommend to visit our annual festival.*

## VOCABULARY  Word pairs

**1** Read about word pairs. Then read the examples and match the word pairs to the meanings.

> Word pairs are two words that are joined by a conjunction (usually *and*), although they often have a similar meaning or opposite meanings.

1 ***Sooner or later** I'll be making some decisions.*
2 *My dreams are becoming **more and more** unlikely.*
3 *However, **now and then** I get the feeling she'd rather have done something different.*
4 ***One or two** have decided on medicine or law.*
5 *Their futures are **more or less** decided*

**a** almost or approximately
**b** sometimes, but not very often
**c** a few
**d** eventually
**e** increasingly; as time passes

**2** Complete the sentences with words from the box.

> down    later    less    more (x3)    now
> one    over (x2)    round (x2)    sooner
> then    two    up

1 We speak online ............ and ............ , but in general, we're not in touch any more.
2 We walked ............ and ............ the park for over an hour, but couldn't find you.
3 You should think about it now. ............ or ............ you'll need to make a decision.
4 James has ............ or ............ decided. He's almost definitely going to university.
5 When she heard the news, she started jumping ............ and ............ with excitement.
6 It's becoming ............ and ............ expensive to do a degree.
7 I've got ............ or ............ ideas about my future. But I'm far from certain.
8 I rang the number ............ and ............ again, but got no answer.

## LISTENING

**1** You will hear an interview with a boy called Aiden Cass who started up his own T-shirt business. Read the questions and underline the words that might help you when you listen.

Aiden Cass runs Unique Tees

1 What gave Aiden the idea for his T-shirt business?
  A One of his parents suggested it.
  B His neighbours couldn't supply him with enough goods.
  C He realised selling T-shirts could be very profitable.

2 The most significant problem that Aiden first encountered was that
  A he ran out of space to keep the T-shirts in.
  B there weren't enough good T-shirts to sell.
  C the T-shirts took too long to repair.

3 How does Aiden's business work now?
  A His brother designs the T-shirts that he sells.
  B He imports T-shirts from other countries.
  C He sells T-shirts with original designs.

4 What does Aiden say about paperwork?
  A He's looking for someone to help him with it.
  B He wishes he were better at it.
  C He does most of it himself.

5 The hardest thing for Aiden about combining school and work is that
  A he doesn't always do his best at school.
  B he often finds his business more interesting.
  C his school isn't very flexible.

6 In general, what do Aiden's friends think of his business?
  A They sometimes make useful suggestions.
  B They are fed up because they never see him now.
  C They don't really take much notice.

7 Summer jobs taught Aiden
  A how hard work was the key to success.
  B how to deal with people well.
  C the importance of money.

**2** ▶3.11 ⬤ Listen to the interview. For questions 1–7, choose the best answer (A, B or C).

**3** ▶3.11 Listen again and check.

## SPEAKING   Agreeing and disagreeing

**1** Work in pairs. Look at the pictures of summer jobs. Answer the questions.
  1 What are the good and bad things about each job?
  2 Would you like to do this as a job? Why? / Why not?

**2** ▶3.12 Listen to Paul and Ana discussing five of the jobs in the photos. Answer the questions.
  1 Which jobs do they talk about?
  2 Do they take turns to talk?
  3 Do they ask each other's opinions?

**3** ▶3.12 Read the *Prepare* box. Who uses each phrase? Listen again and write *P* (Paul) or *A* (Ana).

### Prepare to speak – Agreeing and disagreeing

**Agreeing**
I'm with you on that.
Absolutely!
That's a good point.
Fair enough.

**Disagreeing**
I'm not sure about that.
I can't really see the point of …
I'm not convinced.
I agree up to a point, but …

**4** ⬤ Discuss the questions. Use phrases from the *Prepare* box to agree or disagree with each other.
  1 What kind of things might you learn from the summer jobs in exercise 1?
  2 Which would you most or least like to do?
  3 Do you think it's a good idea for teenagers to do summer jobs? Why? / Why not?

# Culture
## Fair play

**1** Look at the photos. What are the people doing? Who is and isn't behaving appropriately?

**2** Read the text. Which two types of rule must athletes obey?

### The IMPORTANCE OF *playing fair*

Established in 1963, the International Committee for Fair Play is devoted to the promotion of responsible, ethical behaviour in sport around the world. It collaborates not only with professional teams and associations, but also with coaches and trainers, most especially those who work with young children. The committee's primary goal is for those in the world of sports to show and support respect for other people, as well as for the sports that they play.

**RESPECTING OTHERS:** Competition and rivalry are very important elements of sport, but acceptance of team spirit and friendship are equally vital. This means athletes should show respect for their opponents, as well as for their team-mates, coaches, referees and fans. However, the principles of fair play should apply to everyone. Fans, for example, should show respect for the members of opposing teams and for their own team as well, if they lose.

**RESPECTING THE SPORT:** Playing fair means obeying the written and unwritten rules of the game. Athletes and coaches should never lie or cheat to gain an unfair advantage. If they do, it only ruins the game for everyone involved. Referees must also apply the rules fairly and they should be respected in turn, even when we don't agree with their decisions.

**AWARDS:** Every year, the International Fair Play Committee hands out awards to athletes, teams and associations that have helped to advance the values of fair play in the world of sports. There are three different types of award for:

1 individual actions that demonstrate a commitment to fair play

2 people who have shown fair play throughout their careers

3 people who promote fair play through educational activities

### Fair Play

#### Fair Play Charter for Youth

1 Fair Play is the only way.

2 I will devote the best of my physical, intellectual and moral abilities during both training and competition.

3 I will observe the written and the unwritten rules of my sport.

4 I will treat my opponents in the same way that I would like to be treated.

5 My aim is to defeat my opponents, not to humiliate them.

6 I will respectfully accept the decisions of the judges.

7 I will accept victory and defeat with dignity.

8 My greatest gratitude is towards my parents, teachers and trainers. Without them, I would not be here.

9 I am ready to help someone in need, even if I put my own victory at risk by doing so.

10 I represent my country with humility.

11 I would like to be a role model for the youth in my country and for my sport.

**3** Read the Fair Play Charter for Youth. Which points do you think are most important?

**4** Discuss the questions in pairs or small groups.

1 Why does the Committee pay special attention to school coaches and trainers?

2 Do you agree that competition and friendship are equally important in sport?

3 In what ways do some athletes cheat in order to gain an unfair advantage?

4 Why is it important or useful for people to receive special awards for fair play?

5 Do you think the Fair Play Charter for Youth is realistic? Why? / Why not?

**5** ▶3.13 **Listen to a conversation about Fair Play Award winners. Are the sentences true or false?**

1 Monti was competing for Austria at the 1964 Olympics.
2 Monti helped two other teams to win gold medals.
3 Monti's own team came in second place in both races.
4 Indurain got a Fair Play award for his work in 2004.
5 Indurain won the Tour de France four times in a row.
6 Indurain was known for treating other people with respect.

**6** ▶3.14 **Complete the texts with words from the box. Then listen and check.**

> championship   diversity   encouraging   expand
> fell down   generosity   launched   lost   racism   symbol

**In 2006, a Turkish girl** named Hilal Coşkuner won a Fair Play Award for (1) ............ towards a rival. Hilal was competing in a (2) ............ that she had a good chance of winning. However, when another girl (3) ............ during the race, Hilal stopped to help her get up. In doing so, Hilal (4) ............ the race, but became a (5) ............ of fair play.

**For the EURO 2008 finals,** the Union of European Football Associations (UEFA) (6) .......... the RESPECT campaign against (7) .......... . The campaign won a Fair Play award for (8) .......... tolerance and for promoting respect for ethnic and cultural (9) .......... . Since then, the campaign has continued to (10) .......... and grow in popularity.

**Project**

Find information about an athlete who demonstrates or encourages fair play.
Write a biography of his/her career.

1 Who is the person you chose?
2 What sport does he/she play?
3 What are his/her achievements?
4 How does he/she support fair play?
5 Does he/she work with any associations?
6 Has he/she taken part in a fair play campaign?

## VOCABULARY   Opinions and beliefs

**Your profile**

Do you have strong opinions and beliefs?
What issues concern you the most at the moment?

**1** ▶3.15 **Listen and match the conversations to the pictures.**

**2** **Match the sentence halves.**

1  You have to **bear in mind**
2  I've never been
3  They could,
4  Are you **in favour of**
5  I'm **totally against** students
6  I'd **go along with**

a  **convinced by** that argument.
b  allowing mobile phones in schools?
c  that their careers are short.
d  using their phones at school.
e  that view.
f  **to my mind**, easily get another job after playing.

7  What are your **views on**
8  It's **hard to deny** that it
9  **As far as I'm concerned**,
10  **I suspect** this is true,
11  **There's no doubt**
12  **I firmly believe in**

g  that you're more independent when you're older.
h  enjoying yourself while you've got the chance.
i  people just need to eat less meat.
j  vegetarianism?
k  must be better for you.
l  to be honest.

**3** ▶3.15 **Listen again and check.**

**4** **Work in pairs. Look at the pictures again. What is your opinion on these issues? Discuss your opinions. Use phrases from exercise 2.**

**EP Word profile *mind***

You have to bear in mind that their careers are short.

They could, to my mind, easily get another job after playing.

I think you have to keep an open mind about this.

page 138

## READING

**1** **Read the article quickly, ignoring the gaps. According to the article, which statement is true?**

1  Teenagers need to spend less time thinking about their emotions.
2  Teenagers' brains have some advantages and disadvantages over adult brains.
3  The differences between adult and teenage brains are now well understood by scientists.
4  Adults need to make more of an effort to understand the way teenagers think.

**2** ● **Six sentences have been removed from the article. Choose from the sentences A–G the one which fits each gap (1–6). There is one extra sentence which you do not need to use.**

A  This is the area we use for thinking carefully about something in order to make a decision.
B  Dramatic conclusions might make good headlines in the press, but the evidence for any truth in them is weak.
C  They argue that if teenagers spend more time with adults, there is more opportunity for them to learn how to make thoughtful decisions.
D  It is able to absorb huge amounts of information and the opportunity is there to make the most of this by putting energy into learning and new experiences.
E  Everyone was asked to identify the feelings their expressions represented.
F  The researchers concluded that teenagers' emotions are developing much faster than the parts of the brain that help them manage their emotions.
G  However, a number of recent studies using brain scanning equipment have led to the belief that the typical teenage brain is as unique as this phase itself.

# Explaining your brain

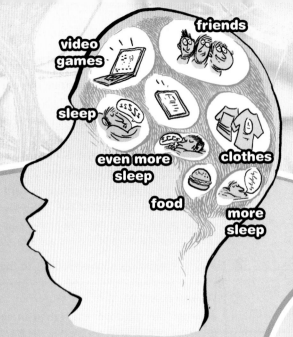

Being a teenager is unique to humans. Animals develop directly from childhood to being an adult. They skip the teenage years altogether. So why do humans go through this stage? Scientists have proposed several explanations for this: some believe long human lifespans have simply made room for this growth phase. Others think these years are needed to learn about the complex ways in which humans behave socially. The truth is that no one really knows.

By the age of 12, our brains are fully grown in size and scientists once firmly believed that they were also fully developed by this age. The unusual behaviours of typical teenagers, from unusual sleeping patterns to strong opinions were widely blamed on *hormones*, the chemicals that control the way our body grows and develops. [1 ☐] In short, scientists now think that teenagers' brains work differently from adults' brains.

In one study, teenagers and adults were shown photos of people's faces. [2 ☐] The results surprised the researchers. One of the pictures was of someone with the clear look of fear on their face. All of the adults in the test were able to recognise this correctly, but the teenagers believed the face was either surprised or angry.

Using scanning equipment, scientists could observe which parts of the brain were active during the experiment. The adults used part of their brain called the *frontal cortex*. [3 ☐] In contrast, the teenagers' brain activity was in the *amygdala*, the region that handles our instant reactions, which are often emotional. The older the teenagers in the group, the more they used the frontal cortex. Therefore, it seems that throughout these years, the brain is still developing.

Another study asked groups of teenagers and their parents to discuss their opinions on controversial subjects, such as homework and the amount of freedom that teenagers should be given. The researchers found that young people with a larger *amygdala* are likely to have stronger opinions on these subjects and, as a result, they are more likely to end up in conflict with their parents. [4 ☐] And that this might explain why teenagers' reactions to seemingly small events can seem very strong.

Incredibly, some 'experts' have used this research to suggest that it is biologically unhealthy for teenagers to play video games or watch a lot of TV. [5 ☐] However, most scientists stress that while considerable progress has been made in our understanding of the teenage brain, our overall knowledge is limited. Drawing too many conclusions, they warn, is both irresponsible and potentially dangerous.

What is clear is that the stage of being a teenager is a significant one for brains and it is not altogether negative. The brain has a tremendous amount of power during this stage. [6 ☐] This may be by studying, by gaining new skills such as creating music or art, or by exploring the world. All in all, it seems that the teenage years are a time of great change for the brain and a time when young people can start to develop to their full potential as they move towards adulthood.

**3** Match the highlighted words in the article to the meanings.

**adjectives**

1 happening immediately
2 causing disagreement
3 difficult to understand

**nouns**

4 strong disagreement
5 the particular ways that something is often done
6 stage

**verbs**

7 experience a difficult or unpleasant situation or event
8 emphasise something in order to show that it is important
9 watch someone or something carefully

**Talking points**

" In what ways do teenagers and adults think differently? What can scientists learn by studying people's brains? "

## GRAMMAR  Subject-verb agreement

**1** **Read the examples and choose the correct verb forms.**

1 *However, <u>a number of studies</u> **has / have** now led to the belief that …*

2 *The truth is that <u>no one</u> really **know / knows**.*

3 *<u>One of the pictures</u> **was / were** of someone …*

4 *<u>Drawing too many conclusions</u> **is / are** both irresponsible and potentially dangerous.*

5 *Considerable <u>progress</u> **has / have** been made in our understanding of the teenage brain.*

**2** **Match the examples in exercise 1 to the rules.**

> We use a singular verb:
>
> **a** when the subject of the verb is an *-ing* form.
>
> **b** with uncountable nouns than end in *-s*, e.g. *news*.
>
> **c** after words such as *everyone, someone, anyone*, etc.
>
> **d** after the expression *one of*.
>
> We use a plural verb:
>
> **e** after the expressions *both of, all (of), plenty of, a couple, a number of*.
>
> With collective nouns, we can use a singular or plural verb, e.g. *My family live/lives in Spain*.
>
> But the noun *police* always takes a plural noun, e.g. *The police are looking for two men.*

→ Grammar reference **page 166**

**3** **Complete the first part of an article with the present simple singular or plural of the verb in brackets.**

## YOU'VE CHANGED MY MIND!

You've just been to the cinema and all of your friends [1] ........... (agree) that the film was brilliant. But one of you [2] ........... (feel) differently. You! Do you express your real views, or go along with the crowd? Plenty of us [3] ........... (do) the latter – everyone [4] ........... (tell) a little white lie from time to time. Now news [5] ........... (come) from an experiment in the US that agreeing with people like this actually [6] ........... (have) a strong effect on your mind and can even change it permanently!

### Corpus challenge

**Find and correct the mistake in the student's sentence.**

*Each one of these have its advantages and its disadvantages.*

**4** **Read the second part of the article and correct six mistakes with subject-verb agreement.**

> If we think someone look attractive, a region of our brain called the orbitofrontal cortex becomes active. In the experiment, a number of people was shown photos of faces and gave scores based on how attractive the faces were. Next, all the people was told they had given much lower scores than a nationwide survey of the same faces. The process of scoring the faces were repeated and the scientists observed the activity in the orbitofrontal cortex. The scores on this occasion were higher than the first time and the activity in the orbitofrontal cortex was also higher. Therefore, one of the researchers' conclusions were that following the opinion of a larger group lead to people changing their own opinion.

**5** **Work in groups. Find something that …**

1 all of you are in favour of.

2 a number of you firmly believe in.

3 one of you is against.

4 no one believes in.

## VOCABULARY  Plural nouns

**1** **The bold nouns in the example are always plural. Can you think of any other nouns that are always plural?**

*He spent his **savings** on lots of new **clothes**.*

**2** **Read the sentences. Which nouns should be plural? Change the nouns, then match them to the meanings.**

0 It's hard to tell the difference between advanced ~~graphic~~ and actual photographs.  *graphics*

1 This term in English, we've been looking at the lyric of popular music.

2 Look in the content at the beginning and find the unit about money.

3 We'd like you to remain in the room for a moment, as we're serving refreshment soon.

4 Leaving my belonging all over the house is guaranteed to drive my parents mad.

5 I'm against zoos because research has shown animals are more content in their natural surrounding.

a a list in a book that tells you what the book contains

b the place where someone lives and the conditions they live in

c images shown on a computer screen  *graphics*

d food and drinks that are available on a journey, at a meeting, etc.

e the words of a song

f the things that someone owns

# WRITING  An essay (4)

**1** What time does your school start and finish each day? Should it start or finish earlier or later?

**2** Read the task and answer the questions.

Students who are 15 and older should start and finish school an hour later. Do you agree?

**Notes**

Write about:

1 health
2 learning
3 ... transport ... (your own idea)

> **1** The student has added their own idea. What other ideas could you add?
>
> **2** What advantages and disadvantages can you think of to do with health, learning and transport?

**3** Read the essay. Which of your ideas are mentioned? What other ideas are mentioned?

Changing the timing of the school day is a complex issue. However, such a policy might benefit teenagers, who are often so busy with after-school activities and homework that they are rarely in bed before 11 pm.

In my country, students need to get up by 7 am in order to arrive at school for 8 am. As a result, teenagers are getting fewer than 8 hours' sleep, when the recommended minimum is 9.5 hours per night. This may well start to affect their health. In addition, while some manage to eat breakfast before they leave home, others arrive at school hungry and consequently, do not always pay full attention in lessons. Some even pretend to be ill to gain more time in bed, therefore missing important work in class. Starting later would help in this respect.

On the other hand, other problems might occur. Teenagers who rely on their parents for transport could experience difficulties, as the parents might have already left for work. Furthermore, even though teachers might support the change, their working hours would be longer.

On balance, despite the drawbacks, it seems worth experimenting in selected schools. A decision could then be made based on the results.

**4** Read the *Prepare* box. Find examples of the different kinds of linkers in the essay.

### Prepare to write — Linking words (2)

We use linking words to link clauses and make sentences longer. Linking words can express:

- contrast: *although, even though, whereas, despite*
- purpose: *so, so that, in order that*
- reason: *because, as, since, for this reason*
- result: *consequently, therefore*

**5** Choose the correct linking words in the sentences.

1 He left early *so / despite* he could catch the last bus.
2 *So that / Even though* she left early, she missed the bus.
3 I got home very late and *because / consequently* I felt exhausted the next day.
4 I was late for school, *as / although* I overslept.
5 I got a bad mark in the exam, *despite / since* all the work I did.
6 Some people work well in the mornings, *therefore / whereas* others work better later in the day.
7 I couldn't get a lift to school, *as / in order that* my parents had already left for work.
8 *In order that / Since* the exam has to be fair, everyone does it at exactly the same time.

**6** Read the task and add some information for each note.

A lot of homework discourages students from wanting to learn. Do you agree?

**Notes**

Write about:

1 the time that homework takes to do
2 how useful homework is
3 ............ (your own idea)

**7** 🔵 Write an essay using all the notes in exercise 6 and giving reasons for your point of view.

- Organise your ideas into paragraphs (see page 13).
- Use language to compare and contrast (see page 57).
- Use linking words to link clauses and make your sentences longer.
- Check your grammar and spelling.
- Write 140–190 words.

## VOCABULARY  Idioms

**1** Look at the list of idioms. Which meanings do you think are the most likely? Why?

**1** break the ice

  **a** make people feel more relaxed in a social situation

  **b** explain why people feel a certain way

**2** break someone's heart

  **a** make someone feel nervous

  **b** make someone feel extremely sad

**3** take your breath away

  **a** make you feel anxious and impatient

  **b** make you feel surprise and admiration

**4** be a piece of cake

  **a** be sweet and tasty

  **b** be very easy

**5** cross your mind

  **a** come into your thoughts for a short time

  **b** make you change your mind

**6** have an eye for something

  **a** want something very much

  **b** be good at noticing certain things

**7** be a pain

  **a** be very sore

  **b** be a nuisance

**8** lose track of time

  **a** not be aware of what time it is

  **b** not be able to find time for something

**2** ▶3.16 Listen and choose the correct meanings in exercise 1.

**3** Discuss the questions.

  **1** What do you think is the best way to break the ice when you meet new people?

  **2** Have you ever seen something that took your breath away? What was it?

  **3** Do you find anything a piece of cake that your friends find difficult?

  **4** When was the last time you were late because you had lost track of time?

**4** Write a paragraph using as many idioms as possible.

## READING

**1** Look at the picture on page 113. What do you think the people are doing? What might the article be about?

**2** Read the article quickly and check your guesses. Then answer the questions.

  **1** Why do teenagers have an influence on language change?

  **2** What examples does the text give of how English has changed lately?

  **3** What are the standard question tags for these questions?

    **a** *You texted me, ............?*

    **b** *You like this game, ............?*

  **4** How does the language of texting differ from standard English?

  **5** How does texting affect texters?

  **6** How does the saying 'Everything rolls on, nothing stays still.' relate to languages?

**3** Match the highlighted words in the article to the meanings.

  **1** relating to language

  **2** the ability to read and write

  **3** learn a new skill or language by practising it rather than being taught it

  **4** informal language that is only used by people who belong to a particular group

  **5** use someone or something instead of another person or thing

**4** Discuss the questions.

  **1** Do you use slang when you are speaking to your friends? Give some examples.

  **2** Do you sometimes get complaints if you use the 'wrong' language? In what situations?

  **3** Think of examples of words in English and in your own language that

    **a** are borrowed from other languages.

    **b** are often shortened.

    **c** come from technological developments.

# 'TEEN-SPEAK'
## WE LOVE IT!

Do you vary how you speak depending on who you're with? Perhaps you use certain words or expressions with your friends, others with your family and yet others in more formal contexts? And do you get complaints if you use the 'wrong' language in a particular situation? Teen-specific slang is common in most languages, as are complaints about it from older people. However, in spite of what adults tend to assume, teenagers making changes to standard grammar and vocabulary isn't a new phenomenon. Plenty of objections to young people's language have been recorded since the time of the Ancient Greeks.

Groups with a common interest always tend to adapt language to suit their purposes; think of the specialist words used in law or medicine, for example. We call this *jargon* and it marks the members of the group who use it as 'different'. When you're a teenager, of course, you want to stress the difference between your age group and the older generation, and changing the language you use is a great way to do this.

One way in which teens change their language is to introduce new vocabulary or change the meaning of existing words. Some recent examples of teen-speak show how big these changes in meaning can be. *Wicked* suddenly changed its meaning from *very bad* to *wonderful*, *bad* suddenly meant *good* and *sick* took on the meaning of *very cool*. These uses don't last for long, though. They change again very quickly, so it can be hard to keep up.

Young people also make changes to grammar. One example of a teen-led change to the grammar of the language is the fashionable use among some young people of *innit* (a shortened form of *isn't it*) as a substitute for all question tags, e.g. *You texted me, innit?* or *You like this game, innit?* Some experts have suggested that this simplification is a by-product of texting and instant messaging. Although some people are concerned that this trend towards 'text-speak' is harming the language, Professor David Crystal doesn't agree. According to him, the fact that teens use 'text-speak', shortened words and even emoticons ☺, does not mean the end of the language. 'Texting is just a new type of English that has evolved as a result of internet technology. It

hasn't had any impact on the rest of the language, and there is definitely no evidence that it is damaging the language. All the recent research shows the standard of language used by young people is generally good and the best texters are actually the best spellers. The more they text, the better their literacy is, as it gives them the practice in reading and writing they wouldn't otherwise have.'

Although teenagers are often criticised for ignoring linguistic rules and ruining the language, we should bear in mind that languages are not fixed. They all change naturally over time, albeit at different rates, for a lot of reasons. New vocabulary evolves as speakers need new words to match the new things in their lives. Where would we be without all those new words such as *internet* and *wifi* that have come into the language as a result of modern technologies? Grammar also changes over time, which explains why many present-day speakers find Shakespeare's sixteenth-century plays difficult to read. Our use of language changes naturally as we go through life too; we continue to pick up new words and phrases all through our lives and integrate them into our speech.

Adults may not like the way teens speak to each other, but realising that language change is normal – unavoidable – and that teens are integral to this process might help the older generations to sleep better at night. They have always complained that standards in general are declining among the younger generation, but as the Greek philosopher Heraclitus observed more than 2,500 years ago, 'Everything rolls on, nothing stays still.'

## EP Word profile *standard*

Teenagers making changes to standard grammar and vocabulary isn't a new phenomenon.

The standard of language used by young people is generally good.

Standards in general are declining.

page 138

## Talking points

" How have modern ways of communicating changed the way we use language? "

## GRAMMAR   Determiners

**1** Read the examples and choose the correct determiners. Check your answers in the rules.

1 *Do you get **the / –** complaints if you use **the / a** 'wrong' language in **a / the** particular situation?*

2 ***Much / Plenty of** objections have been recorded.*

3 *Languages change for **a bit of / a lot of** reasons.*

4 *This explains why **much / many** speakers find Shakespeare's plays difficult to read.*

5 *Changing the language you use is **– / a** great way to do this.*

> We use:
>
> **a** *a* or *an* before a singular countable noun, for referring to one of many things, or one that is not specific.
>
> **b** *the* before any noun, for referring to something in particular or something already mentioned.
>
> **c** *–* before any noun, for referring to things generally.
>
> **d** *some, any, plenty, a lot, lots* before uncountable and plural countable nouns.
>
> **e** *much, (a) little, a bit, a small/large amount of* before uncountable nouns.
>
> **f** *many, (a) few, several, a small/large number of* before plural countable nouns.

→ Grammar reference   **page 167**

**2** Read the sentences and explain the difference in meaning between the bold words.

0 **a** She has **a little** money to spend.

  **b** She has **little** money to spend.

  *'A little' means a small amount. It is positive. 'Little' means a very small amount and is negative.*

1 **a** They gave me **little** help.

  **b** They gave me **a little** help.

2 **a** **Few** people here can speak Chinese.

  **b** **A few** people here can speak Chinese.

3 **a** I learned it at school, but I speak **little** French these days.

  **b** I learned French at school and I still speak **a little** these days.

4 **a** We get **a little** rain in summer.

  **b** We get **little** rain in summer.

5 **a** Latin is offered by **few** schools these days.

  **b** Latin is offered by **a few** schools these days.

### Corpus challenge

**Find and correct the mistake in the student's sentence.**

*I am keen on singing, but I have very few experience.*

**3** Complete the text with the correct determiners. There may be more than one correct answer.

## FOREIGN ACCENT SYNDROME

Olga Grigorieva, a Russian schoolgirl from Novgorod, passed out one day while she was in ¹ ........... art class. When she came round, a nurse told her to drink ² ........... of water and to get ³ ........... rest. When Olga thanked ⁴ ........... nurse and stood up, she noticed that ⁵ ........... of her classmates were giggling. Olga asked them what was wrong and then she noticed her own voice. She was speaking Russian with ⁶ ........... English accent! Olga was not amused. In fact, like a large ⁷ ........... of people with 'foreign accent syndrome', Olga was extremely upset. A person's speech forms part of their personality. If you suddenly start speaking with ⁸ ........... foreign accent, it can be very frightening. Olga's case was unusual because she didn't speak ⁹ ........... English before her fall – not one word. It was her accent, not the language, that was different. Slowly her old Russian accent returned, but she has learned to say a ¹⁰ ........... things in English as well.

## VOCABULARY   Commonly confused words

**1** Choose the correct words.

1 Which is your favourite *way / means* of transport?

2 What is the best *means / way* to practise English?

3 I'll visit you if the *journey / way* isn't too long.

4 What is the best *way / journey* to the beach?

5 You'll have plenty of *possibilities / opportunities* to meet people at university.

6 There's *a possibility / an opportunity* my sister will be at the party.

7 Why won't you let me play my music? I'm only trying to have *funny / fun*.

8 I never thought that *Mr Bean* was very *fun / funny*.

**2** Complete the sentences with words from exercise 1.

1 Did you have a good ........... or was the traffic bad?

2 I haven't had the ........... to read your blog yet.

3 He told us a very ........... joke!

4 I know the ........... to school from here.

5 There's a ........... I'll be late, I'm not sure yet.

6 I really enjoyed my holiday. It was great ........... .

**3** Complete the sentences with the verbs in the box.

| damage | harm | guess | injure | know | observe |
|---|---|---|---|---|---|

1 How did you ........... your leg?

2 The rain won't ........... you or your equipment.

3 Please don't ........... the furniture.

4 Can you ........... how old I am?

5 The headteacher is going to ........... this class.

6 I have read the essay title, but I don't ........... what it means.

## LISTENING

**1** 🔘 ▶3.17 **You will hear people talking in eight different situations. For questions 1–8, choose the best answer (A, B or C).**

**1** You hear two friends talking about libraries. What does the boy think of libraries?

   **A** Their lending systems aren't modern enough.

   **B** Library staff can be unhelpful in locating books.

   **C** You should be able to borrow books for longer periods.

**2** You hear a girl giving part of a presentation on the subject of endangered languages. What is her main point?

   **A** Languages represent one of man's most important skills.

   **B** The loss of languages reduces our knowledge of social history.

   **C** There will be fewer regional cultures if certain languages die out.

**3** You hear two friends talking about a novel they read for their English class. They agree that

   **A** it was really well-written.

   **B** the main character was realistic.

   **C** it gave a clear picture of a historical period.

**4** You hear a teacher talking to her students about the school holidays. She wants them to

   **A** look after the members of their families.

   **B** catch up on all the work they have missed.

   **C** set aside regular periods of time for something.

**5** You hear two friends talking about languages. According to the boy, if you can speak two languages,

   **A** you can interact with cultures around the world.

   **B** you might have a more efficient brain than other people.

   **C** you should be able to learn a third language without much difficulty.

**6** You overhear part of an interview with a university lecturer. The lecturer advises students starting at university to

   **A** prepare themselves for a different approach to studying.

   **B** find out about entertainment in the city they are moving to.

   **C** make sure their computer is in good condition before they arrive.

**7** You hear two friends talking about a long-distance running race. What is the girl worried about?

   **A** whether she will finish the race or not

   **B** how big a problem her shoes will be

   **C** who will be there to watch her run

**8** You overhear a boy telling a friend about his blog. What does he regard as a priority?

   **A** to control the length of what he produces online

   **B** to keep his readers happy by featuring new topics

   **C** to increase the number of followers that he has

## SPEAKING   Taking turns and negotiating

**1** What techniques do you use to learn new vocabulary?

**2** ▶3.18 **Dan and Sara study Spanish at school. Listen to them talking about learning Spanish vocabulary. Answer the questions.**

   **1** Which would be their three favourite ways of learning vocabulary?

   **2** Which is the best way for them?

**3** ▶3.18 **Read the *Prepare* box. Who uses each phrase? Listen again and write *S* (Sara) or *D* (Dan).**

> ### Prepare to speak – Taking turns
>
> **Taking turns**
> You go first/next.
> It's your turn now.
>
> **Ranking**
> What would be your top …?
> For me, the ones that make the most sense are …
> Well, personally, I'd choose / leave out …
>
> **Negotiating**
> So if you had to choose just one, what would it be?
> I think I'd go for …
> … are all very well if …, but they …
> I'm happy with … as well.

**4** **Look at the list of ways you can learn vocabulary. In pairs, agree which you think is the best way. Use phrases from the *Prepare* box.**

- writing sentences
- categorising words
- mind maps
- vocabulary cards
- translation

**5** **Look at the list of ways of practising English outside the classroom. In pairs, agree the best way for you. Use phrases from the *Prepare* box.**

- visiting English-language websites
- reading graded readers in English
- watching TV shows and films in English
- having a native-speaker pen-friend
- speaking to schoolmates in English regularly

# Economics
## A school business

**1** Read the text. How do the school programmes in Tanzania and Nicaragua help people?

**Wanted:** YOUNG ENTREPRENEURS

SCHOOL ENTERPRISE CHALLENGE

Do you and your classmates have an idea for a school business? Then sign up for the School Enterprise Challenge! You can earn money, learn new skills, get business experience and win prizes too! Your hard work can also make a difference in your local community.

The School Enterprise Challenge is a two-step competition. The first step is to design a business plan for a school business. The second step is to put your plan into action, making money for your school and making a difference in your community. More than 400 schools in 41 different countries have already participated in the challenge. Here are just two examples of businesses that have been started:

### Nicaragua: Crafty helpers

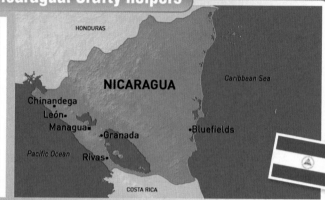

Students at Esther del Río las Marías Secondary School in Nicaragua have started a new business, making and selling craft products, such as party decorations, fashion accessories and jewellery. The new project not only earns money to support the school, but also helps students to develop their artistic skills and learn valuable business and life lessons. The craft products, which are sold at the school shop, are made from natural or recycled materials, in order to protect the environment.

### Tanzania: A sweet idea

In Tanzania, students at Ilowala Secondary School have set up a bee-keeping business, which lets them raise funds by selling honey, as well as candles made from beeswax. In the process, students also learn about biology, chemistry and geography. In order to save money, the students used recycled wood to build their beehives. After the first year, the school spent 40% of the profits to help needy students and then used the rest to build more beehives for local people who need jobs.

### ? FREQUENTLY-ASKED QUESTIONS

**What kind of enterprise should we develop?**
Your business should be socially responsible, helping people to live better lives. It should also be a long-term project that will continue to earn money in the future. Finally, your business should be environmentally friendly, helping to protect our world's resources. Just remember the Three Ps: People, Profit and Planet.

**What can we do with the profits that we make?**
You can use your profits in a number of ways:
*   to improve and maintain school buildings
*   to make donations to charitable organisations
*   to buy classroom supplies and equipment
*   to continue developing your school's business
*   to help classmates who need assistance
*   to help other schools start their own business!

**What prizes can we win for our enterprise?**
There are lots of ways to win! There are prizes of $500 to $5,000 for the best plans and the most successful enterprises. There's also a $2,000 award for the most inspirational teachers. In addition, the most enterprising and hardworking students can win individual prizes, such as cameras and laptop computers!

**2** Choose the correct words to make questions about the text. Then answer the questions.

1 What did the students in Tanzania sell in order to *earn / pay off* money?
2 How did the Nicaraguan students *win / raise* funds for their school?
3 What kind of enterprise should schools *make / set* up?
4 How can schools *do / make* a difference in their own communities?
5 What prizes can individual students *gain / win* for their hard work?

**3** Answer the following questions with information from the text and your own ideas.

1 Why is it important for schools to complete both steps of the challenge?
2 In your opinion, which school project from the article is …
   **a** more academic?   **b** more creative?   **c** more challenging?   **d** more important?
3 Why are the Three Ps important? Do you think one is more important than the others?
4 How do the two schools in the reading text meet the Three Ps? Which project is better?

**4** Work in pairs. Imagine your school earns $1,000 from running a business. What should it do with the profits?

**5** ▶3.19 Read the 'Bags to Books' business idea. Then listen to two students presenting the plan. Do you think it will be successful? Why? / Why not?

**Business idea:** Students will make and sell home-made cotton shopping bags.
• **People** Students will learn about sewing, economics and the importance of books.
• **Profit** The business will earn money to buy school books and offer reading lessons.
• **Planet** Cotton shopping bags are more environmentally friendly than plastic ones.

**6** ▶3.19 Complete the 'Bags to Books' plan with steps a–g. Listen again to check you answers.

# Bags to books

**A Preparation**
1 Visit cotton suppliers to compare prices.
2 *c) Get donations to rent sewing machines.*
3 Find a company to print logos on the bags.
4 ...................................................................

*a) Try to sell the bags at supermarkets and shops.*

*b) Have sewing classes before production starts.*

*c) Get donations to rent sewing machines.*

**B Getting started**
5 Order the cotton cloth from the best supplier.
6 Have a contest to design a business logo.
7 ...................................................................

*d) Put the students into teams to sew the bags.*

*e) Give a prize the person who sold the most bags.*

*f) Collect the bags and take them to be printed.*

**C Production**
8 ............
9 Give a prize to the team that makes the most bags.
10 ...................................................................

*g) Calculate the production costs and final price.*

**Project**
Design and plan your own school business.
1 What type of business will you start?
2 How will your business make a profit?
3 How will it be able to help people?
4 What will you do to protect the planet?
5 Who will participate in the project?
6 What will the steps in your business plan be?

**D Promotion and sales**
11 ............
12 Ask the local newspaper to write about the project.
13 ...................................................................

# Review 5
## Units 17–20

## VOCABULARY

**1** Complete text with the words in the box.

> be honest    chill out    comment on    date
> go along    gossip    keep    keeping
> making fun    mind

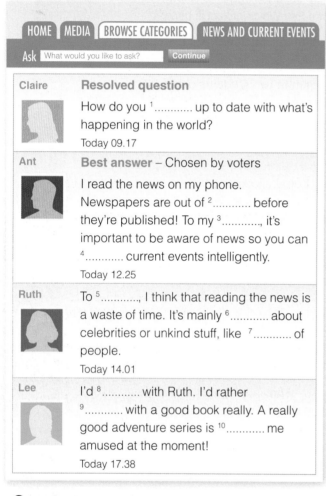

HOME | MEDIA | BROWSE CATEGORIES | NEWS AND CURRENT EVENTS

Ask [ What would you like to ask? ]    Continue

**Claire**

Resolved question

How do you ¹............ up to date with what's happening in the world?

Today 09.17

**Ant**

Best answer – Chosen by voters

I read the news on my phone. Newspapers are out of ²............ before they're published! To my ³............, it's important to be aware of news so you can ⁴............ current events intelligently.

Today 12.25

**Ruth**

To ⁵............, I think that reading the news is a waste of time. It's mainly ⁶............ about celebrities or unkind stuff, like ⁷............ of people.

Today 14.01

**Lee**

I'd ⁸............ with Ruth. I'd rather ⁹............ with a good book really. A really good adventure series is ¹⁰............ me amused at the moment!

Today 17.38

**2** Complete the sentences with the jumbled verbs in the box.

> ahctc    evela    igrnb    kbac    okol    teg

1 I hate to ............ this up, but you owe me £10.
2 My holiday gave me time to ............ up on sleep.
3 Please help me make a list for the party. I might ............ out something important.
4 I tried to ............ my point across at the meeting, but I'm not convinced people understood.
5 When I tell Mum about the stain, will you ............ me up that it wasn't my fault?
6 Can you ............ into borrowing a stove for our camping trip?

**3** Match the two parts of the phrases.

| | | |
|---|---|---|
| 1 be your | a | working hours |
| 2 do something | b | shifts |
| 3 be | c | manual work |
| 4 take lots | d | for foreign travel |
| 5 work | e | of time off |
| 6 have flexible | f | well-paid |
| 7 do | g | own boss |
| 8 have opportunities | h | creative |

**4** Complete the sentences with the idioms. Make changes to the idioms as necessary.

> take your breath away    lose track    be a pain
> cross your mind    break my heart    be a piece of cake

1 I finished the test 15 minutes early. It ............ .
2 Is it two o'clock yet? I've ............ of time.
3 My phone's battery rarely lasts the whole day. Having to recharge it during the day ............ .
4 It ............ when the last series of that programme ended. I used to love it so much.
5 The view from out hotel room ............ . We could see right across the whole city.
6 It didn't ............ that Mark and Robert were brothers. They look completely different.

## GRAMMAR

**5** Complete the mixed conditionals with the correct form of the verbs.

1 If I didn't have so much to do this week, I ............ (be able) to come.
2 I wouldn't be here now if Abby ............ (not mention) the game.
3 If we had sorted out the problems earlier, we ............ (not be) in this mess today.
4 I ............ (take) the summer job if it were a bit better paid. But I had to turn it down.
5 Tom could apply for medicine if he ............ (study) biology. But he did maths, physics and chemistry.
6 If my brother ............ (not be) such a pain, I might have invited him to the festival. He's just too young at the moment.

**6** Complete the sentences with the correct form of the verbs. Use the *-ing* form, the infinitive with *to*, or the infinitive without *to*.

1 I hate ............ told what ............ . (be, do)
2 I'd been ............ English for over eight years before I ............ visit the country. (learn, manage)
3 ............ in mind how long it will take ............ there, I think we should leave now. (bear, get)

**4** Despite Ollie ............ the best cook, we took turns ............ the meals on holiday. (be, make)

**5** He denies ............ Joe, but admits he's been ............ about it. (tell, think)

**6** ............ in a shop made me ............ how much I would hate that kind of job. (work, realise)

**7** Choose the correct words.

**1** I like most of my classmates, but a couple *is / are* a pain.

**2** The news about his accident *has / have* really upset me.

**3** I think starting your own business *sound / sounds* like hard work.

**4** One of my friends *work / works* in that café at weekends.

**5** *Is / Are* anything in those film reviews positive?

**6** A number of students *is / are* in favour of banning phones from school.

**8** Choose the correct words. Sometimes there is more than one possible answer.

I've got ¹ *a / the / some* summer work in a local pizza restaurant. ² *A / The / –* job itself is OK and at least I'm earning ³ *some / a little / a few* money. I spend ⁴ *a lot of / several / some* time taking orders over the phone, but I also make ⁵ *a lot / a large number / a bit* of pizzas too. There are always ⁶ *a few / a bit of / several* pizzas left at the end of ⁷ *an / the / –* evening, but I've eaten such ⁸ *a large amount / a lot / a large number* of pizzas in the last few weeks, that I've gone off them! I'll still have ⁹ *few / several / some* weeks of holiday left when I finish, so I'm going away with ¹⁰ *the / – / some* friends.

**Corpus challenge**

**9** Tick the two sentences without mistakes. Correct the mistakes in the other sentences.

**1** I would be grateful if you correct your errors.

**2** Almost all of us like shopping!

**3** I don't enjoy to shop all the time.

**4** I really enjoyed spending time to go sightseeing.

**5** Life nowadays is so full of things to be done, that people forget that their health are important.

**6** I firmly believe that it would be better if the swimming pool opened earlier.

**7** Whilst spending a few time in Barcelona, I have been looking for different kinds of activities which you could do in a single week.

**8** Eating too much sugary or oily things has a bad affect on the body.

**10** ⬤ Read the article and decide which answer (A, B, C or D) best fits each gap. There is an example at the beginning (0).

**The world's best summer job?**

When an international holiday company advertised a job for someone to test their waterslides, they didn't expect such an incredible **(0)** ...C... . Over 2,000 people applied, but lucky Seb Smith, a British student, **(1)** ............ them all.

The advertisement said that potential **(2)** ............ needed to be 'mad about waterparks', '**(3)** ............ to travel' and 'happy to get wet at work'. Seb backed **(4)** ............ his application with a funny video of himself testing a slide in his local park.

He will now spend three months travelling the world and **(5)** ............ waterslides at the company's 20 water parks. **(6)** ............ in mind all Seb's accommodation and travel expenses are free, the job isn't badly paid either: Seb will earn £20,000.

'I'm absolutely over the **(7)** ............,' said Seb, 'and I can't wait to get started'. A spokesman for the company said Seb's enthusiasm made him the ideal person for the **(8)** ............ of waterslide tester.

| | | | | | | |
|---|---|---|---|---|---|---|
| **0** | A reply | B answer | C response | D feedback |
| **1** | A broke | B won | C hit | D beat |
| **2** | A candidates | B contestants | C opponents | D substitutes |
| **3** | A agreeing | B opening | C willing | D enjoying |
| **4** | A up | B off | C on | D in |
| **5** | A guessing | B deciding | C determining | D judging |
| **6** | A Taking | B Crossing | C Bearing | D Catching |
| **7** | A sun | B moon | C Earth | D world |
| **8** | A piece | B role | C character | D function |

# Exam profile 1

## Reading and Use of English Part 7  Multiple matching

**What is Part 7?**
- One text divided into sections or several short texts
- Ten questions

**1** Look at questions 1 and 2. Which is asking about an opinion? How do you know?
Identify the answers by reading the highlighted parts of texts A and B below.

Which teenager

1  arranges additional matches as part of his fitness plan?

2  disapproves of an aspect of his fellow players' behaviour?

3  is confident that he can overcome a weakness in his performance?

4  admits that a chosen form of physical exercise could be risky?

5  praises the advice and support he has been given on diet?

**2** In this exam task, some 'distraction' for each question will appear in another text. Underline
the distraction for question 1. Which words are used in both the question and text?

> **Now you try Reading and Use of English Part 7**
> - Read the questions first and underline important words.
> - Scan the texts quickly to find the information you need.

**3** Look at questions 3–5 and find the answers. Highlight the parts of the texts that
give you the answers.

# Teenage tennis players and their fitness

## A  Mats

Being part of the top college team means I have to
stay in great shape, so however hard I'm studying,
not a day goes by without some form of exercise,
although I might only actually hit a ball in practice
three times a week. Swimming and long-distance
running suit me better than arranging extra matches,
allowing me to build up my strength. These activities
also provide useful thinking time for essays, so my
brain gets a proper workout. Our fitness trainer keeps
an eye on general food intake and comes up with
really smart suggestions about what to eat when. Not
all the guys listen to him though, which shows little
respect for what he's contributing to the team effort.
That's poor. Then again, I tend to ignore advice on
sleep patterns, while the others are pretty good at
observing the early nights rule, so I maybe shouldn't
criticise them.

## B  Tomas

Our team practices are scheduled after classes and
focus on movement around the court and general
technique. I also set up regular sessions on court
with friends, so there's no shortage of tennis! Some
players do other sports to keep fit, but that's not my
thing. I do lift weights, but my body's still growing, so
I need to watch out there, even though it's evidently
good preparation for long matches. Up to a point,
taking in high-energy products on court controls
this lack of stamina, but I can't deny that as time
goes on, it's tough to close things effectively and
get the win. I'm doing extra workouts right now to
tackle the matter and I expect to see some benefit
from that soon. Maybe I should seek advice on
eating a balanced diet too. We don't get much official
support on that, which is odd as it could make all the
difference in big matches.

## Reading and Use of English Part 4 Key word transformations

**What is Part 4?**

- Six separate questions each with a first and incomplete second sentence
- A key word in bold which you must use to complete the second sentence

**1** **Read the instructions for this part and then answer question 1, using four words including the word given. Use a phrasal verb and a modal.**

**1** Medical research recommends reducing the amount of salt you consume.

**DOWN**

According to medical research, you ......................................................... the amount of salt you consume.

**2** A majority of students selected Jackie as the best singer in the school's talent competition.

**VOTED**

More students ......................................................... other singer in the school's talent competition.

**3** I'll only phone next week if it is absolutely necessary.

**REALLY**

Next week, I won't phone ......................................................... to.

---

**Now you try Reading and Use of English Part 4**
- Make sure the second sentence means the same as the first.
- Check your spelling and grammar.

---

**2** **Answer questions 2 and 3. Which one tests a collocation?**

## Listening Part 3 Multiple matching

**What is Part 3?**

- Five individual speakers, talking about a common theme
- Five questions, to be matched to eight options A–H (three options aren't used)

**1** ▶3.20 **You will hear five short extracts in which university students are talking about doing voluntary work on conservation projects in different parts of the world. Read options A and B, then listen and choose what Speaker 1 enjoyed most about the experience.**

**A** saving the life of individual animals

**B** getting to see different natural environments

**C** having the chance to do challenging tasks

**D** getting close to a very rare animal

**E** being responsible for collecting important data

**F** using relevant background research

**G** learning more about various local traditions

**H** being able to visit the beautiful surroundings

**2** **Now skim the recording script for Speaker 1. Identify the part that confirms the answer.**

I was working in a rescue centre in South Africa for a month, looking after animals and birds that were hurt or young ones that'd been found wandering about alone – mainly monkeys. It was quite demanding work, with long days, but it was very rewarding, especially when I realised that without my efforts, the animal I was looking after would've died. It was tiring though. Luckily we all slept on site, so we didn't have far to travel to our accommodation at the end of the day.

---

**Now you try Listening Part 3**
- Read the options carefully and underline key words.
- Be careful. Sometimes an option seems possible, but it isn't an exact match.
- Listen a second time to check your answers.

---

**3** ▶3.21 **For Speakers 2–5, choose from the letters A–H what each speaker enjoyed most about the experience.**

121

# Exam profile 2

## Reading and Use of English Part 5 Multiple choice (fiction)

### What is Part 5?
- A fiction or non-fiction text
- Six four-option, multiple-choice questions

**1** Skim the text, which is from a novel about a boy who sings and plays the guitar. What is his name?

**2** Read question 1 below. Then look at the highlighted part of the first paragraph, which confirms the answer – C.

   1 Why was Curtis present at the beach party?

     **A** Shay had asked Nikki to invite him.

     **B** He lived next door to Finch and Nikki.

     **C** Nikki had suggested he should come.

     **D** He wanted to perform his songs with Shay.

**3** Why are A, B and D wrong in question 1?

> **Now you try Reading and Use of English Part 5**
> - Read the relevant paragraph and highlight where you think the answer is.
> - Check that the other three options are wrong.

**4** Now answer questions 2 and 3.

   2 Shay realised nothing would come of Curtis's offer because

     **A** Wrecked Rekords don't sign up schoolchildren.

     **B** Curtis needed the agreement of Shay's parents.

     **C** Wrecked Rekords weren't taking on any new talent.

     **D** Curtis felt Shay's guitar-playing lacked sufficient skill.

   3 Why doesn't Shay's brother Ben play professional football now?

     **A** He hurt himself too badly to ever play again.

     **B** He lost interest after he left the youth squad.

     **C** He acted on his father's advice to give it up.

     **D** He missed his opportunity due to getting an injury.

Finch's mum, Nikki, had heard me play a few times over the holidays, though I'd never thought anything of it – until I met her friend Curtis at our last beach party. Curtis works as a talent spotter for Wrecked Rekords in London and he'd travelled all this way to hear me play, on Nikki's recommendation. In fact, he'd been listening to me for the last hour. He shook my hand and said, 'Shay, isn't it? Nice playing. And they're all your own songs?' I said that they were and Curtis asked if I'd ever recorded anything or if I might like to.

Wrecked Rekords were always on the lookout for new talent. And according to Curtis, I was just the kind of thing they were looking for. It could have been that easy. Curtis said he thought I had something special – raw talent, awesome songs. Plus, I was young and keen. And I had the surf-boy looks. My life could have changed in that moment, but … well, it didn't. The thing is, I'm still at school. Curtis said that was no problem at all, but that obviously my parents would have to be on board with the whole thing. That's when I knew it would never happen.

It's not that my dad doesn't believe in talent – I think he believes in it too much. It's just that as far as Dad is concerned, all of the talent in our family belongs to my brother. Ben is a bit of a legend around here. He's brilliant at sport, football especially … he was playing for a professional club's youth squad by the time he was 14 and a major team took him on when he was 16, but he had an injury and things didn't work out. It wasn't that serious, but it was enough to wipe out Ben's chances of a premier-league career. Dad didn't cope too well when it all went wrong. He couldn't believe you could play so well and work so hard and have it all end in nothing, and I suppose that has made him suspicious of chances and opportunities and promises of fame and fortune. Just my luck …

# Reading and Use of English Part 1  Multiple-choice cloze

**What is Part 1?**
- A short text with eight gaps
- Six four-option multiple-choice questions

**1  Skim the paragraph below to understand its general meaning. What title would you give the text?**

Today, over half of the world's population lives in cities and this percentage is likely to (0) ........... significantly. More and more people are moving to a city in (1) ........... of employment and a better life. There are (2) ........... some negative aspects to city living, such as traffic and pollution. However, those with earning power can (3) ........... the most of their urban experience, for cities generally provide many cultural attractions and excellent shopping (4) ........... , as well as other leisure facilities.

**2  Look at the example. All four options are verbs. Why is A the correct answer?**

  **0  A** rise        **B** widen        **C** go        **D** progress

**3  Now look at the four options in question 1. What part of speech are they? The correct answer is (C) because it is part of the fixed phrase 'in search of'. Did you know this phrase?**

  **1  A** aim        **B** hunt        **C** search        **D** track

> **Now you try Reading and Use of English Part 1**
> - Identify the part of speech in each set of options.
> - Look at the words around the gap, to see if the missing word is part of a phrase or collocation.

**4  Look at questions 2–4. Choose the correct answers.**

  **2  A** absolutely    **B** certainly    **C** fairly    **D** directly
  **3  A** take    **B** get    **C** make    **D** keep
  **4  A** occasions    **B** chances    **C** capabilities    **D** opportunities

# Listening Part 1  Short extracts

**What is Part 1?**
- Eight unrelated extracts of about 30 seconds each
- One or two speakers

**1  ▶3.22  Read question 1. Then listen to the recording. Choose the best answer (A, B or C).**

  **1** You hear two friends discussing a novel. What do they agree is impressive about it?

    **A** how believable the characters are
    **B** how clearly the plot develops
    **C** how well the places are described

**2  ▶3.22  Listen again. What do the speakers agree and disagree about? Why is A the correct answer?**

> **Now you try Listening Part 1**
> - Choose the answer you think is correct at the first listening.
> - Check your answer when the recording is repeated.

**3  ▶3.23  Now listen twice and answer question 2.**

  **2** You overhear a boy talking on the phone about some homework. He is worried because he

    **A** doesn't have the right textbook.
    **B** can't complete everything in time.
    **C** hasn't got enough ideas to include.

# Exam profile 3

## Reading and Use of English Part 3 Word formation

**What is Part 3?**
- A short text with eight gaps
- Eight words beside the text to form the missing words from

**1** Look at gaps 1–4 in the text. Then read the explanations below. Notice that the answers require a suffix, a prefix or both.

| | |
|---|---|
| **IDENTITY AND THE INDIVIDUAL** | |
| The whole concept of (0) ..*personal*.. identity is fascinating. A lot of (1) ............ research has been carried out in this area and (2) ............ continue to spend their working lives exploring its deep questions. Do we remain (3) ............ the same person over time? Given that our childhood experiences are so different to what we encounter as adults, this is very (4) ............ to be the case. | PERSON MEANING PSYCHOLOGY EXACT LIKE |
| Do we even have just one 'self' or (5) ............ 'selves', according to who we are with? A teenage boy's interaction with his elderly grandmother, even if she is (6) ............ and loving, will not be the same as his (7) ............ among other teens. In society, our desire to gain (8) ............ of a group often influences how we are, for better or worse. | VARY FRIEND BEHAVE MEMBER |

Question 1 As in the example, the noun beside the text is used to form an adjective – *meaningful*
Question 2 The plural verb and 'their' shows that the answer must be people – *psychologists*
Question 3 The gap follows a verb and an adverb is needed – *exactly*
Question 4 Here, you must understand the meaning of the whole sentence to know that an adjective with a negative prefix is needed – *unlikely*

**2** Now look at question 5. The word in capitals is a verb. What is needed in the gap, a noun or an adjective? Choose *variety* or *various*.

> **Now you try Reading and Use of English Part 3**
> - Decide what part of speech is needed for each gap.
> - Check your answer makes sense in the text and is spelled correctly.

**3** Write the answers for gaps 6, 7 and 8.

## Writing Part 2 An article

**What is a Part 2 article?**
- 140–190 words long
- Usually written for an English-language magazine for teenagers

**1** Look at this article question. In pairs, list some unexpected events that you could write about and then decide which ones would engage the reader of the magazine.

> You see this advert in an international student magazine.
>
> > **A BIG SURPRISE!**
> > We are looking for articles about surprises or unexpected events that our readers have had. Share your experiences with us!
> > Your article should describe what happened to you and explain in detail how you felt, both at the time and afterwards.
> > The best articles will be published in next month's magazine.

> **Now you try Writing Part 2 An article**
> * Make sure you answer all parts of the question.
> * Write in a lively way to interest your readers.

# Writing Part 1  An essay

### What is a Part 1 essay?
* 140–190 words long
* A compulsory question – you must answer it

**1** Look at the Part 1 essay question. Which of the ideas below (A–C) would be relevant as a third content point?

> In your class you have been talking about sport. Now your teacher has asked you to write an essay for homework.
> Write your essay using **all** the notes and giving reasons for your point of view.
>
> > **All young people should have free use of local sports facilities.**
> > **What do you think?**
> >
> > **Notes**
> > Write about:
> >
> > 1  keeping fit
> > 2  having equal opportunities
> > 3  ............ (your own idea)

**A** developing talent      **B** buying sportswear      **C** meeting friends

**2** Complete these dos and don'ts about the essay question with words from the box.

> conclusion   grammar   introduction   language   paragraphs   plan   spelling

1  DO make a ............ before you begin writing.
2  DO start your essay with an ............ , where you explain what it will cover.
3  DO organise your essay in ............ .
4  DO check your essay for ............ and ............ .
5  DON'T forget to include a ............ at the end.
6  DON'T use any informal ............ .

> **Now you try Writing Part 1 An essay**
> * Choose a relevant third idea to include.
> * Time how long it takes you to write your essay
>   – spend no longer than 40 minutes on it.

# Exam profile 4

## Reading and Use of English Part 6  Gapped text

### What is Part 6?
- A text from which six sentences have been removed
- Seven sentences A–G – one is not needed

**1** Read the title and first paragraph of the text to become familiar with the topic.

> ### How adverts persuade you to buy
>
> Advertisements work in different ways according to how they have been developed. Of course, the objective is the same – to persuade you the consumer to purchase the product – but the techniques employed vary a great deal.
>
> Some adverts are designed to appeal directly to your <u>emotions</u>, both <u>positive</u> and negative. ☐ **1** The suggestion being that <u>if you do so</u>, you will end up as satisfied as them.
>
> On the other hand, witnessing pain and suffering can play on your feelings just as effectively. Showing someone with a heavy cold, who gains instant relief from the product in question, should register in your memory that this is the remedy to seek out the next time you are <u>sneezing helplessly</u>. ☐ **2** In this particular case, the advert would be shown during the peak period of <u>winter</u> illness.
>
> A totally different approach that is adopted for certain adverts, relies on convincing the consumer by means of real scientific evidence or statistics. ☐ **3** This appeal to reason appears to be highly effective where personal health and fitness is concerned.

**2** Now read the second and third paragraphs. Decide which sentences fit in gaps 1 and 2, choosing from A–C. Use the underlined words to help you.

   **A** Another proven technique involves featuring a celebrity giving a personal recommendation for their chosen brand.

   **B** It goes without saying, that commercials like this one are only <u>broadcast at certain times of year</u>.

   **C** A sunny image of <u>smiling</u> teenagers enjoying their favourite soft drink by the pool may well persuade you to <u>follow their example</u>.

> ### Now you try Reading and Use of English Part 6
> - Look for content and language links in the sentences around the gap.
> - Read each paragraph with your answer in place to check it makes sense.

**3** Choose the right sentence for question 3.

   **D** By releasing such an impressive set of facts about this special ingredient, the advertiser expects you to commit to the dish without a second thought.

   **E** So, the orange juice providing 75% of your daily requirement of vitamins will be bought in preference to another soft drink where no such claim is made.

## Listening Part 2 Sentence completion

**What is Part 2?**
- A monologue lasting 3–4 minutes
- Ten sentences, each needing to be completed with a word or short phrase

**1** Look at the title and sentences 1–4. What will the recording be about?

### JAMAL EDWARDS AND HIS MUSIC WEBSITE SBTV

The first video Jamal uploaded to the internet showed **(1)** ............ in London.

Some of Jamal's music videos were filmed in the **(2)** ............ , which people found very original.

Jamal's website has been visited more than **(3)** ............ times.

There are several **(4)** ............ of musicians posted on Jamal's website.

**2** ▶ 3.24 Listen to part of the recording. How many words are needed to complete gap 1? What is the answer?

> **Now you try Listening Part 2**
> - Read the sentences before listening to predict what might be missing.
> - Check all your answers when the recording is repeated.

**3** ▶ 3.25 Listen to the whole recording and complete gaps 2, 3 and 4.

## Reading and Use of English Part 2 Open cloze

**What is Part 2?**
- A short text containing eight gaps
- Each gap requires an answer of one word only

**1** Read the text quickly for its general meaning.

### CROCODILES

Not **(0)** ...*all*... crocodiles in Australia are life-threatening. Freshwater crocodiles, known **(1)** ............ 'freshies', do not attack humans, but Saltwater crocodiles, **(2)** ............ rather, 'salties', are extremely dangerous creatures. Salties are in fact **(3)** ............ largest living crocodiles on our planet. An adult male can grow to a length of seven metres, in **(4)** ............ case its weight may reach 1,000 kilos.

**2** Look at the example and gaps 1–4. What type of word is needed in each gap? Choose from a–f. Find an example in the text of the word types not needed.

**a** conjunction
**b** determiner
**c** modal verb
**d** preposition
**e** pronoun
**f** quantifier

> **Now you try Reading and Use of English Part 2**
> - Complete each gap with a single word.
> - Check your spelling before writing your answers in capital letters on the answer sheet.

**3** Think of the word which best fits each gap 1–4.

# Exam profile 5

## Writing Part 2 A story

**What is a Part 2 story?**
- 140–190 words long
- Usually written for an English-language magazine for teenagers

**1** Read the exam task and then answer questions 1–4 below. They help you to think of ideas for your story.

> You have seen this announcement in an English-language magazine for young people.
>
> > **WRITE A STORY!**
> >
> > We are looking for stories about strong emotions to publish in the next issue of our magazine.
> > Your story must **begin** with this sentence:
> > *Sofie was so furious that she stood up and ran out of the room, slamming the door behind her.*
> > Your story must include:
> > - a secret
> > - a phone

**1** What do you think has happened in the room to cause Sofie to leave?

**2** Where do you think Sofie will go next?

**3** Has someone been unable to keep a secret? Why might Sofie want to use her phone?

> **Now you try Writing Part 2 A story**
> - Decide the best way to continue from the first sentence.
> - Remember to include the two things listed.

## Listening Part 4 Multiple choice

**What is Part 4?**
- An interview or conversation lasting 3–4 minutes
- Seven multiple-choice questions with three options A, B and C

**1** Look at question 1 and the underlined parts of the recording script. Which answer is correct?

**1** Maria's biggest challenge while working on her survey was

   A persuading enough students.

   B analysing all the results thoroughly.

   C preparing suitably worded content.

**Maria:** Well, none of it was easy! First of all, I had to design the survey, improving my questions so that they were clear and asked for the right information. <u>I guess that was the trickiest thing</u>. In terms of finding enough people to take part, <u>I had no trouble</u> with all my social media connections. Analysing all the results <u>took a fair bit of time, though it was quite straightforward</u>, really.

> **Now you try Listening Part 4**
> - Underline any key words in the questions before you listen.
> - Check your answers at the second listening.

**2** ▶ 3.26 Listen to the interview. Answer questions 2 and 3.

**2** What did Maria identify as being of concern to the majority of students regarding their future?

   A being accepted at the right university

   B getting a job that is suitable for them

   C having an adequate standard of living

**3** On the subject of technology, Maria says that many students seem to be

   A unhappy at having to rely on it constantly.

   B dissatisfied with the range of products available.

   C unconvinced about its relevance in the future.

## Speaking Parts 2, 3 and 4  Long turn, shared task and related discussion

**What is Part 2?**

- A one-minute individual turn based on two photographs
- A response on the other candidate's turn

**1** The photographs show teenagers doing different things in their free time.
Think of ideas for the question below.

What are the advantages and disadvantages of doing these activities?

> **Now you try Speaking Part 2**
> - Compare the two photographs, making sure you answer the printed question.
> - Use a range of vocabulary, with suitable linking and contrast phrases.

**2** ▶3.27 **Now listen to Ludmila comparing the photographs. How many of your ideas does she include?**

**What are Parts 3 and 4?**

- Part 3 – a shared task lasting three minutes, with written prompts
- Part 4 – a discussion on the same topic as Part 3

**3** ▶3.28 **Read the task. Imagine that a museum wants to attract more teenage visitors. Look at the task and listen to Ludmila and Oleg. Which two things do they decide the museum should provide?**

> I'd like you to imagine that a town is deciding whether or not to spend money keeping its museum open for people to visit.
>
> Here are some ideas being considered and a question for you to discuss.
>
> Talk about whether towns and cities should provide museums for people to visit.

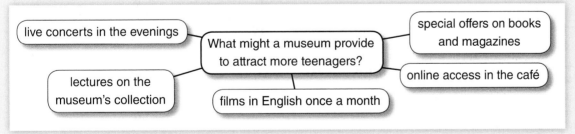

live concerts in the evenings

special offers on books and magazines

What might a museum provide to attract more teenagers?

lectures on the museum's collection

online access in the café

films in English once a month

**4** ▶3.29 **Now read these Part 4 questions and listen to Ludmila and Oleg again. What ideas do they mention?**

Do you enjoy visiting museums? (Why? / Why not?)
How important are museums in the 21st century? (Why?)
Is it easier to learn about history by visiting a museum or by finding the information
you need online? (Why?)
Do you think places like museums and art galleries should have free admission? (Why? / Why not?)

# Pairwork

## UNIT 8 PAGE 49   Speaking

> ● **The photographs show two cities.**
> **Student A:** Compare the photographs and say which city you would prefer to live in and why.
> **Student B:** Talk briefly about your ideal place to live.

## UNIT 9 PAGE 54   Key for quiz

**What was your score?**

All the statements are characteristics of optimistic people. Optimists have a belief that things will always turn out well. They believe they are in control of their future and when things go wrong, they tend to see others as the reason, rather than themselves. They look for new opportunities and see themselves as very able people in everything they do. They are goal-oriented and often determined to achieve their goals.

The more statements you agreed with, the more optimistic you are.

**35–40: Very optimistic**

You always look on the bright side of a situation. The positive attitude you bring to everything you do means your friends probably see you as someone whose presence cheers everyone up.

**28–34: Quite optimistic**

For the most part, you're someone who makes the most of things and looks forward to the future, but there is still a part of you that holds back. Perhaps a bit of realism is useful, though?

**21–27: Realistic**

For you, it's not about hoping for the best in situations or seeing the worst in people. It's about using reason to make decisions. You might not have the most exciting time, but your realism means you usually have a fairly accurate idea of what new experiences will be like.

**14–20: Quite pessimistic**

You aren't a complete pessimist, but you tend to avoid new experiences, as generally speaking you think that something might happen.

**8 (minimum score)–13: Very pessimistic**

If something can go wrong, your belief is that it will. And if you can blame yourself for the problem, you probably will too. Even if something good happens, you'll probably believe that it was only because of good fortune that things went well.

**What was your score?**

All the sentences are qualities of good leaders.

**24–30:** Wow! You're the kind of person that people look up to and you're on your way to becoming a great leader.

**17–23:** You're doing OK, but you probably have the potential to be even better. Look at the questions you scored the least on – is there anything you could do to improve your leadership skills?

**10 (minimum score)–16:** You're probably not a natural leader, but there's nothing wrong with that. All teams need good, positive team members!

# UNIT 16 PAGE 93   Speaking

> **The photographs show two advertisements.**
>
> **Student B:** Compare the photographs and say who the adverts might be aimed at.
>
> **Student A:** Talk briefly about which of these games you would prefer to play.

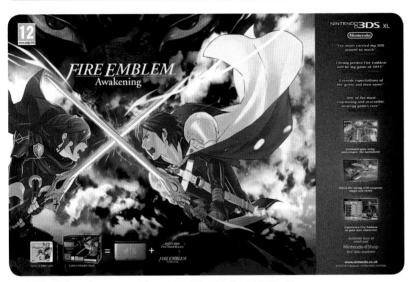

# Word profiles

## UNIT 1
### WORD PROFILE: *not* /nɒt/

| | |
|---|---|
| not even | *She doesn't even get nervous before exams.* |
| not half as good/ bad/exciting, etc. | *The director's latest film isn't half as good as the last one.* |
| not only … but also | *Nancy has not only completed the books, but also translated them into Chinese herself.* |
| not quite | *I'm not quite ready to go out yet.* |
| not to mention | *This resort has great indoor sports facilities, not to mention some of the best skiing in the region.* |

**1 Match the sentence halves.**

1 She not only composed the soundtrack,
2 I thought the film wasn't
3 Sara loved the book, but I'm
4 The author must have made a fortune from the books,
5 I've never seen any of the TV series,

a half as bad as the reviews said it was.
b not even the first one.
c not quite sure I understood the plot.
d but also had one of the lead roles.
e not to mention the films.

## UNIT 2
### WORD PROFILE: *point* /pɔɪnt/

| | |
|---|---|
| make a point | *Sam made a very good point just now about pollution.* |
| be no point (in) + -ing | *There's no point in inviting Sally, as she never comes to parties.* |
| get to the point | *I wish he'd hurry up and get to the point!* |
| miss the point | *I think you've missed the point.* |
| The point is, … | *The point is, if you don't claim the money now, you might never get it.* |
| up to a point | *You're right up to a point, but it's more complicated than you say.* |

**1 Replace the underlined parts of the sentences using the phrases in the box. Make any other changes you think are necessary.**

> You made a good point    get to the point
> You've missed the point of    There's no point in
> up to a point    The point is

1 <u>It's a waste of time</u> asking him to help, because he never does anything for other people.
2 I thought you were never going to <u>explain what you really meant</u>.
3 I agree with most of your theory, <u>but not all of it</u>.
4 <u>I really agreed with what you said</u> about school. I had never thought of it like that.
5 <u>The important thing is</u>, it's not worth spending too much money on clothes.
6 <u>You haven't understood anything about</u> this film.

## UNIT 3
### WORD PROFILE: *smart* /smɑːt/

| | |
|---|---|
| STYLISH | *You're looking very smart in that dress!* |
| CLEVER | *Why don't you fix it if you're so smart?* |
| TECHNOLOGY | *Smart packaging shows when the food in your fridge has become unsafe to eat.* |

**1 Match the uses of *smart* in the questions to the meanings in the *Word profile* box. Then ask and answer the questions.**

1 a What smart devices do you own?
  b What smart devices would you like to own?
2 On what occasions do you think it's important to wear smart clothes? Why?
3 a Is being smart simply a question of academic performance?
  b Who do you consider to be smart? Why?
  c Do you think it's possible to get smarter? How?

**2 Write five sentences with *smart*. Can your partner match your sentences to the definitions?**

# UNIT 4
## WORD PROFILE: *control* /kənˈtrəʊl/

| HAVE POWER OVER | You can't *control* how much homework you are given. |
|---|---|
| STAY CALM | Simon must *control* his temper more. |
| LIMIT | Parents should *control* the number of hours children spend online every day. |
| POWER | The police are in *control* of the situation. |
| EQUIPMENT | Where's the volume *control* on your tablet? |
| out of control | Sally's behaviour is *out of control* at the moment. |
| beyond my control | Tonight's performance has been cancelled due to circumstances *beyond our control*. |
| under control | If stress was just about deadlines, we would probably be able keep it *under control*. |

**1** Look at the *Word profile* box and match the pairs of sentences.

1 'Turn it down!'
2 'Mrs Parsons is a lot better than our last teacher.'
3 'Were you annoyed when she told you?'
4 'Have you sorted out the food? Have you reminded Daisy to bring some music?'
5 'What happened to your leg?'
6 'I feel really dizzy.'
7 'How would you tackle traffic problems?'
8 'Do you think you did OK in the exam?'

a 'Yes, he had no control over the class.'
b 'We must control the number of cars on the roads.'
c 'Don't worry. It's all done. Everything's under control.'
d 'OK! Where's the TV control?'
e 'I don't know. Anyway, it's beyond our control now!'
f 'Very! But I controlled myself and took a deep breath.'
g 'A dog bit me in the park yesterday. It was completely out of control.'
h 'Sit down and try to control your breathing.'

# UNIT 5
## WORD PROFILE: *take* /teɪk/

| take it/things easy | Why don't you *take things easy* for a while? |
|---|---|
| take into account | We should *take into account* the fact that we've all been busy on other projects. |
| take the/this opportunity to | I'd like to *take this opportunity to* tell you about our exhibition next month. |
| take for granted | Most of us *take* our freedom *for granted*. |
| take turns | We usually *take turns* to tidy up. |

**1** Look at the *Word profile* box and complete the note using phrases with *take*.

Dear Mr Peters,
I'd like to ¹............ thank you again for helping us out with the football match this weekend. We really appreciate your help. As you know, my brother and I usually ²............ to be the referee, with me doing one game and him doing the next. We relied on him, but I think I was ³............ him ............ . When he went back to university after the holidays, I'd forgotten to ⁴............ his university term dates and all of a sudden, we needed extra help. Life used to seem so much simpler! We used to play a match every weekend and apart from that we'd just ⁵............, but now there's too much to think about.
All the best,
Simon Carr

**2** Answer the questions.

1 Do you take anyone for granted? Who? Do you feel guilty about it? Why? / Why not?
2 When do you tend to take things easy? What do you usually do?
3 Have you ever taken the opportunity to write a thank-you note? Who to and why?

# UNIT 6
## WORD PROFILE: *thing* /θɪŋ/

| the whole thing | *The whole thing was ruined by the rain.* |
|---|---|
| the thing is … | *I'd love to go surfing, but the thing is, I haven't finished my essay.* |
| it's a good thing | *It's a good thing that we booked our tickets early.* |
| not a single thing | *There wasn't a single thing I could do to check you were alright.* |
| the main thing | *You're happy at the new school and that's the main thing.* |
| among other things | *Among other things, small children tend to be scared of monsters and the dark.* |
| no such thing | *Some people think there's no such thing as scoliophobia.* |

**1** Look at the *Word profile* box and choose the correct phrase, a or b.

1 I'd normally be keen to come, but ............ ,
   I've been going out a lot recently and I haven't got any money left.
   a   the thing is
   b   it's a good thing

2 I've tried telling her there's ............ as monsters, but she insists on leaving a light on.
   a   not a single thing
   b   no such thing

3 ............ I'm not a sensitive person or his email might have offended me.
   a   The main thing
   b   It's a good thing

4 Don't worry about the car. ............ is that you're alright.
   a   The main thing
   b   It's a good thing

5 I'd describe my brother, ............ , as an optimistic person.
   a   the thing is
   b   among other things

6 I can't understand why she's so furious with me.
   ............ has got out of control.
   a¯  The thing is
   b   The whole thing

7 It was incredibly dark outside and we couldn't see ............ .
   a   no such thing
   b   a single thing

# UNIT 7
## WORD PROFILE: *patient* /ˈpeɪʃənt/

| (im)patient | *Freddy has a lot of exciting ideas for the exhibition and he's impatient to get started.* |
|---|---|
| (im)patiently | *We were waiting impatiently for the show to begin.* |
| (im)patience | *His patience with small children is incredible.* |

**1** Look at the *Word profile* box and complete the sentences.

1 Looking after the elderly can require a lot of ............ .
2 Can you hold on for just a minute? I waited ............ for you while you tried on all those clothes.
3 The children were growing ............ with the delays.
4 Are you listening to me? I'm beginning to lose my ............ with you!
5 As he continued talking, I felt a growing ............ and realised I was in danger of losing my temper.

# UNIT 8
## WORD PROFILE: *make* /meɪk/

| make a difference | *It would make a big difference if you learned some Turkish.* |
|---|---|
| make sense | *It makes sense to go to the bookshop after we've had a coffee.* |
| make no sense | *It makes no sense to pay more than you need to.* |
| make the most of | *You can make the most of the city's beaches.* |
| make use of | *The staff encouraged us to make use of all the gym equipment.* |
| make your way | *We slowly made our way down the river.* |

**1** Complete the sentences with the correct form of the phrases with *make*.

1 I got your text, but it didn't ............ . Can you explain?
2 While I'm away, you might as well ............ my tablet. I won't be able to use it.
3 When you arrive, ............ to the reception desk and ask for the director.
4 Thank you for your calls. They ............ big ............ when I was feeling down.
5 ............ your holidays because you'll be back at school next week.
6 'Turn left!' 'No, it ............ to turn left! We turned left a few minutes ago and we arrived back here!'

# UNIT 9
## WORD PROFILE: *hold* /həʊld/

| hold a/the record | *Danny holds the record for the most goals scored this season.* |
|---|---|
| hold on | *I can get it on my phone … Hold on …. Yeah, here it is.* |
| Hold on! | *Hold on! If the flight's at midday, why do we need to leave so early?* |
| get hold of sb | *I couldn't get hold of Sara yesterday – is she away?* |
| get hold of sth | *The novel is out of print, but Sally got hold of an old copy online.* |
| hold your breath | *How long can you hold your breath under water?* |
| catch/get/grab/take hold of sth/sb | *I just managed to grab hold of Tom before he fell.* |

**1** Complete the sentences with the correct form of *hold* and any other words that are needed.

1 **A** He really gets on my nerves.
 **B** ............! Didn't you just say you always try and see the best in people?
2 I was so scared that I was ............, terrified of making even the tiniest sound.
3 **A** I can't undo this.
 **B** Here, let me have a go. You just have to ............ the lid tightly and press down while you turn it.
4 **A** Can you hurry everyone up? I want to go.
 **B** Would you mind ............ for a moment? We're not in a rush.
5 Do you know where I can ............ some 1960s-style clothes? We need some for our school play.
6 Dennis Kimetto currently ............ for the men's marathon.

# UNIT 10
## WORD PROFILE: *expect* /ɪkˈspekt/

| THINK | *I didn't expect to see you until Saturday.* |
|---|---|
| BEHAVE | *Everyone on the team is expected to attend training twice a week.* |
| expected/ unexpected | *The news about closing the hospital was completely unexpected.* |
| expectation | *The resulting advert more than lived up to everyone's expectations.* |
| unexpectedly | *He called in unexpectedly last week.* |
| be expecting sb/sth | *We're expecting him to arrive within the next five minutes.* |
| I expect | *Tom: Presumably he was late … Rachel: I expect so!* |

**1** Complete the sentences with the correct form of words or phrases from the *Word profile* box.

1 We did really well in the competition – beyond all our ............ .
2 They didn't really advertise the event, so they only ............ a few hundred people to come.
3 I should go. My parents will ............ me home soon.
4 ............ you've finished all the homework, haven't you?
5 You'd better warn her. She won't appreciate you turning up ............ .
6 We're ............ to learn our presentations by heart before we give them.

**2** Answer the questions.

1 What's the most unexpected thing that's happened to you all week?
2 Are you expected to do homework every night at your school?
3 In your experience, what kinds of things never live up to expectations?

# UNIT 11
## WORD PROFILE: *all* /ɔːl/

| in all | *They wrote around 200 letters in all before Carolina became Mrs Yamamoto.* |
|---|---|
| all of a sudden | *But now, all of a sudden, Rachana Shah is talking about moving to Thailand.* |
| all over again | *I had to go through the instructions all over again because no one had heard me.* |
| all along | *Max had known about the plan all along, but kept it secret.* |
| all in all | *The tournament was a great success, all in all.* |
| all over the place | *There were books and papers all over the place and the room looked a complete mess.* |

**1** Look at the *Word profile* box and complete the sentences with phrases with *all*.

1 I told you it was a bad idea. I knew ............ that it was a mistake to have a family party.
2 There were dirty dishes ............ .
3 ............ , my dad came bursting in through the door.
4 Some of the children came, so there were 15 of us ............ .
5 The family holiday could have been a disaster, but ............, it went pretty well.
6 I forgot to save my work, so after the computer crashed I had to start ............ .

## UNIT 12
## WORD PROFILE: *as* /æz/

| as a matter of fact | I'm not from Cambridge – I was born in Bristol, *as a matter of fact.* |
|---|---|
| as far as I know | *As far as I know,* James hasn't *passed his driving test.* |
| as a result of | *The bridge was damaged as a result of the recent floods.* |
| as far as sb is concerned | *As far as Ben is concerned, music is the most important thing in life.* |

**1** Look at the *Word profile* box and complete the sentences with phrases with *as.*

1 ............ , you can do whatever you like. I really don't mind.
2 ............ , they promote their business with newspaper ads, but I'm not absolutely certain.
3 Unemployment has risen ............ the financial crisis.
4 Sam isn't in school today. ............ , I haven't seen him all week.

## UNIT 13
## WORD PROFILE: *lead* /liːd/

| CONTROL | *Ernest Shackleton led three expeditions to the South Pole.* |
|---|---|
| WINNING | *With two laps of the race to go, she led by over eight seconds. It was only in the final 100m that he took the lead.* |
| leader | *You're on your way to becoming a great leader.* |
| leading | *... the teenagers work with leading experts in relevant areas to develop their ideas.* |
| lead to | *Reducing speed limits should lead to fewer road accidents.* |
| lead into/to/ towards, etc. | *We followed the path which led to a small house.* |
| lead a busy/normal/ quiet, etc. life | *Debbie leads a quiet life these days.* |

**1** Complete the sentences with the correct form of the words or phrases from the *Word profile* box.

1 Everyone looks up to Josie. She's a natural ............ .
2 Sally's constant criticism ............ us falling out ages ago.
3 The teacher asked me to ............ the project.
4 Research shows that young people ............ far busier lives these days than they ever used to.
5 My cousin has been offered a job at a ............ advertising company.
6 Barcelona ............ by three goals at half-time, but the match ended in a draw.
7 This road eventually ............ the motorway.
8 Chelsea took the ............ through an early goal.

## UNIT 14
## WORD PROFILE: *break* /breɪk/

| break sth in two/ half | *We broke the last snack bar in two and shared it.* |
|---|---|
| break a record | *If he scores five more goals this season, he'll break the school record.* |
| break an agreement, a promise, etc. | *Sally agreed not to tell anyone, but she has broken her promise.* |
| break the law | *He was breaking the law by using a mobile phone while driving.* |
| break the ice | *On the first morning, we played a game which helped learn each other's names and break the ice.* |
| break sb's heart | *It breaks my heart when I listen to the news on Ebola.* |
| break off (sth) or break (sth) off | *I had to break off my trip early because I ran out of money.* |

**1** Match the sentence halves.

1 One of my teeth broke
2 Nate started to say something, but then broke
3 The boys knew they would be breaking
4 I was so fast I must have broken
5 Jim organised a few games to break
6 It breaks
7 I have to go now or I'll break

a my promise to be back by ten.
b the ice when people first arrived.
c in half while I was chewing something.
d off in the middle of his sentence.
e my heart sometimes when I listen to the news.
f a record cycling here this morning.
g the law if they went inside the building.

# UNIT 15
## WORD PROFILE: key /kiː/

| FOR LOCKS | I can't open the door – I've forgotten my key. |
|---|---|
| ANSWERS | Look at the key on page 124. |
| METHOD | Practice is the key to success. |
| KEYBOARD | Type in the amount, then press the Return key. |
| IMPORTANT | Andy is a key player on the school football team. |
| be key | Our drama teacher was key in our group's application to perform at the arts festival. |
| key in sth or key sth in | Key in your name and address. |

**1** Complete the sentences and match them to the meanings in the *Word profile* box.

1 Wait a moment while I ........... my password.
2 Holding debates is a ........... aspect of our organisation.
3 Have you lost your ........... ?
4 I think the delete ........... is broken.
5 Plenty of practice is the ........... to fluency in English.
6 I've done the quiz. Where's the ........... ?
7 You ........... to the success of this project. We're all relying on you.

**2** Make five sentences using *key*. Can your partner match them to the uses?

# UNIT 16
## WORD PROFILE: no /nəʊ/

| no matter what | I refuse to believe the adverts, no matter what they say. |
|---|---|
| no need | There's no need to give us a lift tonight as we can go with Jen. |
| no wonder | No wonder we couldn't find the remote – it's under the sofa. |
| no good | It's no good making excuses – admit it, you forgot my birthday! |

**1** Look at the *Word profile* box and complete the sentences with phrases with *no*.

1 I never manage to lose weight, ........... I do.
2 Boots are ........... if they aren't waterproof.
3 I understand why she was angry but there was ........... to be rude.
4 It's ........... you're excited if it's the first time you've been abroad.
5 We'll still support him, ........... he's done.
6 This text is in Icelandic. ........... you don't understand it.
7 It's ........... pretending, we know the truth.
8 There's ........... to shout! Just calm down.

# UNIT 17
## WORD PROFILE: date /deɪt/

| date back (to) | Many objects in the museum date back to the 14th century. |
|---|---|
| date from | The invention dates from 1720 and is largely the same today. |
| out of date | This website is so out of date! |
| up to date | Make sure you download regular upgrades, so that your device is always up to date. |

**1** Look at the *Word profile* box and complete the sentences with phrases with *date*.

1 This house ........... to 1850.
2 These movie reviews are really old and ........... now.
3 The castle ........... the 11th century.
4 I stay ........... with the news by reading it on my phone.
5 Your music collection is seriously ........... .
6 This software isn't very ........... .
7 Our problems ........... to when we first started at this college.
8 Some of these poems ........... the First World War.

## UNIT 18
## WORD PROFILE: *balance* /ˈbæləns/

| WEIGHT | I lost my balance and fell off the bike. |
|---|---|
| EQUAL IMPORTANCE | It isn't easy to find the right balance in our lives. |
| MONEY | I always pay off the balance on my credit card. |
| NOT FALLING | The waiter balanced a tray of glasses on each hand. |
| on balance | On balance, she feels that qualifications gave her more options when she was ready to decide. |

**1 Match the sentence halves.**

1 On balance, I think that
2 She lost her balance
3 Having a summer job will definitely
4 It's important to keep a balance
5 We had to balance

a help my bank balance.
b between studying and having a social life.
c Spain is the best place for a holiday.
d our plates of food on our knees.
e and fell off the chair.

## UNIT 19
## WORD PROFILE: *mind* /maɪnd/

| bear (sb/sth) in mind | Bear in mind that there's a public holiday next week. |
|---|---|
| to my mind | To my mind, the film was rather disappointing. |
| cross your mind | To be honest, it has never even crossed my mind that I eat too much meat. |
| have/keep an open mind | It's important to keep an open mind and consider all the facts before making a decision. |
| be in two minds | I'm in two minds about whether to go out tonight. |
| put your mind to sth | If you really put your mind to it, I think you could be one of the best. |

**1 Match the phrases in the *Word profile* box to the meanings.**

1 used to emphasise that you are giving your own opinion
2 come into your thoughts as a possibility
3 remember to consider something
4 wait until you know all the facts before you form an opinion about something
5 give your full attention to something and try very hard to do it
6 have difficulty making a decision

**2 Complete the sentences with the correct form of the phrases with *mind*.**

1 I'll try and speak if you call, but ............ that I'll be at a party!
2 The acting was awful and ............ the plot made no sense.
3 Jess ............ about what to study at university. She enjoys languages, but she also likes the idea of medicine.
4 I'm desperate to learn how to play the guitar. I'm going to ............ it over the summer.
5 The police are ............ about the possible causes of the fire, claiming it is too early to draw any conclusions.
6 It ............ yesterday that you might need my help at the weekend.

## UNIT 20
## WORD PROFILE: *standard* /ˈstændəd/

| QUALITY | The hotel offers a very good standard of service. |
|---|---|
| BEHAVIOUR | My grandmother had very high moral standards. |
| USUAL | White is the standard colour for this model of fridge. |
| standard of living | Canada offers a good standard of living and beautiful countryside. |

**1 Match the questions to the meanings in the *Word profile* box. Then ask and answer the questions in pairs.**

1 Has the standard of your work improved this year? In what ways?
2 What is the standard way of dealing with bad behaviour in your school?
3 In what ways have standards of dress changed from your parents' generation to your generation?

| | | | |
|---|---|---|---|
| *adj* = adjective | *adv* = adverb | *n* = noun | *v* = verb |
| *pv* = phrasal verb | *prep* = preposition | *phr* = phrase | *id* = idiom |

## UNIT 1

**bestseller** /best'selə/ *n* a very popular book that many people have bought

**blog** /blɒg/ *n* a record of your activities or opinions that you put on the internet for other people to read and that you change regularly

**cast** /kɑ:st/ *n* ACTORS all the actors in a film, play or show

**character** /'kærɪktə/ *n* IN A STORY a person represented in a film, play or story

**the charts** /ðə tʃɑ:ts/ *phr* an official list of the most popular songs each week

**classic** /'klæsɪk/ *n* a piece of writing, a musical recording or a film which has been popular for a long time and is considered to be of a high quality

**comment** /'kɒment/ *n* THING SAID something that you say or write that expresses your opinion

**compose** /kəm'pəʊz/ *v* MUSIC to write a piece of music

**critic** /'krɪtɪk/ *n* ARTS someone whose job is to give their opinion about something, especially films, books, music, etc.

**director** /daɪ'rektə/ *n* FILM/PLAY someone who tells the actors in a film or play what to do

**editor** /'edɪtə/ *n* a person who corrects or changes text, film, etc., or a person who is in charge of a newspaper or magazine

**form** /fɔ:m/ *v* START to start an organisation or business

**lyrics** /'lɪrɪks/ *n* the words of a song

**novelist** /'nɒvəlɪst/ *n* a person who writes books about imaginary people and events

**post** /pəʊst/ *v* WEBSITE to leave a message on a website

**presenter** /prɪ'zentə/ *n* someone who introduces a television or radio show

**review** /rɪ'vju:/ *v* GIVE OPINION to give your opinion in a report about a book, film, television programme, etc.

**scene** /si:n/ *n* FILM, BOOK, ETC. a short part of a film, play, or book in which the events happen in one place

**series** /'sɪəri:z/ *n* BOOKS a set of books published by the same company which deal with the same subject

**soundtrack** /'saʊndtræk/ *n* the music used in a film or a television programme

**version** /'vɜ:ʒən/ *n* FORM one form of something that is slightly different to other forms of the same thing

**voice** /vɔɪs/ *n* SOUNDS the sounds that are made when people speak or sing

## UNIT 2

**addicted (to)** /ə'dɪktɪd/ *adj* LIKING liking something very much

**adventurous (with)** /əd'ventʃərəs/ *adj* willing to try new and often difficult or dangerous things

**apologise (for)** /ə'pɒlədʒaɪz/ *v* to tell someone that you are sorry about something you have done

**aware (of)** /ə'weər/ *adj* knowing that something exists, or having knowledge or experience of a particular thing

**bothered (about)** /'bɒðəd/ *adj* If you are bothered about something, it is important to you and you are worried about it.

**cautious (about)** /'kɔ:ʃəs/ *adj* taking care to avoid risks or danger

**compared with** /kəm'peəd wɪð/ *v* used when saying how one person or thing is different from another

**cope (with)** /kəʊp/ *v* to deal successfully with a difficult situation

**critical (of)** /'krɪtɪkəl/ *adj* OPINIONS saying that someone or something is bad or wrong

**decisive (about)** /dɪ'saɪsɪv/ *adj* able to make decisions quickly and confidently, or showing this quality

**depend on** /dɪ'pend ɒn/ *pv* NEED to need the help and support of someone or something in order to exist or continue as before

**do without** /du: wɪ'ðaʊt/ *pv* to manage without having something

**have heard of** /həv hɜ:d əv/ *v* If you have heard of someone or something, you know that that person or thing exists.

**hopeless (at)** /'həʊpləs/ *adj* BAD AT SOMETHING very bad at a particular activity

**impressed (by)** /ɪm'prest/ *adj* feeling admiration or respect for someone or something

**jealous (of)** /'dʒeləs/ *adj* WANTING SOMETHING unhappy and angry because you want something that someone else has

**laugh at** /lɑ:f ət/ *pv* to show that you think someone or something is stupid

**loyal (to)** /'lɔɪəl/ *adj* always liking and supporting someone or something, sometimes when other people do not

**mean (about)** /mi:n/ *adj* NOT KIND unkind or unpleasant

## UNIT 3

**advise** /əd'vaɪz/ v to make a suggestion about what you think someone should do or how they should do something

**agree** /ə'griː/ v DECIDE to decide something with someone

**agree** /ə'griː/ v SAY YES to say you will do something that someone asks you to

**agreement** /ə'griːmənt/ n SAME OPINION when people have the same opinion or have made the same decision

**beg** /beg/ v STRONG REQUEST to make a very strong and urgent request

**belief** /bɪ'liːf/ n IDEA an idea that you are certain is true

**concentration** /kɒnsən'treɪʃən/ n THOUGHT the ability to think carefully about something you are doing and nothing else

**creativity** /kriːeɪ'tɪvɪti/ n the ability to produce new ideas or things using skill and imagination

**determination** /dɪtɜːmɪ'neɪʃən/ n when someone continues trying to do something, although it is very difficult

**development** /dɪ'veləpmənt/ n CHANGE when someone or something grows or changes and becomes more advanced

**encourage** /ɪn'kʌrɪdʒ/ v GIVE CONFIDENCE to give someone confidence or hope

**expect** /ɪk'spekt/ v THINK to think or believe that something will happen

**expect** /ɪk'spekt/ v BEHAVE to think that someone should behave in a particular way or do a particular thing

**force** /fɔːs/ v GIVE NO CHOICE to make someone do something that they do not want to do

**fortune** /'fɔːtʃuːn/ n LUCK the good or bad things that happen to you

**help** /help/ v MAKE BETTER to make something better

**intelligence** /ɪn'telɪdʒəns/ n the ability to learn, understand and think about things

**intend** /ɪn'tend/ v HAVE PLAN to have as a plan or purpose

**nature** /'neɪtʃə/ n LIFE the force that is responsible for physical life

**persuade** /pə'sweɪd/ v MAKE SOMEONE AGREE to make someone agree to do something by talking to them a lot about it

**plan** /plæn/ v DECIDE to think about and decide what you are going to do or how you are going to do something

**pretend** /prɪ'tend/ v to behave as if something is true when it is not

**refuse** /rɪ'fjuːz/ v to say that you will not do or accept something

**remind** /rɪ'maɪnd/ v to make someone remember something, or remember to do something

**success** /sək'ses/ n If you achieve success, you are recognised and admired by many people for your skills and achievements or wealth.

**tend** /tend/ v BE LIKELY To be likely to behave in a particular way or to have a particular characteristic

**warn** /wɔːn/ v to make someone realise a possible danger or problem, especially one in the future

## UNIT 4

**appetite** /'æpɪtaɪt/ n FOOD the feeling that makes you want to eat

**bad-tempered** /bæd'tempəd/ adj describes a person who becomes angry and annoyed easily

**come down with (sth)** /kʌm daʊn wɪð/ pv to become ill, usually with a disease that is not very serious

**cut down on (sth)** /kʌt daʊn ɒn/ pv CUT BACK ON STH to do less of something or use something in smaller amounts

**faint** /feɪnt/ v to suddenly become unconscious for a short time, usually falling down

**feel dizzy** /fiːl 'dɪzi/ phr to feel as if everything is turning round, so that you feel ill or as if you might fall

**get (sb) down** /get daʊn/ pv to make someone feel unhappy

**get over (sth/sb)** /get 'əʊvə/ pv to get better after an illness, or feel better after something or someone has made you unhappy

**go over (sth) in your mind** /gəʊ 'əʊvər ɪn jɔː maɪnd/ pv to think repeatedly about an event that has happened

**lose** /luːz/ v NOT HAVE to stop having something that you had before

**lose your temper** /luːz jɔː 'tempə/ phr to suddenly become angry

**panic** /'pænɪk/ n a sudden, strong feeling of worry or fear that makes you unable to think or behave calmly

**pass out** /pɑːs aʊt/ pv to become unconscious

**stay up** /steɪ ʌp/ pv to go to bed later than usual

**upset stomach** /ʌpset 'stʌmək/ n an illness in the stomach

## UNIT 5

**ancestor** /ˈænsestə/ *n* a relative who lived a long time ago

**most days/weeks/months** /məʊst deɪz wiːks mʌnθs/ *phr* almost every day/week/month

**citizen** /ˈsɪtɪzən/ *n* TOWN/CITY someone who lives in a particular town or city

**civilisation** /sɪvəlaɪˈzeɪʃən/ *n* human society with its well developed social organisations, or the culture and way of life of a society or country at a particular period in time

**constantly** /ˈkɒnstəntli/ *adv* all the time or often

**decade** /ˈdekeɪd/ *n* a period of ten years, especially a period such as 1860 to 1869, or 1990 to 1999

**from time to time** /frəm taɪm tə taɪm/ *phr* sometimes but not often

**inhabitant** /ɪnˈhæbɪtənt/ *n* a person or animal that lives in a particular place

**kingdom** /ˈkɪŋdəm/ *n* COUNTRY a country ruled by a king or queen

**launch** /lɔːntʃ/ *v* NEW PRODUCT If a company launches a product or service, it makes it available for the first time.

**myth** /mɪθ/ *n* STORY an ancient story about gods and brave people, often one that explains an event in history or the natural world

**occasionally** /əˈkeɪʒənəli/ *adv* sometimes but not often

**(every) once in a while** /ˈevri wʌns ɪn ə ˈwaɪl/ *phr* sometimes but not often

**rarely** /ˈreəli/ *adv* not often

**regularly** /ˈregjʊləli/ *adv* OFTEN often

**seldom** /ˈseldəm/ *adv* not often

**tribe** /traɪb/ *n* a group of people who live together, usually in areas far away from cities, and who share the same culture and language and still have a traditional way of life

## UNIT 6

**anxious (about)** /ˈaŋkʃəs/ *adj* WORRIED worried and nervous

**bad-tempered (about)** /bædˈtempəd/ *adj* angry and annoyed

**bright** /braɪt/ *adj* HAPPY happy or full of hope

**cheerful** /ˈtʃɪəfəl/ *adj* HAPPY happy and positive

**concerned** /kənˈsɜːnd/ *adj* WORRIED worried

**content (with)** /kənˈtent/ *adj* pleased with your situation and not hoping for change or improvement

**definitely** /ˈdefɪnətli/ *adv* without any doubt

**depressed** /dɪˈprest/ *adj* UNHAPPY unhappy and without hope for the future

**down (about)** /daʊn/ *adj* unhappy and depressed

**fed up (with)** /fed ˈʌp/ *adj* annoyed or bored with something that you have experienced for too long

**frequently** /ˈfriːkwəntli/ *adv* often

**furious** /ˈfjʊəriəs/ *adj* extremely angry

**irritated** /ˈɪrɪteɪtɪd/ *adj* annoyed

**optimistic** /ɒptɪˈmɪstɪk/ *adj* always believing that good things will happen

**over the moon (about)** /ˈəʊvər ðə muːn/ *id* very pleased

**pessimistic** /pesɪˈmɪstɪk/ *adj* always believing that bad things are likely to happen

**petrified (of)** /ˈpetrɪfaɪd/ *adj* extremely frightened

**relieved (about)** /rɪˈliːvd/ *adj* happy that something unpleasant has not happened or has ended

**scared** /skeəd/ *adj* frightened or worried

## UNIT 7

**before (very/too) long** /bɪˈfɔː lɒŋ/ *phr* soon

**bounce** /baʊns/ *v* to move somewhere in a happy and energetic way

**burst open** /bɜːst ˈəʊpən/ *pv* to open suddenly

**charge** /tʃɑːdʒ/ *v* MOVE FORWARD to move forward quickly and violently, especially towards something that has caused difficulty or anger

**for hours/weeks on end** /fər aʊəz/ wiːks ən ˈend/ *phr* for hours/weeks without stopping

**for some time** /fə sʌm ˈtaɪm/ *phr* for a long period of time

**in no time** /ɪn ˈnəʊ taɪm/ *phr* very soon

**kneel down** /niːl daʊn/ *pv* to go down into, or stay in, a position where one or both knees are on the ground

**lean** /liːn/ *v* to (cause to) slope in one direction, or to move the top part of the body in a particular direction

**mumble** /ˈmʌmbl/ *v* to speak too quietly and not clearly enough for someone to understand you

**mutter** /ˈmʌtə/ *v* to speak quietly so that your voice is difficult to hear, often when complaining about something

**rush** /rʌʃ/ *v* HURRY to hurry or move quickly somewhere, or to make someone or something hurry or move quickly somewhere

**shake** /ʃeɪk/ *v* FEAR If you are shaking, your body makes quick short movements, or you feel as if it is doing so, because you are frightened or nervous.

**sigh** /saɪ/ *v* to breathe out slowly and noisily, often because you are annoyed or unhappy

**slap** /slæp/ *v* to hit someone with the flat, inside part of your hand

**swing open** /swɪŋ ˈəʊpən/ *pv* MOVE SIDEWAYS to open easily and without interruption

**tap** /tæp/ *v* to knock or touch something gently

**the week before last** /ðə wiːk bɪˈfɔː lɑːst/ *phr* the week before the one that has just finished

**wander** /ˈwɒndə/ *pv* WALK SLOWLY to walk around slowly in a relaxed way or without any clear purpose or direction

**whisper** /ˈwɪspə/ *v* to speak extremely quietly so that other people cannot hear

**whistle** /ˈwɪsl/ *v* to make a sound by breathing air out through a small hole made with your lips, or through a whistle

**yell** /jel/ *v* to shout something very loudly

# UNIT 8

**close** /kləʊs/ *adj* RELATIONSHIP seeing or communicating with someone a lot

**diverse** /daɪˈvɜːs/ *adj* varied or different

**industrial** /ɪnˈdʌstriəl/ *adj* connected with industry, or having a lot of industry and factories, etc.

**inner city** /ˈɪnə ˈsɪti/ *n* the central part of a city where people live and where there are often problems because people are poor and there are few jobs and bad houses

**relaxed** /rɪˈlækst/ *adj* SITUATION A relaxed situation or place is comfortable and informal.

**remote** /rɪˈməʊt/ *adj* FAR AWAY describes an area, house, or village that is a long way from any town or cities

**residential** /rezɪˈdentʃəl/ *adj* WHERE PEOPLE LIVE A residential area has only houses and not offices or factories.

**rural** /ˈrʊərəl/ *adj* relating to the countryside and not to towns

**urban** /ˈɜːbən/ *adj* belonging or relating to a town or city

**welcoming** /ˈwelkəmɪŋ/ *adj* friendly or making you feel welcome

# UNIT 9

**achieve** /əˈtʃiːv/ *v* to succeed in doing something good, usually by working hard

**active** /ˈæktɪv/ *adj* BUSY doing a lot of things, or moving around a lot

**beneficial** /benəˈfɪʃəl/ *adj* helpful, useful or good

**competition** /kɒmpəˈtɪʃən/ *n* EVENT an organised event in which people try to win a prize by being the best, fastest, etc.

**effective** /ɪˈfektɪv/ *adj* successful or achieving the results that you want

**emotional** /ɪˈməʊʃənəl/ *adj* EMOTIONS relating to emotions

**encouragement** /ɪnˈkʌrɪdʒmənt/ *n* something that makes someone more likely to do something

**enjoyment** /ɪnˈdʒɔɪmənt/ *n* when you enjoy something

**friendship** /ˈfrendʃɪp/ *n* when two people are friends

**go wrong** /gəʊ rɒŋ/ *pv* to develop problems

**goal** /gəʊl/ *n* AIM an aim or purpose

**have a go at (sth)** /hæv ə gəʊ ət/ *pv* to try to do something you have not done before

**look bright** /lʊk braɪt/ *phr* to appear full of hope for success or happiness

**majority** /məˈdʒɒrəti/ *n* more than half of a group of people or things

**make a (big) difference** /meɪk ə ˈdɪfərəns/ *phr* to improve a situation (a lot)

**make the best of (sth)** /meɪk ðə best əv/ *phr* to make an unsatisfactory situation as pleasant as possible

**make the most of (sth)** /meɪk ðə məʊst əv/ *phr* to take full advantage of something because it may not last long

**personality** /pɜːsəˈnæləti/ *n* CHARACTER the type of person you are, which is shown by the way you behave, feel and think

**practical** /ˈpræktɪkəl/ *adj* REAL relating to experience, real situations or actions rather than ideas or imagination

**put an end to (sth)** /pʊt ən end tuː/ *phr* to make something stop happening or existing

**relationship** /rɪˈleɪʃənʃɪp/ *n* CONNECTION the way in which two things are connected

**remarkable** /rɪˈmɑːkəbl/ *adj* very unusual or noticeable in a way that you admire

**responsibility** /rɪspɒnsəˈbɪləti/ *n* DUTY something that it is your job or duty to deal with

**satisfaction** /sætɪsˈfækʃən/ *n* FEELING a pleasant feeling which you get when you receive something you wanted, or when you have done something you wanted to do

**see the best in (sb)** /siː ðə best ɪn/ *phr* to look for the good qualities that someone has

**see the worst in (sb)** /siː ðə wɜːst ɪn/ *phr* to look for the bad qualities that someone has

**strength** /streŋθ/ *n* GOOD QUALITIES a good quality or ability that makes someone or something effective

**take an opportunity** /teɪk ən ɒpətjuːnəti/ *phr* use an occasion to do or say something

**valuable** /ˈvæljʊbl/ *adj* IMPORTANT Valuable information, advice, etc. is very helpful or important.

**weakness** /ˈwiːknəs/ *n* NOT EFFECTIVE a particular part or quality of someone or something that is not good or effective

# UNIT 10

**at fault** /ət fɒlt/ *phr* responsible for something bad that has happened

**at risk** /ət rɪsk/ *phr* being in a situation where something bad is likely to happen

**be at your best** /bi: ət jɔ: best/ *phr* to be as active or intelligent as you can be

**boiling** /ˈbɔɪlɪŋ/ *adj* very hot

**bright** /braɪt/ *adj* HAPPY happy or full of hope

**by accident** /baɪ ˈæksɪdənt/ *phr* without intending to

**by chance** /baɪ tʃɑːns/ *phr* LUCK when something happens because of luck, or without being planned

**flood** /flʌd/ *v* FILL to fill or enter a place in large numbers or amounts

**freeze** /friːz/ *v* NOT MOVE to suddenly stop moving, especially because you are frightened

**have something in common with (sb)** /hæv ˈsʌmθɪŋ ɪn kɒmən wɪθ/ *phr* to share interests, experiences, or other characteristics with someone or something

**hit** /hɪt/ *v* AFFECT to affect something badly

**in advance** /ɪn ədˈvɑːns/ *phr* before a particular time, or before doing a particular thing

**in all** /ɪn ɔːl/ *phr* used to show the total amount of something

**in detail** /ɪn ˈdiːteɪl/ *phr* including or considering all the information about something or every part of something

**in public** /ɪn ˈpʌblɪk/ *phr* in a place where other people, especially people you do not know, can hear you and see what you are doing

**in secret** /ɪn ˈsiːkrət/ *phr* without telling other people

**keep in touch** /kiːp ɪn tʌtʃ/ *phr* to communicate or continue to communicate with someone, for example by email or telephone

**learn by heart** /lɜːn baɪ hɑːt/ *phr* learn so that you can remember all of something

**out of character** /aʊt əv ˈkærɪktə/ *phr* unusual in terms of someone's personality

**out of nowhere** /aʊt əv ˈnəʊweə/ *phr* If someone or something appears out of nowhere, it appears suddenly or unexpectedly.

**weigh up** /weɪ ʌp/ *pv* CONSIDER CAREFULLY to consider something carefully, especially in order to make a decision

# UNIT 11

**badly-behaved** /bædli bɪˈheɪvd/ *adj* behaving in a way that is accepted as incorrect

**count on (sb)** /kaʊnt ɒn/ *pv* to be confident that you can depend on someone

**fall out with (sb)** /ˈfɔːl aʊt/ *pv* to argue with someone and stop being friendly with them

**finish with (sb)** /ˈfɪnɪʃ wɪð/ *pv* to end a romantic relationship with someone

**go off (sb/sth)** /gəʊ ɒf/ *pv* to stop liking or being interested in someone or something

**grown-up** /grəʊn ʌp/ *adj* If you say that someone is grown-up, you mean that they are an adult or that they behave in a responsible way.

**high-tech** /haɪ ˈtek/ *adj* using or involved with the most recent and advanced electronic machines, computers, etc.

**hit it off** /hɪt ɪt ɒf/ *pv* If people hit it off, they like each other and become friendly immediately.

**last-minute** /lɑːst ˈmɪnɪt/ *adj* done at the latest possible opportunity

**let (sb) down** /let daʊn/ *pv* to disappoint someone by failing to do what you agreed to do or were expected to do

**long-distance** /lɒŋ ˈdɪstəns/ *adj* travelling or communicating between two places that are a long way apart

**look down on (sb)** /lʊk daʊn ɒn/ *pv* to think that you are better than someone

**look up to (sb)** /lʊk ʌp tuː/ *pv* to admire and respect someone

**middle-aged** /mɪdl ˈeɪdʒd/ *adj* in the middle of your life before you are old

**self-confident** /self ˈkɒnfɪdənt/ *adj* feeling sure about yourself and your abilities

**short-term** /ʃɔːt tɜːm/ *adj* lasting a short time, or relating to a short period of time

**stick together** /stɪk təˈgeðə/ *pv* If people stick together, they support and help each other.

**take after (sb)** /teɪk ˈɑːftə/ *pv* to be similar to an older member of your family in appearance or character

**well-balanced** /wel ˈbæləntst/ *adj* FOOD A well-balanced diet or meal includes all the different types of food that the body needs to be healthy.

**well-built** /wel ˈbɪlt/ *adj* having a large, strong body

**well-organised** /wel ˈɔːgənaɪzd/ *adj* planned and arranged in a good way, to a high or satisfactory standard

**well-paid** /wel ˈpeɪd/ *adj* earning a lot of money

## UNIT 12

**amuse** /əˈmjuːz/ v MAKE LAUGH to make someone laugh or smile

**cheer (sb) up** /tʃɪər ʌp/ pv If someone cheers up, or something cheers them up, they start to feel happier.

**congratulate** /kənˈgrætjʊleɪt/ v to tell someone that you are happy because they have done something good or something good has happened to them

**express** /ɪkˈspres/ v to show what you think or how you feel using words or actions

**inspire** /ɪnˈspaɪə/ v ENCOURAGE to make someone feel that they want to do something and can do it

**persuade** /pəˈsweɪd/ v to make someone do or believe something by giving them a good reason to do it

**promote** /prəˈməʊt/ v ADVERTISE to advertise something

**stimulate** /ˈstɪmjʊleɪt/ v MAKE EXCITED to make someone excited or interested about something

## UNIT 13

**adventurous** /ədˈventʃərəs/ adj willing to try new and often difficult or dangerous things

**appreciation** /əpriːʃiˈeɪʃən/ n when you understand how good something or someone is and are able to enjoy them

**cautious** /ˈkɔːʃəs/ adj taking care to avoid risks or danger

**come up** /kʌm ʌp/ pv MOVE TOWARDS to move towards someone

**in my own company** /ɪn maɪ əʊn ˈkʌmpəni/ phr alone

**criticism** /ˈkrɪtɪsɪzəm/ n saying that something or someone is bad

**doubt** /daʊt/ v to not feel certain or confident about something

**fairly** /ˈfeəli/ adv IN THE RIGHT WAY If you do something fairly, you do it in a way which is right and reasonable and treats people equally.

**influence** /ˈɪnfluəns/ n POWER the power to affect how someone thinks or behaves, or how something develops

**keep up** /kiːp ʌp/ pv SAME SPEED to move at the same speed as someone or something that is moving forward

**live up to** /lɪv ʌp tuː/ pv to be as good as someone hopes

**make (sth) up** /meɪk ʌp/ pv to say or write something that is not true

**motivated** /ˈməʊtɪveɪtɪd/ adj enthusiastic and determined to succeed

**set up** /set ʌp/ pv ORGANISATION to start a new company, organisation, system, way of working, etc.

**speak up** /spiːk ʌp/ pv to speak in a louder voice so that people can hear you

**stand out** /stænd aʊt/ pv EASY TO SEE to be very easy to see or notice

**strict** /strɪkt/ adj PERSON A strict person makes sure that children or people working for them behave well and does not allow them to break any rules.

**sympathetic** /sɪmpəˈθetɪk/ adj PROBLEMS showing that you understand and care about someone's problems

**target** /ˈtɑːgɪt/ n AIM something that you intend to achieve

**turn up** /tɜːn ʌp/ pv to arrive or appear somewhere

## UNIT 14

**agree** /əˈgriː/ v SAY YES to say you will do something that someone asks you to

**break down** /breɪk daʊn/ pv NOT WORKING when a vehicle or machine stops working for a period of time

**confess** /kənˈfes/ v to admit that you have done something wrong or something that you feel guilty or bad about

**cool down** /kuːl daʊn/ pv to become or cause something to become slightly colder

**criticise** /ˈkrɪtɪsaɪz/ v to say that someone or something is bad

**drive off** /draɪv ɒf/ pv to leave in a car or other vehicle

**enquire** /ɪnˈkwaɪə/ v to ask someone for information about something

**hold up** /həʊld ʌp/ pv DELAY to make something or someone slow or late

**insist** /ɪnˈsɪst/ v SAY FIRMLY to say firmly that something is true

**insist** /ɪnˈsɪst/ v DEMAND to demand that something must be done or that you must have a particular thing

**keep up with (sb or sth)** /kiːp ʌp wɪð/ pv to move at the same speed as someone or something that is moving forward so that you stay level with them

**make out** /meɪk aʊt/ pv SUCCEED to see, hear, or understand something or someone with difficulty

**persuade** /pəˈsweɪd/ v to make someone do or believe something by giving them a good reason to do it

**point out** /pɔɪnt aʊt/ pv to tell someone about some information, often because they do not know it or have forgotten it

**pull into** /pʊl ˈɪntuː/ pv If a vehicle pulls in or pulls into somewhere, it moves in that direction and stops there.

**pull out** /pʊl aʊt/ pv If a train pulls out, it starts to leave a station.

**pull over** /pʊl ˈəʊvə/ *pv* If a vehicle pulls over, it moves to the side of the road and stops.

**pull up** /pʊl ʌp/ *pv* If a vehicle pulls up, it stops, often for a short time.

**recommend** /rekəˈmend/ *v* ADVISE to advise someone that something should be done

**run over** /rʌn ˈəʊvə/ *pv* If a vehicle or its driver runs over someone or something, the vehicle hits and drives over them or it.

**slow down** /sləʊ daʊn/ *pv* to become slower, or to make someone or something become slower

**slow down** /sləʊ daʊn/ *pv* If someone slows down, they become less active.

## UNIT 15

**ban** /bæn/ *v* to forbid something, especially officially

**ban** /bæn/ *n* an official order that prevents something from happening

**collect** /kəˈlekt/ *v* GET MONEY to ask people to give you money, or sometimes food or clothes, for something, for example a charity

**collection** /kəˈlekʃən/ *n* when money, food or clothes are collected for something, for example a charity

**cooperate** /kəʊˈɒpəreɪt/ *v* WORK TOGETHER to work together with someone in order to achieve the same aim

**cooperation** /kəʊɒpərˈeɪʃən/ *n* when you work together with someone or do what they ask you

**criticise** /ˈkrɪtɪsaɪz/ *v* to say that someone or something is bad

**criticism** /ˈkrɪtɪsɪzəm/ *n* when you say that something or someone is bad

**elect** /ɪˈlekt/ *v* to choose someone for a particular job or position by voting

**election** /ɪˈlekʃən/ *n* a time when people vote in order to choose someone for a political or official job

**in all** /ɪn ɔːl/ *phr* used to show the total amount of something

**in general** /ɪn ˈdʒenrəl/ *phr* considering the whole of someone or something, and not just a particular part of them

**in progress** /ɪn ˈprəʊgres/ *phr* happening or being done now

**in public** /ɪn ˈpʌblɪk/ *phr* in a place where other people, especially people you do not know, can hear you and see what you are doing

**in secret** /ɪn ˈsiːkrət/ *phr* without telling other people

**in turn** /ɪn tɜːn/ *phr* one after another

**support** /səˈpɔːt/ *v* AGREE to agree with an idea, group, or person

**supporter** /səˈpɔːtə/ *n* OF IDEA OR PERSON someone who supports a particular idea, group or person

## UNIT 16

**be aimed at** /biː eɪmd ət/ *v* If information is aimed at a particular group of people, it is made known in a way that influences them or makes them interested in something.

**commercial break** /kəˈmɜːʃəl /breɪk/ *n* a short interruption of a television or radio programme to broadcast advertisements

**constantly** /ˈkɒnstəntli/ *adv* all the time or often

**consumer** /kənˈsjuːmə/ *n* a person who buys goods or services for their own use

**ecologically** /iːkəˈlɒdʒɪkli/ *adv* in a way that relates to ecology or the environment

**environmentally friendly** /ɪnvaɪərənˈmentəli frendli/ *adj* not harmful to the environment

**financially** /faɪˈnænʃəli/ *adv* in a way that relates to money or how money is managed

**globally** /ˈgləʊbəli/ *adv* in a way that relates to the whole world

**incredibly** /ɪnˈkredɪbli/ *adv* EXTREMELY extremely

**launch** /lɔːntʃ/ *v* NEW PRODUCT If a company launches a product or service, it makes it available for the first time.

**logo** /ˈləʊgəʊ/ *n* a design or symbol used by a company to advertise its products

**on offer** /ɒn ˈɒfə/ *phr* If goods in a shop are on offer, they are being sold at a lower price than usual.

**sample** /ˈsɑːmpl/ *n* SMALL AMOUNT a small amount of something that shows you what it is like

**scientifically** /saɪənˈtɪfɪkli/ *adv* using scientific methods

**sponsor** /ˈspɒnsə/ *v* to give money to someone to support an activity, event, or organisation, sometimes as a way to advertise your company or product

**well-balanced** /wel ˈbælənst/ *adj* A well-balanced diet or meal includes all the different types of food that the body needs to be healthy.

# UNIT 17

**achievement** /əˈtʃiːvmənt/ *n* something very good and difficult that you have succeeded in doing

**back (sb) up** /bæk ʌp/ *pv* to support or help someone

**bring (sth) up** /brɪŋ ʌp/ *pv* to start to talk about a particular subject

**catch up on** /kætʃ ʌp ɒn/ *pv* to learn the newest facts about something

**celebrate** /ˈselɪbreɪt/ *v* PRAISE to express admiration or approval for someone or something

**chill out** /tʃɪl aʊt/ *pv* to relax completely, or not allow things to upset you

**clear (sth) up** /klɪər ʌp/ *pv* to give or find an explanation for something, or to deal with a problem or argument

**comment (on)** /ˈkɒment ɒn/ *v* to give your opinions about something

**current events** /ˈkʌrənt ɪˈvents/ *n* events that are being reported in the news

**follow up** /ˈfɒləʊ ʌp/ *pv* to find out more about something, or take further action connected with it

**get (sth) across** /get əˈkrɒs/ *pv* to manage to make someone understand or believe something

**gossip (about)** /ˈgɒsɪp/ *v* to talk about other people's private lives

**highlight** /ˈhaɪlaɪt/ *v* to emphasise something or make people notice something

**keep (sb) amused** /kiːp əˈmjuːzd/ *phr* to help someone feel interested and happy

**keep (sb) up to date** /kiːp ʌp tə deɪt/ *phr* to give someone the latest information

**leave out** /liːv aʊt/ *pv* to not include someone or something

**look into** /lʊk ˈɪntuː/ *pv* to examine the facts about a problem or situation

**make fun of** /meɪk fʌn əv/ *pv* to make a joke about someone or something in a way that is not kind

**need (for sth)** /niːd fɔː/ *n* something that it is necessary to have or do

**performance** /pəˈfɔːməns/ *n* ENTERTAINMENT acting, dancing, singing, or playing music to entertain people

**review** /rɪˈvjuː/ *v* GIVE OPINION to give your opinion in a report about a book, film, television programme, etc.

# UNIT 18

**be your own boss** /biː jɔːr əʊn bɒs/ *phr* to work for yourself, not for an employer

**creative** /kriˈeɪtɪv/ *adj* producing or using original and unusual ideas

**flexible** /ˈfleksɪbl/ *adj* ABLE TO CHANGE able to change or be changed easily according to the situation

**foreign** /ˈfɒrən/ *adj* OTHER COUNTRIES relating to or dealing with countries that are not your own

**manual** /ˈmænjuəl/ *adj* PHYSICAL WORK involving physical work rather than mental work

**more and more** /mɔːr ən mɔː/ *phr* increasingly, as time passes

**more or less** /mɔːr ɔː les/ *phr* almost or approximately

**now and then** /naʊ ænd ðen/ *phr* If something happens now and then, it happens sometimes but not very often.

**one or two** /wʌn ɔː tuː/ *phr* a few

**opportunity** /ɒpəˈtjuːnəti/ *n* CHANCE a situation in which it is possible for you to do something, or a possibility of doing something

**over and over (again)** /ˈəʊvər ən ˈəʊvə/ *phr* happening or done many times

**personally** /ˈpɜːsənəli/ *adv* NOT SOMEONE ELSE affecting you and not anyone else

**professional** /prəˈfeʃənəl/ *adj* JOB describes the type of job that is respected because it involves a high level of education and training

**rewarding** /rɪˈwɔːdɪŋ/ *adj* making you feel satisfied that you have done something important or useful

**round and round** /raʊnd ən raʊnd/ *phr* moving in a circle

**shift** /ʃɪft/ *n* When people work shifts, they work for set periods of time during the day or night.

**sooner or later** /suːnər ɔː leɪtə/ *phr* used to say that you do not know exactly when something will happen, but you are certain that it will happen

**take time off** /teɪk taɪm ɒf/ *n* to stop work, in order to do something else

**up and down** /ʌp ən daʊn/ *adv* rising and falling

**well-paid** /wel peɪd/ *adj* earning a lot of money

**working hours** /ˈwɜːkɪŋ aʊəz/ *n* the amount of time someone spends at work during a day

# UNIT 19

**as far as I'm concerned** /əz fɑːr əz aɪm kənˈsɜːnd/ *phr* in my opinion

**be against** /biː əˈɡenst/ *phr* NOT AGREE to disagree with a plan or activity

**be in favour of** /biː ɪn ˈfeɪvər əv/ *phr* to support or approve of something

**bear in mind** /beər ɪn maɪnd/ *phr* to remember a piece of information when you are making a decision or thinking about something

**believe in** /bɪˈliːv ɪn/ *pv* to be confident that something is effective and right

**belongings** /bɪˈlɒŋɪŋz/ *n* the things that a person owns, especially those which can be carried

**contents** /ˈkɒntents/ *n* BOOK a list in a book that tells you what different parts the book contains

**convince** /kənˈvɪns/ *v* to persuade someone or make them certain

**deny** /dɪˈnaɪ/ *v* NOT TRUE to say that something is not true

**firmly** /ˈfɜːmli/ *adv* STRONGLY strongly

**go along with (sth/sb)** /ɡəʊ əˈlɒŋ wɪð/ *pv* to support an idea, or to agree with someone's opinion

**graphics** /ˈɡræfɪks/ *n* images shown on a computer screen

**lyrics** /ˈlɪrɪks/ *n* the words of a song

**refreshments** /rɪˈfreʃmənts/ *n* food and drinks that are available at a meeting, event, on a journey, etc.

**surroundings** /səˈraʊndɪŋz/ *n* the place where someone lives and the conditions they live in

**suspect** /səˈspekt/ *v* THINK LIKELY to think that something is probably true, or is likely to happen

**there's no doubt** /ðeəz nəʊ daʊt/ *phr* used to emphasise that what you are saying is true or likely to happen

**to my mind** /tə maɪ maɪnd/ *phr* used to emphasise that you are giving your own opinion

**totally** /ˈtəʊtəli/ *adv* completely

**view** /vjuː/ *n* OPINION your opinion

# UNIT 20

**be a pain** /biː ə peɪn/ *id* to be annoying

**be a piece of cake** /biː ə piːs əv keɪk/ *id* to be very easy

**break (sb's) heart** /breɪk hɑːt/ *id* If an event or situation breaks your heart, it makes you feel very sad.

**break the ice** /breɪk ðiː aɪs/ *id* to make people feel more relaxed in a social situation

**cross (sb's) mind** /krɒs maɪnd/ *id* If something crosses your mind, you think about it for a short time.

**damage** /ˈdæmɪdʒ/ *v* to harm, break or spoil something

**harm** /hɑːm/ *v* to hurt someone or damage something

**have an eye for (sth)** /hæv ən aɪ fɔː/ *id* to be good at noticing a particular type of thing

**injure** /ˈɪndʒə/ *v* to hurt a person, animal or part of your body

**lose track of time** /luːz træk əv taɪm/ *id* to not be aware of what time it is

**means** /miːnz/ *n* METHOD a method or way of doing something

**observe** /əbˈzɜːv/ *v* WATCH to watch someone or something carefully

**opportunity** /ɒpəˈtuːnəti/ *n* CHANCE a situation in which it is possible for you to do something, or a possibility of doing something

**possibility** /pɒsəˈbɪləti/ *n* MAY HAPPEN/BE TRUE a chance that something may happen or be true

**take (sb's) breath away** /teɪk breθ əˈweɪ/ *id* to make you feel surprise and admiration

# Grammar reference

## UNIT 1

## SIMPLE, CONTINUOUS OR PERFECT

### Present perfect

- We use the **present perfect** (*has/have* +past participle) for events which happened some time before or up to the present <u>if we do not mention when they happened.</u>
  We often use it with *still ... not, not ... yet, just, already, before, ever, never, the first (second etc.) time, since* and *for*.
  They **still haven't** repaired my bike.
  I'**ve just had** lunch.
  They **have never eaten** spicy food.
  We **haven't seen** him **since** last week.
  They **haven't repaired** my bike **yet**.
  The plane **has already left**.
  **Have** you **ever ridden** a motorbike?
  This is **the first time** I'**ve tried** this dish.

### Past perfect

- We use the **past perfect** (*had* + past participle) for events which happened some time before or up to a point in the past. Like the present perfect, we often use it with *still ... not, not ... yet, just, already, before, ever, never, the first (second* etc.*) time, since* and *for*.
  I phoned the shop, but they **still hadn't** repaired my bike.
  I'**d just had** lunch, so I didn't go for a swim.
  They'**d never eaten** such spicy food, but they really enjoyed it.
  We **hadn't seen** him **since** the previous week and were very relieved when he turned up.

### Past simple

- We use the **past simple** (regular form: verb + *-ed*) for completed events in the past which answer the question *when?*
  I **visited** China twice **last year**.
  I **stayed** there **for three weeks**.
  I **swam every day last summer**.

### Practice

**1** Complete the answers with the correct form of the verb in brackets, present perfect, past perfect or past simple.

1 Where did you get the idea for that painting?
   I ........................ (want) to do a landscape that ........................ (look) like a place no one ........................ (see) before.

2 How old were you when you started learning the guitar?
   I think I ........................ (be) eleven because I ........................ (already/start) secondary school.

3 What do you think of my car?
   I ........................ (never see) anything like it! Where ........................ (find/you) it?

### Present continuous

- We use the **present continuous** (*am/is/are* + verb + *-ing*) for events which are happening now; for temporary or changing situations; with *always* to express annoyance or for repeated events.
  He'**s making** coffee.
  The price of coffee **is going** up.
  My brother **is always borrowing** my phone.

### Past continuous

- We use the **past continuous** (*was/were (not)* + verb + *-ing*) for past events which are happening at the same time; for events happening around the time of another past event (in the past simple); with *always* to express annoyance; for temporary or changing situations and for plans which didn't succeed or were changed later.
  He **was making** coffee and I **was opening** the biscuits.
  I **was opening** the tin when I cut my finger.
  My sister **was always borrowing** my phone.
  We **were staying** at the Grand Hotel before we found this house.
  They **were hoping** to win the election, but no one voted for them.

### Practice

**2** Underline the verbs in sentence beginnings (1–6) and endings (a–f) and then match the halves.

1 We want to move house because ☐
2 I'm taking sandwiches to school this week because ☐
3 My brother was sailing round Ibiza while ☐
4 When my parents got home ☐
5 I want to get a new phone because ☐
6 I was planning to take a holiday after my exams, but ☐

a this one is always crashing.
b his school friends were doing exams.
c I didn't have enough money.
d the traffic is getting so bad round here.
e we were all eating pizza in the kitchen.
f the kitchen is closed for repairs.

**3** Match each sentence in exercise 2 with the different uses A–F.

A for past events which are happening at the same time
B for an event happening around the time of another past event
C continuous tense with *always* to express annoyance
D for plans which didn't succeed
E for a temporary situation
F for a changing situation

# UNIT 2

## PRESENT PERFECT SIMPLE AND CONTINUOUS

We use the **present perfect simple** and **present perfect continuous** for events which happened some time before or up to the present (we do not mention when).

We use the **present perfect simple** to talk about:

- a completed action, especially one which has a present result.
  *She's designed this computer game. What do you think of it?*
  (the game is ready to play)
- how often something has happened before now.
  *I've visited that shop three times.*

→ **See Unit 1 for form of present perfect**

We use the **present perfect continuous** (*has/have (not) been* + past participle) to talk about:

- an action that may or may not be complete, where the focus is on the action more than the result.
  *He's been designing a computer game.*
  (we don't know if it's ready to play, perhaps he's still working on it)
- how long something has been happening, up to and possibly including the present moment.
  *She's been trying to find a bag like yours for weeks.*
  (we don't know if she's found one yet)

**NOTE** We do not use the present continuous to say how long something has been happening.
~~She's trying to find a bag like yours for weeks.~~

Some common verbs describe actions which normally last for a period of time, so their meanings are not usually different in the present perfect simple or continuous. They include: *live, stay, study, wait, work*.

*I've worked in the fashion industry for 30 years.*
*I've been working in the fashion industry for 30 years.*

## Practice

**1** Complete the sentences with the present perfect continuous of the verbs in brackets.

0 The students *have been doing* (do) research on British fashion in the 1960s.

1 ........................ (you/wait) long?

2 You ........................ (not listen) to what I ........................ (tell) you.

3 My brother ........................ (mend) his bike in the kitchen. It's a terrible mess!

4 I ........................ (walk) round the shops all morning looking for a present for my mum.

5 The bathroom floor is very wet. ........................ (the children/play) in there?

6 We don't know where Erin is. She ........................ (not live) at this address for some time.

**2** Which pairs of sentences mean the same and which are different? Where they are different, explain why.

1 I haven't worked here since last May.
  I haven't been working here since last May.

........................................................................

2 I've cleaned the car.
  I've been cleaning the car.

........................................................................

3 Have you been living in Africa for a long time?
  Have you lived in Africa for a long time?

........................................................................

4 I've cooked lunch.
  I've been cooking lunch.

........................................................................

5 I haven't driven that car.
  I haven't been driving that car.

........................................................................

**3** Choose the correct form of the verbs. In some places, both forms are correct; which are they?

I'm working on my final art project at the moment and **(1) I've nearly finished / I've nearly been finishing**. For the past six weeks, **(2) I've designed / I've been designing** men's clothes for a variety of occasions, such as a wedding, a job interview and a trip to see a football match. **(3) I've looked / I've been looking** at websites of famous designers to see how they present their work. **(4) I've also visited / I've also been visiting** the Costume Museum in Bath twice, to get ideas from historical costumes. **(5) I haven't spent / I haven't been spending** too much money on the fabric samples. I love all kinds of interesting patterns and textures and **(6) I've collected / I've been collecting** fabrics since I was quite young, so I had plenty to choose from.

**4** Write sentences about yourself or a friend, using the words given and putting the verb into the present perfect continuous.

1 live / my present address for …

........................................................................

2 study / English since …

........................................................................

3 support / … football team for …

........................................................................

4 wear / these clothes since …

........................................................................

# UNIT 3

## PHRASAL VERBS

A phrasal verb is a verb + particle(s). A particle is an adverb or a preposition.

### Phrasal verb patterns

**verb + adverb with no object**

- These phrasal verbs never have an object.
  *Most of the musicians were fairly good, but the drummer really stood out.*

**verb + adverb + object / verb + object + adverb**

- These phrasal verbs always have an object.
- The object can go after the adverb or between the verb and the adverb.
  *I had lots of good ideas, but the boss turned all my suggestions down.*
  *I had lots of good ideas, but the boss turned down all my suggestions.*
- When the object is a pronoun, it must go between the verb and the adverb.
  *I had lots of good ideas, but the boss turned them down.* **NOT** … ~~but the boss turned down them.~~

**verb + preposition + object**

- These verbs always have an object.
  The object must go after the preposition, even if it is a pronoun.
  ***Look after this document** carefully, it's very important.* **NOT** ~~Look this document after carefully, …~~
  ***Look after it** carefully, it's very important.* **NOT** ~~Look it after carefully,…~~

**verb + adverb + preposition + object**

- These verbs always have an object.
- The object must go after the preposition, even if it is a pronoun.
  *I missed a lot of classes, so it's hard to **catch up with** the other students.*
  *I missed a lot of classes, so it's hard to **catch up with** them.*
- If you look up a phrasal verb in a good dictionary, it will tell you which pattern it follows and give you examples of different meanings.

### Phrasal verb meanings

- The meaning of some phrasal verbs is easy to understand.
  *The boy **picked up** the box.*
  *The students **handed in** their work to the teacher.*
- The meaning of many phrasal verbs is less easy to guess, but the context may help.
  *You can't **count on** Nigel in an emergency.*
  *In the end, it **turned out** that we didn't need his help.*
- Some phrasal verbs have more than one meaning.
  *I don't know what the boys are doing, they've **gone off** somewhere.*
  *She set her alarm to **go off** at 5.30 as she didn't want to oversleep.*
  *There was bad storm and all the lights **went off**.*
  *Put the milk in the fridge, or it'll **go off**.*
  *She used to enjoy yoga, but she's **gone off** it recently.*

## Practice

**1 Rewrite the sentences, replacing the words in bold with a pronoun in the correct position.**

0 He doesn't want to go to the dentist but he can't put off **the appointment** again.
   *He doesn't want to go to the dentist but he can't put it off again.*

1 I borrowed £15 from Mum and I promised I'd pay back **the money** at the weekend.

2 Is this an idea you've heard from someone else or did you make up **the story** yourself?

3 We've decided to go to Holland for a few days and we're really looking forward to **our holiday**.

**2 Replace the verbs in bold with the correct form of a phrasal verb from the box.**

> break down    come across    get down
> get into    go by    pass on    think about
> ~~stand by~~    take up

Dear Joe,

I'm writing to say thank you for **(0) supporting** *standing by* me these past few weeks.

When my friendship with Peter **(1) ended** ............ , I never expected him to accuse me of those things .

I may **(2) seem** ............ as if I'm calm now, but really I'm not. As you can imagine, the whole business has really **(3) made** ............ me ............ .

Other friends tell me to **(4) start** ............ some new hobby, but I can't **(5) become interested in** ............ anything yet. Perhaps when a few months **(6) have passed** ............ , I may **(7) consider** ............ it.

Please **(8) give** ............ my best wishes to your brother.

See you soon I hope,
Mike

**3 Complete these sentences with your own ideas.**

0 No one has the right to look down on
   *people who have less money than them.*

1 Police officers sometimes have to put up with

2 Have you ever given someone a present to make up for

3 Emotional maturity means being able to face up to

4 Working in the hotel business, I have to get on with

5 The children of successful parents may have trouble living up to

# UNIT 4

## MODALS (1): NECESSITY, OBLIGATION, PROHIBITION AND ADVICE

### Necessity, obligation, prohibition

**Necessity** = The speaker believes it is necessary to do this: *need to / need* + verb

You *need to* take a fitness test to join the team.

*Do I need to / Need I* take a fitness test before I join the team?

*I don't need to / I needn't* take a fitness test before I join the team.

**NOTE** *need* is not used alone in positive statements, you can't say ~~I need pass a fitness test~~.

**Obligation** = The speaker believes it is obligatory to do this, there is no choice: *must / have to / 've got to* + verb

- We can often use any of these forms:
  You *must / have to / 've got to* pass a fitness test to join the team.

- We usually prefer *must* or *'ve got to* when the idea comes from the speaker, to give an order or express a feeling.
  You *must* show me your new boots!
  *I've got to* buy some new shorts, these are too small.

- We usually prefer *have to* when the obligation is not the speaker's idea, for example to explain a rule.
  She *has to* wear a red sweatshirt for training.
  We *have to* play until the whistle is blown.

**NOTE** for the past of *must* we use *had to*.

**Lack of obligation** = The speaker believes it is not necessary to do this, although it is possible. There is a choice: *don't have to / haven't got to / don't need to / needn't* + verb

You *don't have to / haven't got to / don't need to / needn't* pass a fitness test to join the team.

**Prohibition** = The speaker believes you are not allowed to do this: *mustn't*

You *mustn't* play football in the classroom.

### Practice

**1** **Choose the correct verbs in the email.**

> When I leave school I want to study sports science, so I'm working in a fitness club twice a week. I **(1) must / had to / needed** have an interview before I began work but I **(2) didn't have to / mustn't / haven't got to** have any experience. I **(3) have / need / got** to be at the club by six pm and I finish at nine, so it's not bad. I **(4) must / have to / had to** stand behind the desk and check the members' cards when they come in. They **(5) don't have / mustn't / needn't** to bring anything with them except sports clothes and trainers because we supply towels. Sometimes I **(6) need / must / needn't** to remind them about the club rules. They **(7) haven't got to / mustn't / don't have to** wear outdoor shoes in the gym, for example, because they damage the floor.

### Advice

**Giving advice** = The speaker believes it is the right thing to do.

- *Should(n't) / ought(n't/not) to* + verb can usually be used in the same way.
  You *should / ought to* discuss your training programme with your sports teacher.
  You *shouldn't / ought not to* miss football practice if you're in the team.

**Asking for advice** = The speaker wants to know someone's opinion about what to do.

- *Should I / Ought I to* + verb?
  *Should I / Ought I to* see the doctor before I play in a match?
  How much money *should we / ought we to* take with us?

### Practice

**2** **Complete these questions asking for advice, using *should*, then using *ought to*.**

1 buying new shoes for a party
   Which pair ........................ buy?
   Which pair ........................ buy?

2 choosing a present for a cousin you don't know well
   What ........................ get for my cousin?
   What ........................ get for my cousin?

3 eating a healthy diet
   What kinds of food ........................ eat and what kinds ........................ avoid?
   What kinds of food ........................ eat and what kinds ........................ avoid?

**3** **Write three pieces of advice for a friend who wants to be a professional sportsman or woman.**

1 You should ....................................................
2 You ought not to .............................................
3 You shouldn't .................................................

**4** **Write new sentences with the same meaning. Use a modal verb. Can you write more than one new sentence for some of them?**

1 You can bring your own towel but it's not necessary.
   You can bring your own towel but ........................

2 I advise you to talk to your teacher.
   You ........................................................

3 You are not allowed to bring food into the shop.
   You ........................................................

4 This school insists that students wear uniform.
   Students at this school ....................................

5 Do you advise me to phone my brother?
   ........................ I ........................ ?

6 I insist that you allow me to help you.
   You ........................................................

151

# UNIT 5

## PRESENT AND PAST HABITS

### Present habits

- We often use the **present simple** with an adverb of frequency to talk about present habits.

  He **drinks** coffee in the morning **once in a while**.

  He **doesn't always/usually/often/normally drink** coffee in the morning.

  **Does he drink** coffee in the morning **all the time**?

- We use **always**, **constantly** and **continually** with the **present continuous** to express a complaint or a criticism.

  She'**s always using** my phone and she never offers to pay for her calls.

  He'**s constantly leaving** dirty dishes on the table.

### Past habits

- We use the **past simple** with an adverb of frequency to talk about past habits.

  She **hardly ever visited** her sister when she was in Milan.

  **Did she visit** her sister **once in a while** when she was in Milan?

  She **didn't always/usually/often/normally visit** her sister when she was in Milan.

- We use **always**, **constantly** and **continually** with the **past continuous** to express a complaint or a criticism.

  They **were continually asking** for more money.

- We can also use **would** to describe a past habit.

  He **would always tidy** his desk before leaving the room.

  They **wouldn't normally put** their bags on the table.

- We use **used to** to describe a habit or state in the past.

  He **always used to tidy** his desk before leaving the room.

  They **didn't normally use to put** their bags on the table.

  She **used to live** in Brighton. **NOT** ~~She would live in Brighton.~~

## Practice

**1** Rewrite the sentences with the adverbs in the correct position.

0 The children go to bed before their parents. (seldom)

...The children seldom go to bed before their parents.

1 My dad would have a snack in the afternoon. (regularly)

....................................................................

2 I didn't use to sleep more than six hours when I was young. (often)

....................................................................

3 Do you get enough sleep during the week? (usually)

....................................................................

4 A doctor wouldn't prescribe sleeping tablets for someone as young as you. (normally)

....................................................................

5 The factory workers were short of sleep and injured themselves as a result. (frequently / sometimes)

....................................................................

6 The students were yawning during lectures because they went to sleep before midnight. (continually / never)

....................................................................

7 I sleep very soundly but I have nightmares and wake up shouting. (normally / from time to time)

....................................................................

8 Did you use to sleep in your parents' bed when you were little? (all the time)

....................................................................

**2** Write sentences criticising these people, using a continuous tense and the adverbs given.

0 A driver who crashed his car. (constantly)

...He was constantly crashing his car.

1 A company that advertises special offers. (always)

They ................................................................

2 A student who gave her assignments in late. (always)

She ................................................................

3 A man who shouts at his children. (continually)

He ................................................................

4 A cat that brings mice into the house. (constantly)

It ................................................................

5 A political party that promised jobs for everyone. (always)

They ................................................................

# UNIT 6

## BE/GET/BECOME USED TO

- **be used to** = be familiar with, be accustomed to (a permanent situation)
- **get/become used to** = become familiar with, become accustomed to (a changing situation)
  **Get** is used more often in speaking, **become** is used in more formal situations.
- Any tense of **be/get/become** can be used.
  **I'm used to** ... They **weren't used to** ...
  **You'll get used to** ... She **hasn't got used to** ...
  We **had become used to** ... , etc.
- **be/get/become used to** are followed by a noun or the *-ing* form of a verb.

| | |
|---|---|
| **I'm used to** spicy **food**. | **I'm used to eating** spicy food. |
| They **weren't used to** such hard **work**. | They **weren't used to working** so hard. |
| **You'll get used to** city **life** soon. | **You'll get used to living** in the city soon. |
| She **hasn't got used to** this **laptop** yet. | She **hasn't got used to using** this laptop yet. |
| We **had become used to** interruptions. | We **had become used to being interrupted**. |

  **NOTE** Do not confuse **be/get/become used to** + noun / *-ing* with **used to do**, which is for past.

## Practice

**1** Complete the paragraph with the verbs from the box.

> am used to    can't get used to    had been used to    have got used to
> wasn't used to    were used to    weren't used to

I grew up in Birmingham, in a modern block of flats not far from the city centre.
Two years ago my parents decided to move to an old farmhouse deep in the
countryside. My brothers and I **(1)** ................................................. country life now, but it
was quite a shock at first. We **(2)** ................................................. being so far from shops
and cafés and cinemas and we **(3)** ................................................. spending our free
time with our friends whenever we wanted. Now though, we know we must plan our
social lives. When we first arrived I **(4)** ................................................. the silence of the
countryside at night. All my life I **(5)** ................................................. hearing traffic, so it
made me nervous. However, now I **(6)** ................................................. living somewhere
so quiet, I **(7)** ................................................. the noise when I go to town!

**2** Complete the sentences about the experiences of Max, a medical student.
Use *be/get/become used to* + a noun or *-ing*.

**0** Before he came to medical school, Max had never lived away from his parents.
He ..*wasn't used to living*.. away from his parents.

**1** He still forgets to buy food for himself because his mother always did the shopping.
He ................................................................................. for himself.

**2** He had never stayed up all night, but he often does night duty now.
He ................................................................................. all night.

**3** He usually remembers to tidy his room, but not always.
He ................................................................................. his room.

**4** He found it difficult to talk to patients at first, but now he enjoys it.
When he began his training, he ................................................................................. to patients.

# UNIT 7

## NARRATIVE TENSES

### Past perfect simple vs. past perfect continuous

The **past perfect simple** and **continuous** are both used in describing events which were happening before the time of another past event.

We use the **past perfect simple**:

- to make clear a sequence of events in the past.
  *He didn't call me because he'd lost his phone.*
  (= 1 he lost his phone; 2 he didn't call me)
- to contrast with past events introduced by **by the time**, **before**, **as soon as** or **when**.
  *The band had finished their first song by the time we reached our seats.* (= 1 the band finished their first song; 2 we reached our seats)
- with **already**, **just**, **ever** and **never**.
  *When we arrived, everyone had already started dancing.* (= 1 everyone started dancing; 2 we arrived)
- to say how many times, or how often, something had happened before a point of time in the past.
  *I'd visited LA four times before my tenth birthday.*
  (= 1 I visited LA four times; 2 I had my tenth birthday)

We use the **past perfect continuous** for describing events which were happening before the time of another past event. We use it:

- to focus on the fact that the earlier event may or may not be complete.
  *We could tell that everyone had been having a good time.*
- when we talk about how long the event had been happening.
  *The tourists had been walking for two hours and wanted a chance to sit down.*

## Practice

**1** Complete the sentences with past perfect simple or continuous. Which verbs can be in either tense?

0 Lizzie ..*had been staying*.. with her sister when her exam results came out, so they celebrated together. (stay)

1 Katie phoned her friends as soon as she ........................ the tickets. (book)

2 The fields were covered in water because it ........................ heavily for several days. (rain)

3 We ........................ for the concert for weeks and were very disappointed when it was cancelled. (prepare)

4 I couldn't go to Jane's party because I ........................ to babysit for my aunt. (already agree)

5 When I checked my phone, I discovered Simon ........................ three times. (text)

6 We weren't surprised when we saw Nicky's new bike, because we knew she ........................ to get one for ages. (want)

### Past perfect vs. past simple

- We use the **past simple** and **past perfect** together to show that one event happened before another.
  *When I walked into the room, everyone had stopped talking.* (= 1 they stopped talking; 2 I walked into the room)
  *Everyone had been enjoying the show when the rain started.* (= 1 they were enjoying themselves; 2 the rain started)
- We use two past simple verbs to show that two events happened at the same time.
  *When I walked into the room, everyone stopped talking.* (= they stopped talking at the moment I walked into the room – possibly because I walked into the room)
  *Everyone danced when the band played.*
- We can use **and** to link the two past simple verbs to suggest that one event caused another.
  *I walked into the room and everyone stopped talking.* (= they stopped talking at the moment I walked into the room – probably because I walked into the room)
  *The rain started and everyone went indoors.*

## Practice

**2** Complete the story with the past simple, the past perfect simple or the past perfect continuous of the verbs in the boxes.

> be (x2)   board   delay   give
> go out   hear   move   wait

We had a dreadful journey home last night. There (1) ........................ a thunderstorm earlier in the day which (2) ........................ lots of incoming flights, including our plane. We (3) ........................ for three hours by the time we (4) ........................ the plane. All the passengers (5) ........................ in their seats, the flight attendants (6) ........................ (already) the safety talk and the plane (7) ........................ onto the runway, when we (8) ........................ a bang and all the lights (9) ........................ .

> arrive   be able to   cause   cheer   complete
> eat   enjoy   get out   land   return   turn out

Of course, everyone was terrified. The plane (10) ........................ to the departure building and we all (11) ........................ . Luckily, it (12) ........................ that a small electrical fault (13) ........................ the problem. Once the safety checks (14) ........................ , we (15) ........................ take off.

It was seven hours since we (16) ........................ at the airport and we (17) ........................ anything all that time, so we (18) ........................ the inflight meal more than we had expected to! And when we (19) ........................ safely at the end of the flight, everyone (20) ........................ !

# UNIT 8

## FUTURE (1): REVIEW

### Present tenses with future meaning

- We use the **present simple** for future events in a timetable and for people if they have a fixed schedule.

  *The airport bus **leaves** at ten minutes past every hour.*

  *When **does** the concert **start**?*

- We use the **present continuous** for plans which have already been made.

  *My brother and I **are playing** football this afternoon.* (= We have already arranged this.)

  *What **are** the students **doing** tomorrow?* (= What have they arranged?)

### *going to* and *will*

*Going to* and *will* can often be used in the same place with little or no difference in meaning.

We use ***going to***:

- for plans which have already been made. (This use is similar to the present continuous.)

  *My brother and I **are going to play** football this afternoon.* (= We have already arranged this.)

  *What **are** the students **going to do** tomorrow?* (= What has been arranged?)

- for predictions when we believe we have present evidence for our prediction.

  *Alice is well ahead of the other skiers; she's **going to win** the race!*

  *You don't speak French, so you're **going to have** problems if you go to a French university.*

We use ***will***:

- for actions which we decide as we speak.

  *I'**ll have** a tuna sandwich, please.*

  *I'**ll pay** for the tickets by credit card.*

- for actions which are likely but not certain, often introduced by *I (don't) think*, *I (don't) expect*, *I hope* or with *probably*, etc.

  *I think I'**ll walk** to school tomorrow.*

  *I don't expect it'**ll rain**.*

  *I'**ll probably meet** Andy after school.*

- for predictions which we believe, but cannot prove.

  *You'**ll enjoy** living in Italy.*

  *No one **will notice** if you leave the party early.*

  *The government **will raise** taxes again next year.*

- for future events which we cannot change.

  *The weather **will be** much hotter in three months' time.*

### *be about to*

We use ***be about to***:

- for actions which will happen immediately.

  *Hurry up, the firework display **is about to** start!*

  *Can I phone you back? We'**re about to** have lunch.*

- with ***not***, to suggest that someone does not intend to do something.

  *I've already planned my holiday and I'**m not about to** change it to suit you.*

### Present simple and present perfect after time expressions

When we talk about future events with time expressions *when*, *until*, *before* and *after*, *as soon as* we use:

- the **present simple** for events which happen **at the same time** as another future event.

  *I'll call you when I **get** home.* (**NOT** ~~when I will get home~~)

  *As soon as the guests **arrive**, we're going to light the candles.* (**NOT** ~~As soon as the guests will arrive~~)

- the **present perfect** for events which have already happened.

  *I'll call you when I've **spoken** to my friends.* (= 1 I will speak to my friends; 2 I'll call you)

  *Don't use the machine until you've **read** the instructions.* (**NOT** ~~until you will read~~)

## Practice

**1** **Circle the best form of the verbs in the conversations.**

**A**

**Maria:** (1) **I'm meeting** / **I meet** some friends in a few minutes. Would you like to come? I expect (2) **we'll try** / **we're trying** the new café in town.

**Anya:** Thanks, but I can't. (3) **I'm about to start** / **I'm starting** my packing. My holiday (4) **begins** / **will begin** tomorrow and (5) **I won't be** / **I'm not** ready when the taxi (6) **comes** / **is coming** in the morning.

**Maria:** What time (7) **will the taxi pick** / **is the taxi picking** you up?

**Anya:** Half past four. My flight (8) **leaves** / **is leaving** at seven and the check-in queues (9) **will be** / **are being** very long because tomorrow (10) **is** / **is going to be** a public holiday.

**Maria:** Yes, and the airline (11) **aren't holding** / **won't hold** the flight until (12) **you arrive** / **you'll arrive**!

**Anya:** OK, so (13) **I'll see** / **I'm seeing** you next term, then. Bye!

**B**

**Tom:** We can't look round the theatre now because a rehearsal (1) **is about to start** / **will start**.

**Kai:** Can we come back later when the actors (2) **are going to go** / **have gone**?

**Tom:** I think so. (3) **I'll go** / **I go** and find out.

**Kai:** OK, (4) **I'll get** / **I'm getting** us a drink. What would you like?

**Tom:** (5) **I'm having** / **I'll have** something cold. The weather is so hot today.

**Kai:** Yes, but I think (6) **we're going to have** / **we're having** a storm later. Look at those clouds over the mountains.

**Tom:** I hope the rain (7) **won't start** / **hasn't started** until (8) **we're** / **we'll be** back at our hotel.

**Kai:** No, (9) **we'll be** / **we're going to be** fine, don't worry.

# UNIT 9

## THE FUTURE (2): CONTINUOUS AND PERFECT

### Future continuous

We use the **future continuous** (*will* + *be* + present participle) for:

- an event going on at a point in time or over a period of time in the future.

  *This time next month, we'll be lying on a beach.*

  *When I'm 30, I hope I won't be working here.*

- an event which is already planned for some time in the future.

  *We'll be travelling to Wales on Saturday.*

  *I won't be starting my new job until January.*

  This use is very similar to the present continuous for planned events, but compare these sentences:

  *He's giving a speech at 11 o'clock.* (= He begins at 11.)

  *He'll be giving a speech at 11 o'clock.* (= He begins some time before 11 and finishes some time after 11.)

- a future event which is part of a regular pattern of events.

  *The coach will be talking to the team before the match.* (= He always talks to them before a match, and he will talk to them before the next match as usual.)

### Practice

**1** Complete the sentences with the future continuous of the verbs in brackets.

   1 The information office ........................ early on Friday and it ........................ at all over the weekend. (close) (not open)

   2 A team training session ........................ place on Monday morning. (take)

   3 How's the goalkeeper? ........................ next Saturday? (he/play) No, he ........................ in any matches until he's recovered from his injuries. (play)

### Future perfect and future perfect continuous

- We use the **future perfect** (*will* + *have* + past participle) to talk about an event which will be complete by a time in the future. We often introduce the time with *before*, *by* (*the time*) or use an adverb such as *soon*.

  *By the time we get to the cinema, the film will have started.*

  *I hope the shop won't have sold all the new phones before we get there.*

  *Will the flat have been decorated when you move in?*

- We use the **future perfect continuous** (*will* + *have* + *been* + present participle) to talk about the length of time a future event will continue until a time in the future.

We usually mention the time, often with *before*, *by* (*the time*) or use an adverb such as *soon*.

We also usually mention the duration of the event.

*Very soon, I'll have been studying medicine for five years.*

*How many years will you have been studying Chinese by the time you go to Hong Kong?*

### Practice

**2** Complete the text with the future perfect of the verbs in brackets. Which ones can also be future perfect continuous?

My brother Freddie is 18 and he's going to Spain for a holiday with his friends after their exams.

He's got 200 euros but he **(1)** ........................ (spend) that before the end of the week. When he gets home, he'll have a suntan because he **(2)** ........................ (sunbathe) for hours every day. He may be thinner, because he **(3)** ........................ (not/eat) properly for a week and he **(4)** ........................ (dance) all night every night. He **(5)** ........................ (not miss) us, but Mum hopes he **(6)** ........................ (text) us at least once to say he's OK.

**3** Complete the sentences describing each situation. Use the future perfect or the future perfect continuous. Where can you use either tense?

   1 My uncle and aunt got married in 1980.
     By 2020, they ........................................................

   2 We moved to this house nearly ten years ago.
     At the end of this year, we ..............................

   3 Harry went to sleep at three o'clock.
     He'll get up at seven, so he ..........................................
     ........................................ only four hours.

   4 I'm making a cake, so the kitchen is a bit messy.
     I'll tidy up before lunch.
     By lunchtime, I ..............................................

   5 The team left in a coach early on Saturday morning to go to an away match. They arrive there on Saturday evening.
     When they get off the coach, they ..............................
     ........................................ all day.

**4** Put a tick (✔) if the sentence is correct or a cross (✗) if it is incorrect.

   1 The train will be leaving in 20 minutes. ☐

   2 The train will have left in 20 minutes. ☐

   3 The train will have been leaving in 20 minutes. ☐

   4 He's writing so slowly he won't be finishing his homework before the class begins. ☐

   5 He's writing so slowly he won't have finished his homework before the class begins. ☐

   6 He's writing so slowly he won't have been finishing his homework before the class begins. ☐

   7 Will you be having a break before you start your next assignment? ☐

   8 Will you have had a break before you start your next assignment? ☐

   9 Will you have been having a break before you start your next assignment? ☐

   10 I hope someone will be inventing a cure for flu by the end of the century. ☐

   11 I hope someone will have invented a cure for flu by the end of the century. ☐

   12 I hope someone will have been inventing a cure for flu by the end of the century. ☐

# UNIT 10

## MODALS (2): MODALS IN THE PAST

### would have done

- We use **would have** + past participle to speak about an event or feeling which we imagine in the past but which did not happen.

  *I was so fed up that I couldn't go to the concert. I **would have loved** to see that band.*

  *We missed the match, but our team played really badly, so we **wouldn't have enjoyed** it anyway.*

  *I'm sorry you didn't get an invitation to the wedding. **Would** you **have gone**?*

### should have done

- We use **should have** + past participle to speak about an event in the past that we regret or want to complain about.

  *I didn't know you were allergic to cheese. You **should have told** me.*

  *You **shouldn't have given** your address to that man.*

  *I knew that bike wasn't very good when my friend bought it. **Should** I **have warned** him?*

### needn't have done

- We use **needn't have** + past participle to talk about an action in the past which happened but which was not necessary.

  *My brother had a spare ticket so I **needn't have bought** one. (= I bought a ticket because I didn't know about the spare one, so I wasted my money.)*

### didn't need to do

- We use **didn't need** + **to** infinitive to talk about an action in the past which was not necessary and therefore didn't happen.

  *My brother gave me a spare ticket, so I **didn't need to buy** one. (= I didn't buy a ticket, I used the one my brother gave me.)*

## Practice

**1** Complete the sentences with *would(n't) have, should(n't) have, needn't have* or *didn't need to* and the correct form of the verb in brackets.

1 Alex ............................................... (not shout) at the shop assistant; she was trying to help him and he was quite rude.

2 I'm glad I didn't buy that sweatshirt, it ............................................... (look) right with these jeans.

3 It was Simon's birthday last Friday. I really ............................................... (send) him a card.

4 I don't think Ellie liked that bag I sent her for her birthday. What ............................................... (I/give) her?

5 I spent hours typing up my notes, but I ............................................... (bother) because the teacher never asked to see them.

6 ............................................... (you/give) the taxi driver a tip? He looked a bit disappointed.

7 Jade was nervous about meeting her new supervisor, but she ............................................... (not worry) because he was absolutely charming.

8 We didn't realise Lisa was ill, or we ............................................... (send) her some flowers.

9 I had an interview for art college, but I ............................................... (not take) an exam; they just looked at my drawings.

10 I know you think these curtains are the wrong colour for this room, but what ............................................... (you/choose) instead?

**2** Complete the sentences with your own ideas.

Your friends went to a concert last weekend. You had arranged to go to the beach so you didn't go with them. They saw your favourite singer there and they bought you a T-shirt. Actually, you already have a T-shirt like that.

What did they say when they saw you?

'It was a great concert. You would
(1) ...................................... . We know you had already arranged to go to the beach, but you should
(2) ...................................... . You can go to the beach any weekend, you needn't (3) ......................................'

What did you think when you saw the T-shirt?

'They needn't (4) ...................................... – but I won't say so!'

# UNIT 11

## RELATIVE CLAUSES

**Defining relative clauses:**

- give essential information about things or people.

  *The photo **that** is on the table is the oldest one we have.*

  We need the words ***that is on the table*** to understand which photo the speaker is referring to.

- can begin with a relative pronoun: ***who*** (for people), ***which*** (for things), ***that*** (for things and people).

  *There's the woman **who** is interested in local history.*

  *She showed me a website **which** she uses.*

  *I can email you the link **that** I told you about.*

  *There's the woman **that** I mentioned.*

- can have ***who**, **which*** or ***that*** as their **subject**.

  *The woman **who/that** is in the photo is my great grandmother.*

  or as their **object**.

  *There's the woman **who** I mentioned.*

  *She showed me a website **which/that** she uses.*

- often omit the relative pronoun when it is the object of the relative clause.

  *There's the woman I mentioned.*

  *She showed me a website she uses.*

- are never separated from the rest of the sentence by commas

  (**NOT** ~~There's the woman, who I mentioned.~~

  ~~She showed me a website, that she uses.~~)

**Non-defining relative clauses:**

- give extra information about things or people.

  *This is a photo of my parents, **who** met in 1999.*

  If we take out ***who met in 1999***, we still know that the photo shows the speaker's parents.

- must begin with the relative pronoun ***who*** (for people) or ***which*** (for things).

  *My dad, **who** owns a software company, travels all over the world.*

  *The company, **which** is quite well known, employs about a hundred people.*

- can have ***who*** or ***which*** (but never ***that***) as their subject.

  *My dad, **who** is in this photo, helped my mum set up the business.* (**NOT** ~~that is in this photo~~)

  *The head office, **which** is in the north of England, is extremely modern.* (**NOT** ~~that is in the north of England~~)

  or as their **object**.

  *Some regular customers, **who** my dad knows well, come to our house.*

  *Our house, **which** we like very much, is near the sea.*

- never omit the relative pronoun. (**NOT** ~~Our house, we like very much, is near the sea.~~)

- must be separated from the rest of the sentence by commas.

  *Some regular customers, **who** my dad knows well, come to our house.* (**NOT** ~~Some regular customers who my dad knows well come to our house.~~)

Both **defining** and **non-defining relative clauses:**

- can begin with ***whose*** (instead of *his / her / their*), ***when*** (for times) and ***where*** (for places).

  *My brother, **whose wife is an architect**, has a beautiful house.*

  *Here it is in this photo from the year **when they bought it**.*

  *My parents' house, **where I still live**, is much bigger than my brother's.*

- usually have any prepositions at the end of the clause.

  *This is the desk **which** my grandad worked **at**.*

  *I have a group of friends I go cycling **with**.*

  *Peter, **who** my dad went to university **with**, has his own business now.*

**NOTE** The object pronoun (***her**, **him**, **it***, etc.) is never used in a relative clause.

*I know most of the people that my dad employs.*

(**NOT** ~~the people that my dad employs them~~)

*The next photo shows my aunt Margaret, who my uncle married in 2005.* (**NOT** ~~who my uncle married her in 2005~~)

## Practice

**1 Correct the mistakes in the sentences.**

1 Have you ever visited the island, that your grandparents came from?

   .....................................................................................

2 John's bicycle, that was stolen last week, has turned up in the next street.

   .....................................................................................

3 Is that the coat you wanted to buy it?

   .....................................................................................

4 This is the website who I told you about.

   .....................................................................................

5 The city, where I went to university, is a very lively place.

   .....................................................................................

6 The singer who I like her most is from Argentina.

   .....................................................................................

7 The friend I stayed with her in Geneva is a painter.

   .....................................................................................

**2 Complete the sentences with your own ideas.**

1 I enjoy films which ...........................................................

2 I prefer the kind of food that ........................................

3 I know someone whose .................................................

4 I hate parties where .......................................................

5 A good friend is someone who ....................................

# UNIT 12

## PASSIVE (1): REVIEW

The passive is formed with the correct form of **be** + a past participle.

*Breakfast **isn't served** until 7.30.*

*We **were offered** a choice of rooms.*

*The dining room **hasn't been cleaned** yet.*

*The doors **were being repaired**.*

*We heard the building **had been damaged**.*

***Are** you **being given** enough help?*

The person or thing that does the action is called **the agent**. We use **by** to introduce the agent.

*We **were offered** a choice of rooms **by** the hotel manager.*

*We heard the building **had been damaged by** the storm.*

We use the passive:

- if we do not know the agent.
  *My phone**'s been stolen**!*

- if the agent is unimportant.
  *The new chairs **will be delivered** tomorrow.*

- if the agent is obvious.
  *The thief **was sent** to prison.*

- if we don't want to mention the agent, for example if we want to avoid blame.
  *The ice cream **has** all **been eaten**.*

- to emphasise the subject of the passive verb instead of the agent.
  *The film star **was being interviewed** by a journalist.*

## Practice

**1** Read the email and then complete the blog with verbs in the correct passive tenses.

| | |
|---|---|
| **To:** | Megadeal Corporation Management team |
| **Subject:** | Top Secret – Successful takeover of Smallway & Co |

Yesterday we bought our competitor Smallway & Co. The firm had resisted our offers for three months, but we made a new offer last week and this time we included a special payment for the managing director. He has not told his colleagues about this payment, but he has persuaded them to accept the offer.

We will give a month's notice to all the staff at Smallway & Co and will put our accountant in charge. We are selling the buildings and we will use the money to pay for the new Megadeal Corporation headquarters.

**A. Crookson CEO Megadeal**

---

### Secret deal by Megadeal Corporation revealed
*by Business journalist Zoe Garrett*

Smallway & Co **(1)** ........................ by Megadeal Corporation yesterday. Their offers **(2)** ........................ for three months, but a new offer **(3)** ........................ last week and this time a special payment for the managing director **(4)** ........................ . His colleagues **(5)** ........................ about this payment, but they **(6)** ........................ by him to accept Megadeal's offer.

All the staff at Smallway & Co **(7)** ........................ a month's notice and Megadeal's accountant **(8)** ........................ in charge. The buildings **(9)** ........................ and the money **(10)** ........................ to pay for the new Megadeal Corporation headquarters.

## CAUSATIVE

- We use **have/get something done** when someone else does something for us.
- It is not usually necessary to mention the agent.
- The use of **get** instead of **have** sounds more informal.
  *I**'m going to have/get** the sitting room **painted**.*
  (= Someone **is going to paint** the sitting room for me.)
  *They want to **have/get** their car **fixed**. (= They want a mechanic to **fix** their car.)*
  *I **had/got** my hair **coloured**. (= The hairdresser **coloured** my hair.)*
  *I **had/got** my hair **coloured by my cousin**.*
  (emphasises that my cousin did it for me)

- We use **get someone to do something** when we ask or persuade someone to do something for us.
  *Jenny **got** her dad **to give** her a lift because it was raining.*
  *I**'ll get** my assistant **to show** you the way to the office.*

## Practice

**2** Complete the sentences with *have/get* + past participle or *get* + *to* + verb using the words in brackets.

1 My new phone didn't work, so I ........................ (the shop/replace) it with a new one.

2 My coat has a dirty mark on it, so I ........................ (it/clean) .

3 My brother kicked a football through the neighbour's window and they ........................ (my parents/pay) for a new one.

4 I had to work very late, but I ........................ (my boss/call) a taxi to take me home.

5 My sister was away on Mum's birthday but she ........................ (a bunch of flowers/deliver) to the house.

# UNIT 13

## THE PASSIVE (2): OTHER STRUCTURES

### Passive infinitive

We form the passive infinitive with (**not**) (**to**) **be** + past participle.

I don't like **to be thought** of as mean by my friends.

This envelope is **not to be opened** until your birthday.

Petra asked **to be taken** to the airport.

### verb + passive infinitive

- Some verbs are followed by the passive infinitive, e.g. **aim**, **appear**, **ask**, **begin**, **continue**, **expect**, **hope**, **refuse**, **seem**, **tend**, **try**, **want**, **wish**, **would like**.

  He **aims to be elected** next year.

  We've **asked to be given** a larger room.

  They **hoped to be offered** a refund.

  You **seem to be amused** by that email.

### verb + object + passive infinitive

- Some verbs are followed by an object + the passive infinitive, e.g. **expect**, **intend**, **like**, **prefer**, **want**, **would like**.

  We **expected him to be stopped** at the gate by the guards.

  Do you **want the lettuce to be washed** now?

  I'**d like this jacket to be cleaned**, please.

### modal + passive infinitive without to

- These are **could**, **may**, **might**, **should**, **would** + **be** + past participle.

  Another doctor **could be asked** for her opinion.

  We **might be told** the truth by somebody one day.

### the first, second, only, last, etc. + noun + passive infinitive

- The words **the first**, **the second**, **the third**, etc. and **the last** can be followed by a passive infinitive.

  He was **the first to be chosen** for the team.

  This box was **the last to be delivered**.

- The words **the first**, **the second**, **the third**, etc. and **the only** and **the last** can be followed by a noun or one + passive infinitive.

  This is **the third club to be opened** in our town this year.

  My suitcase was **the only one not to be inspected** by the customs officer.

### -ing passive

We form the -ing passive with **being** + past participle.

I don't remember **being asked** my name.

We enjoyed **being entertained** by the dancers.

### verb + -ing passive

- Some verbs are followed by the -ing passive, e.g. **avoid**, **bear**, **deny**, **forget**, **imagine**, **risk**, **remember**.

  The children **avoided being found** by hiding under a bed.

  Sandy **won't forget being sent** home by the head teacher.

  Can you **imagine being refused** entry to a restaurant?

### verb + preposition + -ing passive

- Some verbs are followed by a preposition + the -ing passive, e.g. **ask about**, **enquire about**, **insist on**, **laugh about**, **look forward to**.

  Let's **ask about being given** a better room.

  He **insisted on being referred to** by his surname.

  Fergus doesn't care what people say. He just **laughs about being told off**.

## Practice

**1** Complete the sentences with the correct passive form (infinitive or -ing form) of the verb in brackets.

1 They don't appear ........................ by your jokes. (amuse)

2 You can laugh about ........................ , but it's not a joke. (tell off)

3 I think we should ........................ a choice of essay topics. (give)

4 They prefer the drinks ........................ very cold. (serve)

5 She was the third woman ........................ (award) a degree by Cambridge University.

6 I'm looking forward to ........................ by my parents after the exams. (treat)

7 My name was the last ........................ . (call)

8 We might ........................ to lead the parade. (choose)

9 I can't bear ........................ by strangers. (hug)

10 I would like ........................ next time you want to use my phone. (ask)

11 Did he deny ........................ in the fight? (involve)

12 The way you drive, we risk ........................ by the traffic police! (stop)

13 These rooms tend ........................ for seminars. (use)

14 They intended the invitations ........................ immediately. (deliver)

15 They enquired about ........................ to use the school hall for a party. (allow)

# UNIT 14

## REPORTED SPEECH

### Tenses in reported speech

We usually change the tense of reported verbs when the reporting verb (e.g. *say, ask*) is in a past tense.

'**I've been swimming** for an hour.' → He **said** he **had been swimming** for an hour.

'What **will you do**?' → She **asked** what **I would do**.

We usually do **not** change the tense of reported verbs:

*   when the reporting verb (e.g. *say, ask*) is in a present tense.

    '**I like** this music.' → He **says** he **likes** this music.

    '**Did you enjoy** the film?' → She'**s asking** whether you **enjoyed** the film.

    'We **won't be** away long.' → They **say** they **won't be** away long.

*   when the reporting verb is in a past tense, but the events reported are not past.

    '**I'm coming** with you this evening.' → She said **she is coming** with us this evening.

    'What time **will you be** home?' → He wanted to know what time **we'll be** home.

*   when the reporting verb is in a past tense, but the events reported are true for any time.

    'The traffic **is** always bad on Fridays.' → She reminded me that the traffic **is** always bad on Fridays.

    'You **can change** money at your hotel.' → He said that we **can** change money at our hotel.

In the examples above, it is not wrong to change the reported verbs to a past tense, but it sounds more formal and it may make the meaning less clear.

*She said* ***she was coming*** *with us this evening.*

*He said that we* ***could*** *change money at our hotel.*

### Practice

**1** Put the sentences into reported speech. Do not change the tenses unless you have to.

**0** 'I'll come skiing with you next weekend.'
Alison has agreed ...*to come skiing with us*... next weekend.

**1** 'We saw Ahmed at the football match.'
They mentioned that ...................................................... at the football match.

**2** 'I hate shopping at weekends.'
My dad claims .......................................................... at weekends.

**3** 'They went to Morocco in the winter.'
He says ............................................................... in the winter.

**4** 'Let me see the report!'
She demanded ........................................................... ........................................................ the report.

**5** 'Where is the ticket office?'
We asked ................................................................ ............................................................................ .

**2** Complete the email with the correct forms of the reporting verbs in the box.

agree   deny   enquire   persuade   praise   suggest

**To:** Drama club supporters

**Subject:** Holiday theatre club project

I've talked to several people about helping us to set up a drama club for local teenagers during the summer holidays and these are the results so far.

The town council has finally (1) ..................... to let us use the old cinema building, which is a big relief. Interestingly, the official I first spoke to now (2) ...................... saying the building wasn't fit to use. So it was worth speaking to all the councillors personally. I met Mr Baktiar, the head of our school, last month and he (3) ...................... us for persevering with the project and (4) ...................... advertising the drama club on the local news website and local radio, so that lots of people hear about it. The local radio station mentioned the club on the breakfast show this week and several people have (5) ....................... about the course since then. Freda Jones, our drama teacher, is going to run some workshops for us and she has (6) ....................... her husband, who is a DJ, to lend us his sound system for our performances!

So, I think that's good progress so far. Has anyone else raised any money yet?

# UNIT 15

## MODALS (3): DEDUCTION

### Deduction in the present and future

- To express deductions about the present and future, we use *may*, *may not*, *might*, *might not*, *could*, *could not*, *can't*, *must* + verb.
- When we think something is **possible**, but we are not sure, we use *may*, *might* or *could*.

  *Where's Nadia?*

  *She **may be** in the garden.*

  *She **could be** in the garden.*

  *She **might be** in the garden.*
- When we think something is **possibly not true**, we use *may not* or *might not*.

  *I want to see her.*

  *She **may not want** to see you.*

  *She **might not want** to see you.*
- When we feel **certain** that something is true, we use *must*.

  *Alan passed his driving test. He **must be** very happy.*
- The opposite of *must be* is *can't/couldn't be* (**NOT** mustn't be).

  *Ben failed his driving test. He **can't be** happy about that.*

  *or He **couldn't be** happy about that.*

### Deduction in the past

- To express deductions about the past, we use *may have*, *may not have*, *might have*, *might not have*, *could have*, *couldn't have*, *can't have*, *must have* + past participle.
- When we think something was **possible** in the past, but we are not sure, we use *may (not) have*, *might (not) have* or *could have*.

  *Where was Nadia when I called?*

  *She **may have been** in the garden.*

  *or She **could have been** in the garden.*

  *or She **might have been** in the garden.*
- When we think something was **possibly not true**, we use *may (not) have* or *might (not) have*.

  *I wanted to see her.*

  *She **may not have wanted** to see you.*

  *She **might not have wanted** to see you.*
- When we feel **certain** that something was true, we use *must have*.

  *Cathy borrowed some money from me. She **must have forgotten** about it.*
- The opposite of *must have been* is *can't/couldn't have been* (**NOT** mustn't have been).

  *She borrowed it last weekend.*

  *She **can't have borrowed** money from you last weekend, she was away.*

  *or She **couldn't have borrowed** money from you last weekend, she was away.*

## Practice

**1** Complete the dialogues using *must/can/could/may/ might/can't/couldn't/may not/might not* + verb.

| | |
|---|---|
| **Marta:** | There's a parcel for you. |
| **Yves:** | It **(1)** ......................... for me. No one knows I'm here. |
| **Marta:** | Someone **(2)** ......................... because it's got your name and this address. |
| **Grandpa:** | Why isn't my phone working? |
| **Jim:** | The battery **(3)** ......................... flat. You know you often forget to charge it. |
| **Grandpa:** | But it **(4)** ......................... flat, I charged it last night. |
| **Jim:** | Well, so you **(5)** ......................... a signal here. |
| **Grandpa:** | There **(6)** ......................... a signal. We're in the middle of a city! It's impossible to be out of range here. |
| **Jim:** | But these buildings are very tall. They **(7)** ......................... the signal. Let's walk to the end of the street. It **(8)** ......................... OK there. |

**2** Match the pairs of sentences.

1 There's the doorbell. ☐
2 Don't wait for me this evening. ☐
3 Chloe left before the end of the show. ☐
4 Otto is very late tonight. ☐
5 Where are the car keys? ☐
6 Josh didn't answer my text. ☐

a She can't have enjoyed the music.
b You could have left them in your bag.
c I may be working late.
d He might not have got it.
e It must be my taxi.
f He must have met some friends.

**3** Choose the correct verbs in the dialogues.

| | |
|---|---|
| **Eva:** | There's no milk in the fridge. Did you finish it? |
| **Fran:** | I can't remember. It **(1) could have been / might be** me, or it **(2) must be / might have been** Jen – she was up early this morning. |
| **Eva:** | No, it **(3) can't have been / must not have been** her. She doesn't drink milk. |
| **Gilda:** | Look at this photo. Who is it? |
| **Kay:** | I'm not sure, **(4) it could be / might have been** my grandparents when they were young. |
| **Gilda:** | But the woman's wearing a long skirt. Your granny **(5) mustn't be / can't be** as old as that! |
| **Kay:** | Oh, of course, it **(6) might be / must be** my great-grandparents. Yes, they **(7) could be / must have been** on their honeymoon. See the signpost? It's in Austria. I know they went there. |

# UNIT 16

## CONDITIONALS (1): REVIEW

### Zero conditional

- We use the **zero conditional** to state general truths.
- *If* and *when* have the same meaning.
  *If/When* + present tense (comma) present tense
  or present tense *if/when* + present tense
  *If/When* you **drive** *fast, you* **use** *more petrol.*
  or *You* **use** *more petrol* *if/when* you **drive** *fast.*

### Practice

**1 Complete the sentences with suitable verbs.**

1 If you ........................ in a hot climate, you don't need many pullovers.
2 Students ........................ bored if they only study grammar.
3 When trains are cancelled, everyone ........................ home late.

### First conditional

- We use the **first conditional** to describe a real possibility.
  *If* + present tense (comma) future tense
  or future tense *if* + present tense
  *If you* **drive** *too fast, I'll* **be** *sick.*
  or *I'll* **be** *sick* *if you* **drive** *too fast.*
- We can also use the imperative + *and/or* + future tense to make offers, promises and threats.
  *Drive* too fast *and* I'll be sick.
  *Drive* more slowly *or* I'll be sick.
- *If* does **not** mean the same as *when* in first conditional sentences. Compare:
  *If* my sister **leaves**, *I'll* be *lonely.* (= The speaker thinks her sister may leave.)
  *When* my sister **leaves**, *I'll* be *lonely.* (= The speaker knows her sister is going to leave.)

### Practice

**2 Match the sentence halves.**

| 1 | Hurry up | **a** | if we're late. |
| 2 | The driver won't wait | **b** | or we'll miss the bus! |
| 3 | If it starts raining | **c** | and I'll call a taxi. |
| 4 | Lend me your phone | **d** | you'll need a coat. |

### Second conditional

- We use the **second conditional** for an imaginary possibility in the present or future, which we believe to be impossible or very improbable.
  *If* + past tense (comma) *would/'d* + verb
  or *would/'d* + verb *if* + past tense
  *If you* **left** *now, I'd* **feel** *sad.* (I believe you're unlikely to leave now)
  *I'd* **buy** *a new car if you* **gave** *me some money.* (but I don't expect you will give me any money)
- We often use *If I were you* to give advice or warnings.
  *If I were you, I* **wouldn't buy** *that car.*
- We sometimes use *I were* instead of *I was* in second conditional sentences.

### Practice

**3 Complete the second sentence so that it means the same as the first.**

1 I advise you to take a smaller suitcase.
  If I ................................................
2 It's a good idea to check the weight limit.
  I'd ................................................
3 It's dangerous to walk along this road at night.
  I wouldn't ................................................
4 You should take a torch with you.
  If I ................................................

### Third conditional

- We use the **third conditional** for an imaginary possibility in the past, which we know to be impossible.
  *If* + past perfect (comma) *would/'d have* + past participle
  or *would/'d have* + past participle *if* + past perfect
  *If the sun* **had shone**, *we'd* **have eaten** *outdoors.*
  (= it did not shine, so we ate indoors)
  *I'd* **have texted** *you if I'd* **seen** *your bag.* (= I didn't see your bag so I didn't text you)

### Practice

**4 Complete the second sentence so that it means the same as the first.**

1 Angie didn't go to the party so she didn't see the band.
  Angie would ................................................
2 Lewis entered the tournament and he won it.
  Lewis wouldn't ................................................
3 Matty felt fine at the end of the race because he had trained carefully.
  If Matty hadn't ................................................

**5 Circle the correct verbs.**

Last week I spent a whole day waiting at home for a new TV to be delivered. If I'd realised that, I **(1) would have asked / wouldn't have asked** the shop to deliver it. I'd have asked my brother to collect it for me. The problem is that I live in a small village and there are few road signs, so people never **(2) find / found** the house if I **(3) don't give / didn't give** them directions. And of course, it **(4) would be / will be** easier if the houses **(5) had / have** numbers like they do in cities.

However, the shop had detailed directions from me so it was their fault. If they **(6) 'd remembered / remembered** to tell the driver, he **(7) wouldn't have got / didn't get** lost. When he eventually arrived he said, 'They always forget to give me directions, they just give a postcode. If the shop manager **(8) didn't forget / hadn't forgotten** so often, we **(9) would save / saved** a lot of time.'

# UNIT 17

## CONDITIONALS (2): MIXED

### Mixed conditional (present affected by past)

We use this mixed conditional to describe an imaginary possibility in the present or future which is affected by the past.

- **If** + past perfect (comma) **would/might/could** + verb

  *If you **had remembered** to book a table, we **would be** in the restaurant now.*

  (= You didn't remember to book a table, so we aren't in the restaurant.)

  *If we **had seen** the beginning of the film, **we might understand** what is happening.*

  (= We didn't see the beginning of the film, so we don't understand what's happening.)

- **would/might/could** + verb **if** + past perfect

  *I **could visit** my grandparents tomorrow if I **hadn't started** tennis club.*

  (= I started tennis club, so I can't visit my grandparents tomorrow.)

  *Where **might** you **live** now if you **hadn't come** to London?*

  (= You came to London, but where else might you have chosen?)

### Practice

**1** Complete the sentences with the verbs in brackets, using **would/might/could** + verb and the past perfect.

1 If my brother ........................ all the pizza, I ........................ so hungry. (not eat, not be)

2 We ........................ to the beach, if it ........................ to rain. (go, not start)

3 If a friend ........................ me a story like that, I ........................ it to everyone I know. (tell, not repeat)

4 How ........................ those games if we ........................ broadband? (play, not install)

5 The students ........................ more out of this trip to Paris, if they ........................ French for longer. (get, study)

6 If I ........................ all my assignments, I ........................ this evening. (finish, relax)

### Mixed conditional (past affected by present)

We use this mixed conditional to describe an imaginary possibility in the past which is affected by the present or by permanent conditions.

- **If** + past simple (comma) **would/might/could** + **have** + past participle

  *If you **were** a better player, they **would have picked** you for the team.*

  (= You aren't a very good player so they didn't pick you for the team.)

  *If I **didn't know** my rights, I **might have lost** a lot of money.*

  (I know my rights, so I didn't lose a lot of money.)

- **would/might/could** + **have** + past participle **if** + past simple

  *They **wouldn't have spent** so much time watching TV **if they were** really busy.*

  (= They spent a lot of time watching TV, so I don't believe they are really busy.)

  *How **could** I **have made** this cake **if** I **was** no good at cooking?*

  (= I am good at cooking, so I could make this cake.)

### Practice

**2** Complete the sentences with the verbs in brackets, using **would/might/could** + **have** + past participle and the past simple.

1 We ........................ to the cinema, if we ........................ some money. (go, have)

2 If the school ........................ up to date, we ........................ the internet to research this project. (be, use)

3 If you ........................ so often, I ........................ the story you told me last night. (not exaggerate, believe)

4 Where ........................ if you ........................ a spare room? (your friends stay, not have)

5 The teacher ........................ us more help if she ........................ more time between lessons. (give, have)

**3** Complete the sentences, using the verbs in brackets to make a mixed conditional structure.

1 I wouldn't be top of the class if I ........................ (not work) every weekend.

2 These politicians ........................ (not be) in power now if voters had known their plans for the economy.

3 ........................ (Rosa / have) more friends if her family hadn't moved house so often?

4 If my parents gave me money every week, I ........................ (save) up for a new phone by now.

5 We ........................ (have) a coffee with our breakfast if the electricity hadn't gone off an hour ago.

6 How many people would have heard of Jane Austen if there ........................ (not be) so many films of her books?

7 If we ........................ (bring) less luggage, we wouldn't be so tired.

8 The boys ........................ (be) at the match now if the bus hadn't broken down.

9 Might the music we listen to now be different if the Beatles ........................ (never exist)?

10 If the roads were safe, the children ........................ (walk) to school every day, but they all had to go by bus.

11 What ........................ (cities / be) like now if cars hadn't replaced horses?

# UNIT 18

## USES OF VERB + -ING

### Verbs + -ing after verbs

- When one verb follows another, the second verb is often the -ing form.

  He **denied stealing** the money.

  They **admitted being** impressed.

  Would you **consider staying** for one more day?

- These verbs can all be followed by the -ing form:

  admit  _advise_  _allow_  appreciate  avoid  begin  can't bear  can't face  can't help  can't stand  carry on  consider  continue  delay  deny  dislike  enjoy  fancy  feel like  finish  _forbid_  give up  hate  imagine  involve  keep  keep on  like  love  mention  (not) mind  miss  _permit_  postpone  practise  prefer  put off  _recommend_  resist  risk  start  suggest

  **NOTE** the underlined verbs are followed by the _to_ form if they have a direct object.

  I advise **leaving** early tomorrow. or I advise **you to leave** early tomorrow.

  (**NOT** ~~I advise you leaving early tomorrow.~~)

- The -ing form is used as part of continuous verb forms.

  They've been **looking** for a solution.

### Practice

**1** Complete the sentences with your own ideas, using the -ing form of a verb and any other words you need.

1 If you have important exams you should avoid

   .................................................................................

2 I'm tired and hungry. Do you fancy ...........................?

3 They have a beautiful house. It's hard to imagine

   .................................................................................

4 If you're short of time, I don't mind ...........................

5 The weather's terrible. I don't think we should risk

   .................................................................................

### Verb + -ing after prepositions and phrases

- We use the -ing form after prepositions, e.g. **by, for, without**.

  You start the machine **by pressing** this lever.

  These cloths are **for cleaning** the tables only.

  Don't leave **without saying** goodbye.

- We use the -ing form after some time prepositions, e.g. **after, before, since, when, while**.

  **After leaving** school, she worked as a lifeguard.

  **Since passing** my driving test, I've been able to drive to work.

- We use the -ing form after some expressions, e.g. **be/get fed up with, have enough of, have (no) difficulty/trouble, pass the time, spend (time), (not) be worth, a waste of time/money**.

  He's **fed up with being told** what to do.

  With your qualifications, you'll **have no trouble finding** a job.

### Practice

**2** A junior chef is talking to some new employees in the kitchen of a famous restaurant. Complete what he says using the words and phrases in the box.

> after    by (x2)    get fed up with
> have no difficulty    it's not worth
> pass the time    since    spend time
> when    without

'OK, so as this is your first day in the restaurant kitchen, I'll just run through the way we do things here.

High standards are very important, so the first thing you do **(1)** ................. arriving is put on a clean apron. For the first week, you do nothing **(2)** ................. being given an order. This is the food processor. It's operated **(3)** ................. turning this handle. Be careful of your fingers **(4)** ................. using it, the blades are very sharp. Chef expects everyone to concentrate on their own work, not to **(5)** ................. chatting. We **(6)** ................. finding people who want to work here, so **(7)** ................. annoying the chef.

You'll get two breaks during the day. You can **(8)** ................. watching the chef as long as you don't get in his way.

If you don't **(9)** ................. working here by the end of the week, we'll give you some more interesting jobs to do. **(10)** ................. starting here two years ago, I've learnt a lot just **(11)** ................. observing what the chef does.'

### Participle clauses

- When two clauses have the same subject, one of them often starts with the -ing form.

- This sometimes replaces a relative clause and can give more information about a noun.

  The teacher, **realising** that we didn't understand, repeated her explanation more slowly.

  (= The teacher, _who_ realised that …)

- It often links an action and its explanation.

  He phoned his brother, **hoping** for some helpful advice.

  (= He phoned his brother _because_ he hoped for …)

  **Not looking** where I was going, I nearly stepped into the road.

  (= _Because_ I wasn't looking where I was going, …)

### Practice

**3** Rewrite the sentences, using the -ing form.

1 I sat at the back of the hall, so I couldn't see the show very well.

   .................................................................................

2 Because I'm not interested in rugby, I didn't go to the match with my cousins.

   .................................................................................

3 My dad, who wanted to know why I wasn't home, phoned the school office.

   .................................................................................

# UNIT 19

## SUBJECT-VERB AGREEMENT

### Singular nouns which end in -s

A number of English nouns end in -s, but take a singular verb. They include:

- some common words: **crossroads**, **means** (= method), **news**.
  *The **crossroads is** about a kilometre further on.*
- some sports: **athletics**, **gymnastics**.
  ***Gymnastics** is a very demanding sport.*
- some academic subjects: **economics**, **maths/mathematics**, **physics**, **politics**.
  ***Maths is** my main subject, but **physics is** also part of the course.*
- some countries which have plural names but take a singular verb because we think of them as individual countries: **the Philippines**, **the United Arab Emirates**, **the United States**.
  *It's not where I was born, but **the Philippines is** my home now.*

### Everyone, anyone, someone, etc.

**Anyone/anybody, everyone/everybody, someone/somebody, no one/nobody:**

- take a singular verb.
  *Can you answer the door if **anybody comes** to the house?*
  ***Someone is** eating all the biscuits.*
  ***Nobody likes** being made to look stupid.*
- but they are usually referred to by plural pronouns.
  *Can you answer the door if anybody comes to the house? Tell **them** I'm not here.*
- *Someone is eating all my biscuits. **They** should buy their own.*

### Clause as subject

When a clause is the subject of a sentence it takes a singular verb.
***Keeping** all my notes up to date **takes** at least an hour every day.*
***Playing** football matches with my mates **is** my way of keeping fit.*

### Both of, all of, plenty of, etc.

- Most expressions with **of** are followed by plural nouns and pronouns and take a plural verb. These include **both of**, **all of**, **plenty of**, **most of**, **a number of**, **a couple of**, **the majority of**.
  ***All of my friends play** computer games.*
- The expression **one of** is followed by plural nouns and pronouns but takes a singular verb.
  ***One of my friends likes** cooking.*
- Some expressions can be followed by a singular or plural noun and take a singular or plural verb. These include **a lot of**, **the majority of**.
  ***A lot of people like** this game.*
  ***A lot of music is** enjoyed by people of different ages.*

### Collective nouns

- Nouns which can take a singular OR plural verb include **band**, **class**, **club**, **family**, **government**, **group**, **staff** and **team**.
  *My **family is** moving house next weekend.*
  *My **team is** playing very well this season.*
- When we think of them as a number of individuals, we usually use a plural verb.
  *My **family** often **argue** about politics.*
  *My **team are** playing very well this season.*

## Practice

**1** Nine of these sentences have mistakes in them. Mark the four correct sentences then correct the mistakes in the others.

1 Nowadays our usual means of communication is texting.
.................................................................................

2 The city is very quiet because everybody are on holiday this week.
.................................................................................

3 Revising for exams were preventing my brother from doing any sport.
.................................................................................

4 The United States is a great place to live if you have plenty of money.
.................................................................................

5 No one has come to see me for ages. I must have done something to upset him.
.................................................................................

6 Spending time with friends has always been very important to me.
.................................................................................

7 A number of my friends is taking part in a riding competition on Saturday.
.................................................................................

8 My phone's dead. Have anyone brought their charger with them?
.................................................................................

9 The majority of people in this town works at the electronics factory.
.................................................................................

10 The class was texting their friends as they came out of the exam.
.................................................................................

11 The swimming club has put up its membership fees.
.................................................................................

12 Learning about other people are an important part of growing up.
.................................................................................

13 Both of my parents works long hours, but we have plenty of fun together at weekends.
.................................................................................

# UNIT 20

## DETERMINERS

### The definite article

**The** is used before any noun:

- when we mention the only one(s).
  *Most young people care about **the environment**.*
- when we refer to the particular one(s).
  *My sister likes shopping in **the local market**.*
- when we refer to a thing or things previously mentioned.
  ***The market** has all kinds of clothes.*
  ***The clothes** are quite cheap.*
- when both the speaker and listener know which thing(s) we are referring to.
  *She's gone to **the park**. (= the park we know)*

### The indefinite article

**A/an** is used before a singular countable noun:

- when we mention one of many things.
  *Most towns in this region have **a market** once a week.*
- when we introduce a new item of information.
  *I want to buy **a rucksack** before I go away.*

### The zero article

We do not use an article before an uncountable noun or a plural countable noun:

- when we refer to all or every kind of that thing in general.
  ***Exercise** is important whatever your age.*
  ***Markets** are good places to look for **bargains**.*
- when the quantity is uncertain or unimportant.
  *Do you want **bread** with your soup?*

### Plenty of, a lot of, etc. + noun

The quantifiers **some**, **any**, **plenty of**, **a lot of**, **lots of** go before:

- a plural countable noun.
  ***Some people** never eat in restaurants.*
- or a singular uncountable noun.
  *There's **plenty of room** for everyone in our car.*

### (not) much, (a) little, etc. + noun

- The quantifiers **(not) much**, **(a) little**, **a bit of**, **a small/large amount of** go before uncountable nouns.
  *I've got **a bit of work** to do before I go out.*
  *There's **not much music** here in the evenings.*
- **Much** is not often used in positive statements; it is rather formal.
  ***Much work** has gone into this project.*
- **Little** is negative; **a little** is positive.
  *I have **little money** to spend on clothes, so I look out for bargains.*
  *I have **a little money**, I can lend you some.*

### Many, (a) few, several, etc.

The quantifiers **(not) many**, **(a) few**, **several**, **a small/large number of** go before plural countable nouns.
*We have **several restaurants** in the city centre.*
*There aren't **many places** for teenagers to go round here.*
**Many** is not often used in positive statements; it is rather formal.
***Many students** find physics difficult, but I enjoy it.*
**Few** is negative; **a few** is positive.
*I have **few friends** in this area, so I get a bit lonely sometimes.*
*I've made **a few friends**, so I don't miss my family now.*

## Practice

**1** Circle the correct alternatives in the email.

Hi Sara,

How are you? We had **(1) a / the** great trip to Turkey. Thanks for recommending **(2) a / the** little hotel by **(3) the / –** harbour. We really liked it. **(4) The / A** staff were so helpful and friendly and **(5) the / –** breakfasts were excellent. We found **(6) several / few** good places for **(7) – / the** dinner nearby. **(8) Some / The** tourists only eat in **(9) the / –** hotels when they go abroad, but not us. Even the smallest cafés had **(10) plenty of / several** choice on the menu and **(11) the / –** Turkish food is absolutely delicious, as you know.

One day we went on **(12) a / –** boat trip. **(13) A / The** boat was quite small but we had **(14) lots of / a few** fun. We were able to jump into **(15) the / a** sea from **(16) the / a** boat and swim to **(17) the / a** sandy beach. There were **(18) few / a few** other tourists there and we soon realised why: there was **(19) a very little / very little** shade and **(20) the / –** sun was extremely hot!

Later we went to **(21) a / the** village where we'd heard there were a **(22) several / number of** carpets at **(23) – / the** good prices. In the end we didn't buy anything, as we hadn't got **(24) plenty of / much** money left. I'd already bought **(25) few / a few** souvenirs anyway.

Write soon and tell me how **(26) the / a** new job is going.

Love, Marta

# Acknowledgements

The authors would like to thank Annette Capel, Diane Hall and Sheila Dignen for their hard work and dedication to *Prepare!* James Styring dedicates this book to Livia Florence Luz Styring. Nicholas Tims thanks Clare, Ismay and Elodie for their endless support and patience.

The authors and publishers are grateful to the following for reviewing the material during the writing process:

Russia: Lorraine Swan; Spain: Laura Clyde.

Development of this publication has made use of the Cambridge English Corpus, a multi-billion word collection of spoken and written English. It includes the Cambridge Learner Corpus, a unique collection of candidate exam answers. Cambridge University Press has built up the Cambridge English Corpus to provide evidence about language use that helps to produce better language teaching materials.

This product is informed by English Profile, a Council of Europe-endorsed research programme that is providing detailed information about the language that learners of English know and use at each level of the Common European Framework of Reference (CEFR). For more information, please visit www.englishprofile.org

William Porter for the text on p. 11(d) adapted from 'An Audience with Syndicate' published by Eurogamer.net 11.10.2012. Reproduced with permission; Cambridge University Press for the text on p. 43 from *Sherlock Level 4 Intermediate Cambridge Experience Readers* by Richard MacAndrew. Copyright © Cambridge University Press 2013. Reproduced with permission; Houghton Mifflin Harcourt for the poem on p. 50 'A Leaf' by Bronislaw Maj from *A Book of Luminous Things: An International Anthology of Poetry.* English translation copyright © 1996 by Czeslaw Milosz and Robert Hass. Reprinted by permission of Houghton Mifflin Harcourt Publishing Company. All rights reserved; Chris Calhoun Agency for the poem on p. 50 'Grand Central'. Copyright © Billy Collins. Reprinted by permission of Chris Calhoun Agency; Random House Group Limited and Henry Holt and Company for the poem on p. 50 'Fireflies in the Garden' from *The Poetry of Robert Frost* edited by Edward Connery Lathem. Published by Jonathan Cape (Random House). Copyright © 1928, 1969 Henry Holt and Company, copyright © 1956 by Robert Frost. Reprinted by permission of Henry Holt and Company, LLC and Random House Group Limited. All rights reserved; Alicia Partnoy for the poem on p. 50 'Communication' first published in *Revenge of the Apple/ Venganza de la manzana.* Cleis Press, 1992. Translated from the Spanish by Richard Schaaf, Regina Kreger and the author. Reproduced with permission of Alicia Partnoy; Penguin Random House LLC for the poem on p. 51 'I broke your heart' from *If there is something to Desire: One Hundred Poems* by Vera Pavlova, translated by Steven Seymour, translation copyright © 2010 by Steven Seymour. Used by permission of Alfred A Knopf, an imprint of the Knopf Doubleday Publishing Group, a division of Random House LLC. All rights reserved; Penguin Books Limited and Darley Anderson Children's Book Agency Ltd for the text on p. 122 from *Chocolate Box Girls: Bittersweet* by Cathy Cassidy (Puffin Books 2013). Copyright © Cathy Cassidy 2013. Reproduced by permission of Penguin Books Ltd and Darley Anderson Children's Book Agency Ltd; We are Family Foundation for the text on p. 77 adapted from *Three-dot-dash. Global teen leaders.* Threedotdash.org. Copyright © We are family Foundation 2014. All rights reserved; British Youth Council for the text on p. 87 'Case Study – Charity Mhende MYP for Solihull 2008-2010'. Adapted from the website www.ukyouthparliament. org.uk. Reproduced with permission of British Youth Council; Loch Lomond & The Trossachs National Park Authority for the listening exercise and logo on p. 95 based on the website http://www.lochlomond-trossachs.org. Copyright © Loch Lomond & The Trossachs National Park Authority. Reproduced with permission; International Committee for Fair Play for the text and logo on p. 106 from the website http://www.fairplayinternational. org/. Reproduced with permission; Text on p.113 adapted from http://www.nsf.gov/news/special_reports/linguistics/change. jsp. Courtesy: National Science Foundation; Newsquest Media Group Limited for the quote by Professor David Crystal on p. 113 from 'texting a great big mwah' by Oliver Evans, *Oxford Mail* 6.3.2012. Copyright © Newsquest Media Group Limited; The School Enterprise Challenge for the logo and text on p. 116 based on the website http://www.schoolenterprisechallenge. org. Reproduced with permission; Daily Mail for the text on p. 119 adapted from 'The world's best summer job? Lucky student lands position travelling the globe as a Water Slide Tester' by Damien Gayle. *Daily Mail* 24.4.2013. Copyright © Associated Newspapers Ltd. Reproduced with permission.

For the sound recording on p. 19, ex 6 & 7, Track 1.6: *Crowd Pleaser,* artist: Elias Music Library. Copyright © Elias Music Library/Getty Images/Music.

For the sound recording on p. 36, Track 1.16: *Room of Pain,* artist: Eric William Johns. Copyright © Sound Express/Getty Images/ Music.

For the sound recordings on p. 62, Track 2.8:

*Bnet Liyoumm,* artist: Bnèt Houariyat. Copyright © Pump Audio/ Getty Images/Music; *China: Quan Bian,* artist: L'ensemble Chaozhou. Copyright © Pump audio/Getty Images/Music; *Não Moro Num País Tropical,* artist: Monica da Silva. Copyright © Pump Audio/Getty Images/Music; *Bluegrass Blues Instrumental,* artist: Round Sky Music/Studio Unicorn. Copyright © Pump Audio/Getty Images/Music; *Sands of India,* artist: Sony/ATV Music Publishing. Copyright © Spin City, from Sony/ATV/Getty Images/Music; *A Reel Dare,* artist: April Vech. Copyright © Pump Audio/Getty Images/Music; *Valenki,* artist: The Russian Folk Ensemble Balalaika. Copyright © Pump Audio/Getty Images/ Music; *Duelling Didgeridoos,* artist: Ah2 Music. Copyright © Ah2 Music/Getty Images/Music.

For the sound recordings on p. 90 ex 1, Track 3.2: *React,* artist: Silver Bullets. Copyright © Silver Bullets Music Library/Getty Images/Music; *He calls me man,* artist: Tom Manche. Copyright © Pump audio/Getty Images/Music; *Relax with me 90,* artist: Elias Music Library. Copyright © Elias Music Library/Getty Images/Music; *Falling Mr X D'n'B Remix,* artist: Get on Down Records. Copyright © Pump Audio.

For the sound recording on p. 95, ex 5-7, Track 3.6: *The enchanted bagpipe,* artist: Film & Music Co. Copyright © Pump Audio/Getty Images/Music.